THE MYSTIC

THE MYSTIC

John E. Knight

iUniverse, Inc.
New York   Bloomington

This is a work of fiction. All of the characters, names, incidents, organizations, and dialogue in this novel are either the products of the author's imagination or are used fictitiously.

iUniverse books may be ordered through booksellers or by contacting:

iUniverse
1663 Liberty Drive
Bloomington, IN 47403
www.iuniverse.com
1-800-Authors (1-800-288-4677)

ISBN: 978-1-4401-9501-3 (sc)
ISBN: 978-1-4401-9502-0 (ebook)

Printed in the United States of America

iUniverse rev. date: 1/20/10

CONTENTS

ACKNOWLEDGEMENTS

I have three expressions of gratitude.

First, to my life partner, Linda, for her encouragement and support. I started writing this book in the summer of 2004. I knew Linda, and we had started dating, but she lived in a different city. In the early morning, I would write a chapter or two and send it to her via email. She would send me a running commentary, and I could feel her excitement about wanting to read the next chapter. Her excitement fed my enthusiasm for the project, and my constantly reinforced enthusiasm kept the writing process alive for this book. She has helped me with a lot of the editing, and I am grateful for her enormous support.

Second, thanks to my philosopher friend, Peter. I am still amazed at how an early morning casual conversation in 2007 with the "gardener" outside my office, evolved into friendship and the person I could count on in the sharing of ideas and philosophy. Peter came to my life as a friend when I needed it to happen, and perhaps I have done the same for him. He has also provided the encouragement, support and critical analysis of my manuscript. We have had some great conversations about parables, and this book has a number of stories that are either extended metaphors or parables.

Third, a thank you to the hundreds of anonymous friends, relatives and acquaintances that I have had over many decades. There a parts of you throughout the book.

One of life's lessons that we all need to learn is that every choice or activity we engage in has not one, but two, levels of purpose. First, the immediate situational, or now moment purpose. Examples could be reading this book, or even routine tasks such as brushing teeth, getting up to go to work, returning phone calls, etc. Our "now moment" tasks can, if allowed, be our entire life focus on purpose. The second level of purpose is the grand design, the reasons for our existence, or the contributions we will make in improving the world we live in. For most people, very few moments are spent reflecting on the larger purpose. And, larger purpose is not some huge life endeavor. It is a compilation of little things – moments of joy, expressions of gratitude, replacing bat habits with good ones, helping others, and, doing something that makes use of your talents.

I have discovered over time that I have a talent for story telling. I also have a talent for viewing complexity and finding and communicating simple explanations of the complexity so that others can better understand a complex situation, issue or subject. This book is making use of my talents while at the same time, reviewing subject areas that fascinate me.

I am fascinated by repetitive and seemingly "chance" encounters. Have you ever seen the same recognizable stranger over and over again? Have you ever wondered what could happen, if you take the first step to introduce yourself to this stranger? What would happen if you connected on some level? Would this stranger somehow help you solve a problem of some kind, without being asked to do so? This musing about the connection of two people resulted in this book. My purpose was to write a short story for my own amusement, and with encouragement from Linda ended up being a book.

I am also fascinated with both mysticism and science and specifically the overlap of the two areas. First, I believe some mystic occurrences and beliefs can be understood in a logical fashion and applied in a practical manner. And second, I believe Einstein's conclusion that the objective world of science has its areas of head scratching illogic and when deeply searching for explanations one can easily transition from scientist to a mystical philosopher. I have acted on a desire to use story telling to explore the fascinating interface of the science of the physical world with the mysticism of the non-physical.

Almost all mature human beings have a desire to create better circumstances for themselves, their families and their communities. Many people at a point in life come face to face with a dark cloud of regret on what could have been, should have been, and would have been if they made different choices at moments in their past. Unfortunately, it is easy to walk into the dark cloud, or stand still while it envelopes your being. However, it is always possible at any moment in your life to walk away from the regret cloud or better yet, stop, smile at it, and with your gentle loving breath blow it away. This book is my method of blowing away the dark cloud, and second, I truly believe the guidance that has been given me as I wrote this book has come from a higher plane, and because of that there will be lessons in this book that will help you create better circumstances in your life.

CHAPTER ONE

GEORGE'S DINER

I am an early riser. This is a habit I developed as a kid growing up on a farm, up at 5:00 AM every day to do the chores. I quite like this early rising habit, and I have no plans to change the routine, even as I enter my mid-fifties. I usually get up between 4:00 and 5:00, and some times I get up really early, such as yesterday when I was awake and up out of bed and dressed at 3:15 AM.It is enlivening to start my day when most of the city is still asleep.

The only constant in my morning routine is getting up early. The rest of the routine changes on a constant basis. For a while I had a gym membership and I went to the gym when it opened at 5 AM. At another stage, I would get up early to take a long walks or to read. Lately, I have been browsing the news and blogs on the Internet. Some people jog in the morning, I blog in the morning. I also go to work early. I am almost always the first one in the office, and I am routinely the last to leave. Label me a workaholic. It has been like this for most of the jobs I have had in my career. I have been in the investment business for 25 years.I have helped my clients make a lot of money, but I have never been wealthy myself. I always lived well, until recently. My life is now mired in a major down cycle. It seems that when the investment business goes well, and I am earning lots of money, my spending habits over-shoot my increased earnings. When my income slips in a down cycle, I am often forced to sell off my assets and possessions, mostly at a loss.

I recently started a new job with a small investment broker on King Street. An old colleague of mine from a company I worked at twenty years ago fortunately hired me after I got caught in another company downsizing. Now, I am ironically working at the latest version of the company that employed me over twenty years ago. However, unfortunately, I am making less money in actual dollars than I made two decades ago, in the mid eighties. At that time, I was married to a career woman, an accountant who was focused on "keeping up with the Jones". She was very materialistic and an obsessive- compulsive with routines and cleanliness. Heaven forbid, if I ever left a dirty cup on the kitchen counter, I would get a nasty call at work and reminded that we had a dishwasher. I don't miss the days of married life. I used to drive "my ex" nuts with my getting up early habit. My routine then didn't include reading, the gym or walks before the sun rose or blogging. It seems funny now, most of the world didn't know that the internet existed in 1985. At that time, the office fax machine was our novelty high-tech apparatus for sending timely correspondence.

In 1985, I went to work early, every day. Before arriving at the office I had the routine of stopping for coffee at a 24-hour diner or coffee shop called George's Diner. The Diner was a relic of the 1950's, but for an early morning person, it was the only coffee shop open when everything else was closed. I vividly remember my routine. When I entered the Diner, I would take a stool at the counter, order a coffee from the waitress and sit there reading the Business section of the Toronto Globe and Mail. George's Diner was three blocks from work, and after finishing the paper I would walk to the office. This was my regular routine for three years, before I got a new job at an investment company located in a different part of the city. I can still recall that every morning when I would go into George's, no matter what time, there would be people in the restaurant. One very strange old guy was always there and he was always sitting in the same chair at the same table. He sat in an alcove by the entrance/exit of the diner at a table with four chairs. This fellow was approximately 60 years old. He would always be at the Diner when I arrived, and always sitting by himself. I could go into George's at 3:30 AM, and he was there. I could go in very late at 7:30 AM and he would be there. I can still remember that every day I went to the \Diner, he was there. I never really spoke to this guy. He would be sitting in his special table, drinking a coffee or tea and writing in a black notebook. When I entered the Diner, he would look up and smile at me. A nice pleasant smile, and then he would go back to writing in his journal. One day when I was leaving George's I was about to toss my newspaper into a garbage bin by the exit door, not far from this man's table and he called out to me – " If you don't mind, could I have your paper please?" "Sure, no problem", would have been my response. He smiled and thanked me. After that day, my routine was to leave him my newspaper, every morning on my way out of the Diner. Every day, he smiled, and said the same thing "thank you, make it a terrific day." I remember smiling at him and saying the same thing, day after day, something like "you too, bye." This routine probably occurred over five hundred times over the course of three years about two decades ago. These were the only words we said to each other. I was always in a rush to read the business news, gulp down my coffee and get to the office.I can't believe I never introduced myself or learned his name. I was too full of myself, being the thirty-something big shot on his way to making millions.

I have been working at Kunlow Investments for three weeks now. The company was called Garriety and Little in 1985 when I was a thirty year old stockbroker. Garriety and Little was my second employer after getting my MBA in 1984. In 1985, I was driving a $50,000 BMW, and thought I had the world by the tail. Now I am driving a 1999 Grand AM, worth about $8,000 and I still owe about $9,000 to pay it off. I owe my current personal financial mess to my idiotic trust in the company Nortel Networks and my insane continuance of purchasing more and more shares in the company with every cent I had, only to watch my net worth evaporate, as the company shares fell further than I thought was possible.

On my way to work this morning I entertained myself by reliving the "good old days". My beat up Grand AM was now my shiny blue, leather interior, BMW. Ah, get into the routine I told myself. And the thought jumped into my mind to take the same route to work that I would have taken twenty years ago. However, the route starts a little different as I am now leaving a seedy apartment building and brushing the snow off my car, instead of pulling out of two-car garage attached to the five-bedroom house in the "la-te-da" part of the city. My ex-wife used to wake up to the garage door opening and closing, and this used to piss her off. Ah, the good old days. In the trip to work this morning, I park my pretend "Beemer" in the underground parking on Bishop Street and set out on my five block walk to Kunlow. It is 6 AM. I have instant recall that my old pattern was to walk down Bishop to Lester, so I could stop at George's for coffee. "Is that old shack still open?" I ask myself out loud. In my current morning routine, I have been making myself coffee in the morning before heading out, and instead of reading the Financial pages of the newspaper, I sit at my computer, sip my coffee and I browse a few financial web-sites, and hit the bookmarks for a few of my favorite blogs. But today, as I relive my old way of going to work, I am eager to see if George's Diner is still around. I actually don't expect the place to be still there. It has probably been torn down, or maybe someone has made it into a bistro. As I turned the last corner, I stepped out toward the street to get a better angle view of the building ahead of me. I am startled to see the George's Diner sign. The joint was still in existence, and not put out of business by Starbucks or a drive through coffee place. I stop outside the door wondering if I should continue the charade. Yeah, why not. As I step inside, it felt like I was like going back in time. The floor was new, the tables and chairs were new, but the diner layout was the same. I couldn't help but break out a big smile when I see that my usual stool by the counter is open. I keep smiling as I think to myself about being caught in a personal time-warp as I go in and sit down at my stool.

"What would you like sir?" the waitress asked.

I quickly respond, "Coffee, with milk please".

However, sitting there I feel naked without my newspaper. I look to the right and see a Globe lying free at the end of the counter. Wonderful. I get up, and walk down to the end, pick the paper up and turn around to go back to my stool. Out of the corner of my eye I see the alcove by the doorway. Yes to the time warp - to my astonishment, the old guy is there! As I look in his direction, he lifts his head and smiles at me. This is 2005 and the guy looks exactly like he did in 1985. He even has what looks to be the same long black winter overcoat. Unbelievable.

An urgent impulse to talk to him overcomes me. He keeps smiling as he watches me walk over to him. A chill runs down my spine. I feel like he is expecting me.

CHAPTER TWO

ADAM

"Hi, I am Ted Gregory", I introduced myself to the smiling stranger.

"Hello Ted, it is nice to see you again".

"And nice to see you......excuse me, but your name is?" I query with a smile.

"Ah, pardon me, impolite for me to not introduce myself. My name is Almeida, Adam Almeida." And the stranger continues to smile broadly as he stands up to shake my hand. His right hand was warm as it gripped my hand, and he placed his left hand lightly on the top of our handshake grip.

"It is my pleasure to finally speak to you Almeida-Adam-Almeida, or should I just call you Triple A.". I really have no idea why I say some of the goofy things I do, the words just come out.

Adam smiled, "Why don't you just call me Adam."

I smiled sheepishly, and felt a slight ache on the side of my rib-cage. The imaginary pain was a silent reminder of the place where my ex-wife used to elbow me when I deployed my sometimes strange sense of humor in public with her at my side.

"I haven't been here for at least fifteen years. First, I can't believe this diner is still here. Second, I can't believe that you are here, and third, let me apologize for interrupting you." I was speaking in a rapid sequence, but still smiling.

Adam maintained his smile, and sat down pointing for me to take a chair and sit with him.

"Why don't you get your coffee Ted, and sit with me a while, or do you have to rush off to work?" I was getting a strong feeling to stay for a chat; there is definitely something very strange, but at the same time, very special about this fellow. I walked over to the counter, paid for my coffee and brought the cup back to Adam's table.

He sat smiling at me, waiting for me to initiate the conversation.

"I guess I should have stopped to say a few words to you when I frequented this diner on early mornings in the mid 1980's. It is funny that I shared my newspaper with you for almost three years and barely said anything to you."

"You were in a rush back then Ted, so I understand. I sincerely appreciated your kindness in leaving me your newspaper, and I am glad to have another opportunity to express my gratitude for your kindness. Thank you for leaving the paper with me." Adam maintained a constant smile.

"Have you been coming to George's every day for the last twenty years?" I asked.

"No, I only recently started coming back here." he said.

"Do you live close by?"

"No, I travel quite a bit."

"Where do you live?"

"It varies. Right now I am staying at the Holiday Inn."

"You live in hotels?"

"Most of the time I stay in hotels, but I also visit friends, and I also go to Bed & Breakfast places."

"No roots, no permanent residence?"

"I don't have a house or an apartment. I have a storage space. But most things I own of any significance fit into two suitcases, and I have a post office box for mail."

"Wow, a modern day Nomad."

"In a way", he smiled.

I couldn't believe I was conducting what must seem like a mini-interrogation of a pleasant old man. But I was driven to continue my questioning.

"If you don't mind me asking, how can you afford living in hotels? That must be expensive."

"Money is no problem for me. I always have what I need."

"Must be nice, I wish that was the case for me"

"Why?" He asked me his first question.

"Well, no money worries…. that would be wonderful. The ideal scenario for me, no debts and I have enough money to retire comfortably." As I said this I glanced down at the table and noticed a small reddish stone shaped like an octagon. It was lying beside a large black notebook.

Adam continued to gaze into my face, "Why?"

"Why?", the single additional Why from Adam confused me. I thought I had explained myself answering his question a moment ago. I said nothing.

"Why do you wish for it?"

"Well doesn't everyone wish they had enough money to do the things they want?"

"I don't know about everybody, but I wonder why you **wish** for something versus actually having it exist now?" he spoke calmly and he still had the nice smile on his face.

"Well you might have a point. I have been really stupid about money, and my investments, and borrowing money, and so on and so on. At my age I should have lots of money, and I shouldn't be wishing for it. It is hard to believe that I have a career in helping others create wealth, and I can't do it for myself." I cut myself off, and I quickly questioned myself as to why I opened up like this with a stranger.

I looked at Adam and for an instant it looked like he was going to give me some words of wisdom, but instead, he said nothing, and he continued to smile at me. A long moment of silence. If anyone else smiled at me for this length of time, it would bother me immensely, but with Adam, it seemed natural. I couldn't explain why I was comfortable.

A spontaneity bubble burst in my mind, an urge to break the silence, and I found myself asking out loud, "Can you give me some advice Adam?"

"Advice about what Ted?"

"Advice on money, on relationships and love, on how I can be healthy and vibrant like you, on being positive again about the big world, and my own little world. I thought I knew all the answers, I have hard so much good fortune, I have always worked hard, but now, everything seems to be crashing down on me. I have nothing to show as a contribution for my existence. I wish my life could be better. Adam, I have always done things on my own, followed my own council, I have never once asked anyone for life guidance, until this moment, and I can't believe I am asking you for this help, but it is like some invisible force has taken over my vocal chords." Again, I couldn't believe I was telling an almost total stranger about my situation and then worse, begging for help. I couldn't believe the sudden desperation in my voice, I had never done this before. I had no idea where my words were coming from.

"Yes". I thought Adam had reverted back to his one word sentences, followed by long silence, but then he spoke again, "Ted, **my advice is to never ever wish for anything**."

I felt like a confusion blanket was thrown on me. "I don't understand…What do you mean?….am I to have no dreams, no desires for something better?"

"That is not what I said – dreams and desires are important. It is the process of **wishing** that is a waste of energy. There is no need to wish for things that you truly desire. You just have to learn to **manifest** your true desires into your current reality, and it is very simple process to do this" He looked down at the table, picked up the little red stone and put it in his pocket, stood up and grabbed his journal and pen.

"Sorry Ted, I must go now. I will see you tomorrow. Make it a terrific day". Adam was smiling broadly, got up from the table, and shook my hand warmly. He turned and left the diner. Everything was in a now in a rush. I assumed he had already paid for his coffee, the waitress didn't seem concerned.

I gulped down the rest of my coffee, and made a mental note to Google the word "manifest". I thought a manifest was a document that went with a truck shipment. I couldn't have been more than half a minute behind Adam, as I left the diner at 6:30 AM, the street was quiet, I looked up and down Lester

Street both sides of the street, and I didn't see Adam. I didn't even see tracks in the fresh snow on the sidewalk.

"Weird", I said out loud. But I knew I had to come back to the Diner tomorrow.

CHAPTER THREE

JIMMY WONG

I was sitting at my desk by 6:50 AM. I couldn't help but think about Adam. There was something powerful drawing me to that very different and ageless man. "Why?" I kept asking myself. I had a strange feeling about him. I decided to find out more about him. What was this manifesting thing he talked about?I scribbled the word "manifest" on my notepad while waiting for my computer to boot-up. On checking my email I see I have a message from Jimmy Wong in Hong Kong. Jimmy has been my "meal ticket" for over twenty years. He has been my largest client and he has fortunately loyally followed me from company to company as I changed employers. Jimmy's portfolio was now worth over $38 million. Jimmy and I have been friends since our MBA days. He inherited his wealth from his father who had made investments in North America prior to the repatriation of Hong Kong by mainland China in 1997. The email confirmed that Jimmy had completed the transfer of his investments to Kunlow. My old employer was creating a lot of fuss about losing the Wong account and transferring Jimmy's assets out of their management. There had been several delays in making the transfer. My previous employer had laid me off in a "times are tough, we've got to save money by firing people, especially those over 50" company restructuring. My old boss, the

President of the company, didn't realize that Crystal Gardens Investments (the holding company owned by Jimmy Wong) was linked so strongly to me. His plan was to keep Crystal Gardens for his personal management (and commissions), after tossing me out.He had even hastily flown to Hong Kong to meet with Jimmy to "sweet talk" him and offer incentives to keep his account with his company. Jimmy had told him very politely and firmly that the only person he trusted to handle his investments was Ted Gregory.Back at the "times are tough" $2,000 per night hotel, the President called me at home at midnight my time, got me out of bed and offered me my old job back. I think he was a little surprised and more than a little disturbed with my "Screw You" or some similar two word response. I have a bad habit of "burning bridges" with old employers, especially the ones that don't appreciate the value of my relationships with clients.

I picked up the phone and called Hong Kong. I have reserved the first button on my speed dial for my number one client. A very soft voice answered the phone with a polite greeting in Chinese. "I don't know many Presidents of multi-million dollar companies who answer their own phone, let alone pick it up on the first ring", I said to Jimmy with a slight smirk in my voice.

"Ahhhh Ted, you know I run a small shop here. How come you are calling me so late, I sent my email to you six hours ago. This is bad service on your part. Maybe I should call that old boss of yours back and tell him I will keep the Crystal Gardens portfolio at his company…" Jimmy was starting to chuckle.

"Go ahead wise guy, and watch that \$38 mil drop back to the original \$15 mil you invested with me in 1988."

"Almost any other broker would have made me ten times my original investment in the same time you have managed it", Jimmy shot back, but he was gently laughing as he said it.

We traded barbs for a few more moments; Jimmy still won't let me forget about my sage advice of not investing in Microsoft and a few other high-tech software companies. I countered with "Remember, that I got you out of your dot com investments before the bubble burst" and a few others. All the quips were in good fun; Jimmy is a terrific person and a good friend. We talked about some changes for the portfolio. I made some notes on his requests and bid him a pleasant farewell.

Jimmy has been a wonderful blessing for me and I value the friendship that I have with him and his wife Rebecca.I met them both in 1983 when I went back to school for my MBA. At a social gathering on the first day, Jimmy and Rebecca were standing quietly at the reception when I bumped into them…literally. I still remember watching in horror as Rebecca's wineglass crashed to the floor after I elbowed her in my smooth move of pulling away from the buffet without looking. Jimmy and Rebecca were newly-weds living in a very modest basement apartment. Jimmy had enrolled as an international student in the University of Western Ontario MBA program.I liked them both immediately, especially after they both unnecessarily apologized for the mess that was created by my clumsiness. At the time I thought this young couple was barely making ends meet, Jimmy was buying used books for school and Rebecca had a part-time job as a cleaning lady.

And even though I could barely afford it, thinking that I could help out, I hired Rebecca to clean my apartment. The three of us enjoyed many week-ends or breaks from school when I took Jimmy and Rebecca in my car to several tourist locations – to Niagara Falls, to New York and many other places they wanted to visit. We had a lot of fun. Jimmy and I got together in the same study group and we became good friends. I majored in Finance and Jimmy majored in Operations. He talked about his dream of being a Plant Manager in a factory some day. After school was finished, the Wongs returned to Hong Kong, yet we stayed in contact, mostly because of Rebecca. She kept sending me letters from them, and for every three letters I received, I managed to send one back.

Jimmy was very happy when I landed my first job in the investment business.It caught me by surprise when Jimmy called me at work one day in early 1988 and asked me to manage some money he had inherited when his father passed away. The "sum" turned out to be $15 million in blue chip stocks and bonds. I vaguely recall almost peeing in my pants from surprised excitement. From that time on, I have communicated with Jimmy and Rebecca an average of once per week. I have endured the Wong jabs about Microsoft over 500 times. I still enjoy telling him my opinion that personal computers, software and the Internet are fads and people investing in stocks in this high-tech sector will regret it some day. Jimmy's Crystal Gardens Investments portfolio is minor compared to the investments that Jimmy has in Hong Kong and China. Crystal Gardens Investments is a safety cushion for Jimmy if the Chinese Communists ever decide to confiscate his 100 million dollars in local China investments. Jimmy's Asian investments are in Real Estate and a variety of manufacturing companies making electronics for the global marketplace. Jimmy is more than living his dream of being a factory manager. He is now the owner of over fifty companies which have a host of factories and world-wide operations.

I clicked the Google icon and typed in "manifest".The search pulls up a variety of listings, mixed, but my eyes stop on a listing for a Wayne Dyer book. *Manifest Your Destiny* - it seemed in line with what Adam was referencing. I see now, this context for the word manifest relates to New Age motivators and profiteers. But I still had a powerful feeling inside me. I need to learn more. I still want to find out more about Adam Almeida.

My boss Greg stuck his head in the door. I gave him the very good news about Crystal Gardens Investments transfer. Most of the day was spent with paperwork. I left work on a real high. The folks in the office wanted to go out for a few celebration drinks about my new big account coming to Kunlow. I begged off and suggested that we could celebrate the addition of our new client at their regular Thursday night get together at the local watering hole. Many of the brokers and support staff didn't need much of a reason to party at the local bar.

I suddenly realized a major behavior change had just occurred. This was the first time in my life I remember declining or postponing a celebration, or a chance to have a few drinks with my working colleagues. I really didn't feel like drinking.

The only thing I wanted to do was enjoy a contemplative drive back home in my "pretend" BMW and dream about "manifesting" a real one.

CHAPTER FOUR

PORRIDGE

I walked into the diner at 4:40 AM. I looked into the alcove area and did not see Adam, but I did see what looked like his coat draped over a chair and the familiar large black journal sitting on the table. As I walked up to the counter I saw Adam coming out of the kitchen with a cereal bowl full of hot food. I could see steam rising from the bowl. Adam was laughing as he was coming out of the kitchen, perhaps sharing a joke with the cook and the front counter waitress. Adam saw me as he came through the kitchen door. "Hi Ted, it is very nice to see you." Adam had a huge grin, I wasn't sure whether it was the remnants of the joke or he was just sincerely happy to see me.

Adam turned his head "Melissa, could you bring Ted a cup of coffee, milk only. Thank you dear." I could see Adam had a bowl of porridge with a little bit of milk and a scattering of raisins on top. He walked briskly over to his table. Adam stood at the table and beckoned me to sit in the same chair I sat in yesterday. He was still smiling.

"A good joke?"

"What is that Ted?"

"You seem full of humor, did you hear a good joke?"

"Oh my no, Gerry in the back asked me if I ate porridge every day. I said, no - not every day, but I have now had por- ridge for breakfast or lunch for 4,126 days in a row."

"Ah, the outrageous number of days is the joke?" I smiled, thinking that Mr. Adam was a bit of an exaggerator. Who in their right mind would believe someone eating porridge three days in a row, let alone over 4,000. I was smiling about it myself.

"No, I am serious about the number of consecutive days I have had porridge" he said, "We were laughing about Gerry wishing he bought shares in Quaker Oats 4,126 days ago."

I was slightly flabbergasted "4,126 days – why Adam, that is over 11 years of eating porridge every single day!"

Adam was still smiling "My, you are good at quick calculations Ted."

Melissa brought over my coffee, it is almost 5 AM in the morning and she was beaming. "Here you go Ted, can I bring you anything else?" Melissa smiled at me and looked lovingly over at Adam.

"No thank you Melissa".

"Alrighty then, you know where you can reach me." Melissa was still smiling as she turned to pick up some dirty dishes at another table on her way back to the counter.

"I think Melissa has the hots for you Adam" I teased him.

"Oh my yes, she looks so much like her great-grandmother it is unbelievable. She is a beautiful young lady."

"You mean her mother or grand mother don't you? You said her **great-grandmother**." I was doing a slight, unimportant and anal correction. This was a habit of mine that annoyed other people unless they were an Engineer or an Accountant.

"Oh no, I do mean her **great-grandmother** Deborah. Back a few decades ago she was a very attractive but a very married woman that had an eye for me, as I did for her, but that is all."

"Okay Adam, let me get my Math skills engaged again. Melissa is say around twenty-five years old, therefore, her mother would be about forty-five, grandmother would be sixty-five, and great-grandmother, Deborah, would be around eighty-five years old. I have used a rule of thumb of a twenty year generational spread. Wow that is a little old isn't it Adam. Fancy the older ones do you?" I was guessing Adam was about sixty years old. He could tell me he was fifty-five or sixty-five and I would believe him either way. I really didn't look at him closely when I encountered him twenty years ago.

"Well Ted that is very good calculating. You guessed Deborah's age on the nose, but Melissa is thirty years old. Her mother, grandmother and great-grandmother had children before they were twenty years old. And Deborah wasn't an older woman for me she was two years my junior. Poor dear, she died in an accident in 1980."

"Say what? You are eighty-seven years old?"

"Good Math Ted"

"But you look like you are sixty!"

"I look that old, hmmm, I better start getting more beauty sleep" Adam laughed. He was methodically eating his porridge as we talked.

I thought of Viggo Mortensen, the forty-something aged actor who played the eighty-seven year old Aragorn in the Lord of the Rings movies. Adam looks exactly like Mortensen as Aragorn. I couldn't tell whether Adam's age claim was bullshit or real. Either conclusion made me slightly nervous.

"How do you do it?"

"Do what Ted?" I made a mental note to stop asking this guy vague, open-ended questions.

"How do you look so young? And money doesn't appear to be a problem for you either."

"There isn't a simple answer to that question Ted. I am blessed. I have manifested abundance in My Life. I have an abundance of Good Health, I haven't been ill in over forty years, not a day. I have an abundance of money, enough money for anything I need and to give to others in need. I have an abundance of wisdom, more or less the rewards of age and experience but also a product of exercising my mind on a daily basis. I have an abundance of love —I love many people, nature and life itself and I receive much love in return. I am truly blessed. I thank the Creator for that, and at the same time I thank myself for the choices I have made." I had a blank look on my face, as I took this all in. Adam initiated the next dialogue.

"What are you thinking about Ted?"

"I think I am going to start eating porridge every day". Adam broke out a hearty laugh and I joined him.

I hesitated for a moment. I had to say something else, and my consciousness was divided into two camps – one voice in my mind shouting 'Time to shut up and leave' and the other more reserved part of my Conscious mind was saying 'This is the reason you are here, you must ask the question.' The quiet voice won. I looked at Adam. "Can you teach me how to manifest abundance?" As I was asking, I thought about all of my opposites to Adam's abundance. Health- how I can't seem to go two weeks in a row without getting sick or having an ache or pain of some sort. Money- my $45,000 in outstanding credit card debts and negative Net Worth while earning over $150,000 a year. Love- a bitter divorce, and a post wife and now ex-girlfriend who took me on an emotional roller coaster, and my last date was over two years ago. Wisdom- yeah I had a near-genius IQ but I had made more errors in judgment and bad choices than the number of bowls of porridge Adam has eaten in his lifetime.

Adam looked intently at me. He was still smiling, that benevolent compassionate kind of smile. "I can help. That is my purpose in Life. We'll talk tomorrow."

CHAPTER FIVE

COMMITMENT

On Wednesday morning I strolled into the diner about 5:00 AM. I had slept in. Adam was sitting in his usual spot in the alcove but didn't notice me when I walked in. He was intently writing in his journal. This was the first time I looked at him when he wasn't smiling. I hesitated before walking over to him, I did not want to disturb him, he seemed very intense in the way he was writing in his book. Melissa saw me, and smiled at me when I saw her. She starting pouring a coffee, and was signalling me to come over to her. I walked over to the counter.

"Good morning Melissa, thank you for the coffee. Hey, I don't think I paid you for the coffee from yesterday." I was scrambling in my pockets looking for change.

"Oh no Ted, no problem, yesterday's coffee is on the house and so is this one."

"Ah, that is mighty nice of you, but I can pay anyway", it was puzzling me why the coffee would be free for me.

"Oh no, you are a friend of Adam's and it would not be right to charge you for the coffee."

I was still a little confused and threw out a blind comment "Ah, so Adam owns this joint".

Melissa continued to smile and didn't say a word, or move her head or give me any indication at all whether what I said was a joke, the truth or anything else. I felt a strong hand touch me on my right shoulder. Normally, this unexpected occurrence would cause me to jump or yelp or have some sort of other startle response. Instead, I felt no fear.

"Good morning my friend", it was Adam's cheerful voice. Again, he had a big smile on his face that made me smile in return. As I turned to face him directly, I noticed smiles on the other customers sitting at the counter. I wondered whether any person tiredly stumbling into the diner at 5 AM either on their way to work or going home from late night shift-work would think we were a bunch of loonies in this place, with all the smiles and laughing and good cheer. Five or six customers was the usual early morning/middle of the night crowd. I wondered why the diner even bothered to stay open 24 hours. Those thoughts ran through my mind in nanoseconds as I started to shake Adam's hand.

"Good morning Adam. I was just in the process of trying to force Melissa to take some of my money for coffee, and she is not being very co-operative. Can you have a word with her?" Melissa stood smiling at us both.

"Oh, Melissa is collecting. Your coffee goes on my tab."

"Why thank you Adam, you don't have to…."

"Ted, not a problem….bring your coffee over to the table… .I have some questions to ask you."

Adam was dropping off what looked to be an empty porridge bowl at the counter and he beat me in our race over to his table. Some race, I was carefully walking, not trying to spill any coffee from the cup into the saucer or worse , on to the floor.Boy this guy is spry for an 87 year old, if indeed he was that age. I hadn't made up my mind about that yet.

As I sat down, I noticed Adam was playing with a small reddish-purple octagonal stone. He had the stone or pebble in his right hand and was gently feeling it with his fingers. It was the same stone I noticed on Monday morning.

" Nice little stone", I said.

Adam was smiling and looking at me, "It is a garnet. This crystal is my daily companion."

" Ah your good-luck stone or your birthstone. Cool." I said.

"In a way…" he said. It looked like he was going to say more but he stopped short. "Shall we overview what we may or may not do with teaching you about manifesting abundance?". Boy he was getting right into it, no messing around. I like that.

"Absolutely." I affirmed softly.

Adam was speaking clearly yet softly and had that nice smile of his engaged. "First, let me say, any transformation process has a time element to it. Let us focus on Big Changes. On one end of the time scale a major transformation or change event can take place quickly – a dramatic occurrence. The high-energy good Big Changes in a hurry occurences are called miracles and the adverse Big Changes in a hurry being cataclysms or disasters."

My first thought was 9-11 and I made a mistake of interupting him, as I raised my right hand and chirped "I vote for miracles". Adam paused and he didn't look distracted or angry, but my immediate feeling was to make a mental note to not interrupt him again.

He picked up the coversation flow at the pause point, "On the other end of the time scale, change or transformation takes place more slowly, call it evolution for progressive or positive change or call it decay for negative change. I mention the time element for only one reason. I am eighty-seven years old, I am already mentoring some people in the evolutionary mode of transformation and if I am going to spend any time with you on this project I would prefer a dramatic brisk transformation process. If you want to go slower, I will guide you by recommending some reading materials and give you some names of people to talk to when you are ready." He paused to guage my reaction. I knew I could speak now.

"Adam, a fast speed is good. I live in a high-paced world. I will work with you in the 'fast-track' training that you will give me."

He looked at me quietly, my instincts were telling me he was going to make a 'yeah, but...' statement.

"Ted, if we are going to proceed, I need your commitment. More important, you need your commitment."

" You have my commitment Adam". My instincts told me that my words didn't seem to be enough for him, so I quickly added a comment... " but first Adam, tell me what is involved, and after listening to it, I will let you know if I can make the total commitment to this project." The corners of his mouth went up a little.

"Okay. Let me give you the outline. First, I lead very full days, my time is precious, and I will be travelling a lot over the next while. I may need you to travel with me." I was going to interupt with the 'but I have a new job...' but the mental note taken minutes ago kicked in and I held back, my face maintained the same expression as he spoke.

"Second, I have coached various individuals in the past and I have found that the same pattern can't be used. Each project, and I am glad you don't mind me using the word project, is unique. I work using my intuition so our sessions may seem sometimes to be disorganized or chaotic. There will be chaos because I can't always remember what we might have talked about, and I will rely on you to tell me when this happens, if you chose to do so. I will also require you to do some assignments on your own, and I expect you will demonstrate your commitment by having the assignments done in the time allotted for them."

"Third, you need to have a completely open mind. Your beliefs must be put in a drawer, and I **don't** want a lot of challenges from you about **why** we are doing certain things."

"Fourth, you need to eliminate all negative behaviours and thoughts. They are toxins that will inhibit your positive transformation." As he said this, the loud-mouth in my conscious mind was shouting "bullshit". Fortunately, the quiet guy in my conscious mind was able to gag him before my body language, or worse, I said the word "bullshit" out loud. This was probably what Adam is talking about in his point number four about negative thoughts.

"Fifth, if we proceed, and we succeed in our goals, you must commit to helping others in need. I sometimes don't say point five, because it is an obvious outcome of a succesfull transformation session." He stopped for a moment.

"There you have it. What do you think?"

I paused. I wasn't sure what to say. I didn't like all aspects of the the life I am leading… My new job is a worry, but at least I had a job, now I might risk losing it. An immediate fear was thinking about how much is all this going to cost me? The loud voice trouble-maker in my consciousness had managed to get the gag off and was machine-gunning all kinds of reasons to not be involved as Adam's 'project'.I closed my eyes and the conscious mind trouble-maker stopped shouting. In closing my eyes, the quiet guy (I am assuming my intuition) spoke gently to me. "Ted, the events of this week have happened for a reason. You deserve the best life you can lead and that includes an abundance of love, wisdom, good health and money. Adam's plan could help you find purpose and he will show you how to use your special talents to help others to lead better lives. This feels right, by the end of today, the practical matters that you are worrying about will be put in order for you to proceed."

I have often wondered if I was schizophrenic. I always had two voices in my mind talking. One voice was loud and obnoxious, but always there to protect me. The other voice was always soft and quiet, and seemed to always contradict the loud voice. My eyes were closed for seconds, and I opened them to find myself staring directly into Adam's bright blue eyes.

It was almost as if Adam was listening to my quiet consciousness voice's advice while I was contemplating.. "Ted it already looks like you practice one of my Life Lessons."

"What do you mean Adam?"

"The lesson is - you can see better with your eyes closed."

He then handed me a piece of paper with a phone number on it. "Call me at 6:00 PM tonight with your answer".But I think he already knew what the answer was.

CHAPTER SIX

FRIENDSHIP

I sat at my desk trying to figure out this 'commitment' I made to Adam. No, in truth, following Adam's direction, a commitment to myself. Suddenly, probably staring directly at my own mortality, I wanted my Life to matter. I had developed a new desire to help people in need. And, I definitely wanted to get out of the struggle that I seemed to be mired in. I began to make mental notes on some key questions. Is the project with Adam going to take a lot of my time? He said we were going to take the "Express" road on this Quest, and I still had no idea on how much of my time this commitment was going to take. Would I be able to keep my job? I definitely want to. I need the money, I like the work, I like the people at this company and best of all, many of my clients are good friends.

I saw that my boss, Greg was in early today. I stopped my mental note taking and popped my head in his office door. "Greg, you got a minute?"

"Sure Ted what's up? Geez, this is your first time coming into my office since I hired you. Ted, I want you to know that you can come into my office at any time. I know I am your boss, but I consider you to be my friend as well, and I am so delighted that you decided to come here and work with us. Please let me know if there are any problems."

"No Greg, things are great here. Three weeks here, and I am already coming to you to tell you that I have a few personal things I need to deal with and I may need some time off."

"Do you have to do any jail time?" Greg was smiling and semi-joking. He had told me about his Enron nightmares in my job interview with him.

"No jail Greg. Don't worry about that. I guess I don't know how to describe what I need to do, or even how much time it is going to take. I may have some travel ahead of me, I just don't know at this point."

Greg was not a guy who pondered responses. "Sounds like another job. Not in the investment business I hope."

"Oh no Greg, I am working on a personal project with an old acquaintance. It is like a one on one coaching seminar for my personal development. He is vague on the time required, and I can't seem to assess how much time I will have to spend with him."

Greg fortunately started to go with the idea, "Hmmm. Well, there might be one approach we could take. I want to keep you working with my company. With our cards face up on the table, we both know I wanted you here because I knew you would bring the Crystal Gardens account with you. There are a lot of bucks in that account. My only worry with this account is the historical transaction activity is light. You know as well as I do that if there is high transaction activity, we both do well on the broker fees."

"Greg, the Crystal Gardens portfolio has been stable for over three years. The account is heavy with long-term bonds. A lot of those bonds are coming due this year, so there will be some huge liquidity. Jimmy is a personal friend of mine, and he gives me a lot of free reign on his account, but I haven't made a lot of stock trades, at least in the last three years. I have been managing his money conservatively for his best interest."

"I know you have Ted. That is why you have built excellent relationships with your clients. With regards to getting you some independence and keeping you working with our company, I have an idea that might be a win for both of us."

"Sure Greg, I'm listening."

"How about we change your compensation from salary plus commission to straight commission. I'll pay a higher rate than your current commission rate, but I won't pay you a base salary like I do now. You don't have to work out of our office; you can work from home or wherever. I'll cover your business costs – phone, fax, cell, internet, and computer. On straight commission, your time is your own. You keep the clients you have now and hopefully you will add some new ones."

I was thinking to myself, this Greg is a clever guy. He knows the Crystal Gardens account has been Warren Buffet style stable, a "hold and prosper" strategy with hardly any transactions. No transactions, no broker fees. If I am hungry, I have to make trades. Generally, the broker makes a lot with portfolios with a lot of equities and clients who like to sell and buy stocks on a regular basis. Greg's idea of a home office, and straight commission was appealing to me. It should align, hopefully, with my project, whatever it will be, with Adam. I decided to talk to Jimmy about this as well. I can't move his account into a new higher-risk, higher-fee management structure without his blessing. Short-term, I could be making a bunch of trades on his account, desperately needing the commissions to pay my rent, car payment and monthly Visa statement.

"Sounds like your idea could work for me Greg. Let's review the details. Can I talk to you later this morning? I have to call Hong Kong."

"Sure Ted, I am really busy until about 11:00. We can review the details then. What's the time difference to Hong Kong?"

"Twelve hours. Jimmy stays at the office until about 8:00 PM. If he goes with a proposed plan to move from bonds into more equities, we have a lot of changes to make in his portfolio."

"Sure Ted. But, make those changes before your commission rate goes up." Spoken like a true boss, but he had a smile on his face and I knew he really didn't care when I made the transactions.

I went back to my office and called Jimmy. Three rings and he answered the phone. We did our usual bantering about Microsoft and other missed opportunities and then I started reviewing the Crystal Gardens portfolio with him, mentioning that over $20 million in bonds were coming due in eight weeks and we would have to have a strategy discussion on his portfolio.

Jimmy was his usual quiet, contemplative self. "Ted, I trust you completely, do what you think is right for the account."

"Well Jimmy, the last few years we have been very conservative. A lot in bonds and preferred shares and the like, do you want to stay in that mode?"

"Ted, whatever you decide is fine with me."

"Jimmy, I appreciate your confidence, but I don't want to move into more equities without your blessing. There is more risk. However, there is an advantage for stocks right now because bond rates suck."

"Ted, I would like two things to happen over the next few months. One, I think you have been too conservative with the funds. I would like you to be more aggressive on the equity side. Be a day trader in half my account if you want. The Crystal Gardens money is never going to leave North America. My two sons will have to figure out what to do with this money when it is their time."

"And the second thing Jimmy?"

"Oh yes, Rebecca and I would dearly love it if you could come and see us. The two boys – Eric and Mark – are ten and eight and you have not met them. It is their money you are playing with, and I think you should meet them. They are very aggressive little guys, they want stocks, not bonds or T-bills." Jimmy was beginning his quiet little laugh.

"My goodness Jimmy, you are right, I need to make plans to visit you and your family. It is really tough because I have some personal projects on the go right now. But, it looks really bad when my old boss has time to see you and I don't. Okay, how does a mid-May trip to Hong Kong sound?

"It sounds absolutely wonderful Ted. Now, let me warn you. I am going to tell Rebecca tonight. She will be excited, and I know she will hound you to book your plane tickets." Jimmy was breaking out into his nice laugh. "Ted, I am not a normal investor. Please do what you think is best with the money. I owe you so much as a friend; you can't do anything that will hurt me. Your friendship is what means everything to me. I think about that Operations 101 report many, many times. I am eternally grateful to you." Jimmy's voice was beginning to quiver. "But now if you will forgive me, I am running late for dinner, and I want to tell the family the good news of your planned visit. Bye for now my friend."

After bidding Jimmy farewell, I was perplexed. The Operations 101 report? I had to think for a moment. What was that? Then it dawned on me. It went back to our first year, in the MBA program. Jimmy and I had recently met at the Business School and we hit it off. We formed a study group with two others, another exchange student, Vincent Chen, and a young Engineer, Karen Fitzpatrick. First year MBA at Western was like an intellectual "boot camp". The Professors threw all kinds of work at their students, tried to embarrass them in class and generally made student life miserable. The International students had a really rough time especially the ones where English wasn't their first language. There was so much reading since all classes were case studies. Class participation was crucial to get good marks. In first year, we had an exam every second Saturday and a report due on the alternate Saturday. I was starting to remember the story around Jimmy's comment. The very first report we had to do was for Operations 101. The Case study on a real-life business problem was given to you 5:00 PM Thursday. The student played the role of a consultant or someone in the business and had to hand in a no more than 1,500 word report typed, double-spaced before noon on Saturday. Less than 36 hours to do everything. The report was a recommendation on how to handle the problem presented in the case. If the report was more than 1,500 words the student was docked marks. If the report was handed in late it was docked one grade or failed outright. This program was tough on new students. The flashback on Operations 101 was now coming back to me vividly. I had finished writing my report about 3 PM on Friday. No personal computers in those days. I had a cracker-jack typist and she had my report typed for me about 8:00 PM Friday night. I wasn't going to be a student star in this program, but I knew I had done a reasonably good job on this report, at least good enough for the average grade. I was just about to head out the door to go downtown to have a few pints with one of my other buddies in the class when the phone rang. It was Rebecca Wong and she was crying. She told me Jimmy hadn't been able to do any of the report and he was in great distress. He had called Vincent Chen for some help with reading some of the sections. Vincent had told him he had no time to help; he was having trouble himself. My heart was tingling. I knew that Jimmy really, really wanted to do well in the Operations course. In our very first conversation he told me of his dream to become a Factory Manager in Hong Kong. Blowing this report would almost certainly mean having a horrible mark in that course and getting a bad grade in the Operations course would devastate him. I changed my plans and decided to drive over to their apartment. I had a reasonably good understanding of the case but I wasn't that interested in being a perfectionist, as this would cut into my week-end drinking time. Jimmy, on the other hand, was a perfectionist and I knew that this was part of his problem. We reviewed the case and I told him what I had written as a recommendation. Jimmy began criticizing my proposed solution to the problem or issue presented in the case. As he was going through his point by point dissection of my report, he suddenly came up with an idea for a solution that seemed to me to be brilliant. It was my gut feeling that Jimmy was sitting on an innovative way to solve the hypothetical problem in the case study, but his proposal would be complex and there would be no way he could describe all the details of his plan in 1500 words or less. Jimmy's idea was brilliant but it involved changing the plant lay-out and process flow in the factory. My solution of firing the plant manager and hiring a new manager from a competitive company seemed simplistic in comparison. As a little trick to get within the 1500 word limit, I suggested he put the all detailed stuff (recommended flows, machine lay-outs, and staffing changes) in a Process Chart, and submit it as an Exhibit to his report. The written proposal would touch on the highlights of the idea and continually reference the exhibit in his report. Jimmy excitedly agreed and started to meticulously make a flow-chart diagram and as he explained the details of the idea. I dictated the report to Rebecca who typed the details into a Word processor. We worked through the night and finished everything around 9 AM on Due-day. Jimmy the perfectionist had to do some fancy coloring on his Exhibit, creating a dead-line crisis. We managed to just make the noon cut-off to drop-off the reports. I had to drive home like a maniac to get my report, I had almost forgotten about it. In our First year MBA boot camp, only ten percent of the class was allocated the highest mark which was a "4 out of 4". Jimmy was one of those guys on the Operations 101 report. He was beaming when he showed me his mark. I showed him my "2", which was the simple passing grade. He hugged me and was crying. I remember finding out later from Rebecca a few other important things. Jimmy's parents had high expectations for him when he left Hong Kong for Canada. The night of writing the Operations 101 report was a personal crisis for him. He was close to quitting the program and going back to Hong Kong, which would be a disgrace (in Jimmy's mind, not Rebecca's). Rebecca was seriously worried that in his state of mind, Jimmy would choose suicide rather than face his father with the embarrassment of failure.I was his life-saver and I had almost forgotten the story behind it. I had made friends for life with the Wongs.

I met with Greg later that morning and we worked out the details for a commission-only compensation package and new contract. The afternoon was spent taking care of some paperwork items for setting up a home office and other practical details.

Just before 6 PM, I called the number Adam gave me. It was the Holiday Inn. The hotel operator put me through to his room.

"Hello Ted", he obviously knew it was me calling.

"Well Adam, I am committed to this thing. Tell me what you need me to do."

"Meet me Friday 6:00 AM at the diner, fill your vehicle up with gas, pack your suitcase, and bring some boots. We are going to drive to northern Michigan."

"Huh?? .....Do we have to rush into a trip already? Omigosh, that must be a six to eight hour drive!"

"Ted – this is test one. Either you are committed or you are not. What is your choice?"

I hesitated. It was a co-incidence I was thinking of First Year of the MBA program and the boot camp analogy. Am I getting into it again? But, I was feeling a rush of excitement.

"You bet I'm committed. I'll see you 6 AM sharp on Friday, and don't make me come over to the Holiday Inn to haul your sleeping ass out of bed."

Adam was laughing. "Wonderful. Ted, even though it doesn't sound like it at first glance, we will have some great fun. See you Friday at 6:00. Park your car in the alley behind the diner"

I had a big smile on my face as I hung up the phone.

CHAPTER SEVEN

KEEPING AN OPEN MIND

I contemplated not stopping at the diner on Thursday morning. But I had formed a new/old habit, morning coffee at George's.I arrived at George's Diner about 4:30 AM. There were four people there. Melissa was laughing and joking with a couple of regulars at the counter. No doubt that those guys came to see Melissa on a regular basis just to be energized by her ever-present and friendly smile. I didn't see Adam, so I sat down at the counter. Melissa poured the coffee and left a small carton of milk for me to select the amount I wanted to mix in to the coffee this morning. I reached into my pocket for some money. She gave a "don't you dare look" with her eyes, obviously not wanting to speak and thus alert her regular customers to my special deal. I had brought along a small notebook with me to scribble down my to do list and any other stuff that might occur to me – you never know, the idea on how to achieve world peace might pop into my head and be lost forever unless I wrote it down. I quickly glanced through the finance section of the newspaper, knowing I would need to select some stocks to research further as new investments to add to Jimmy's portfolio. I was busy writing in my notebook, in full concentration and didn't even notice that someone had sat down beside me at the counter.A break in my concentration and I felt a presence. I turned and saw Adam sitting there looking at me with his "slight smile" facial expression.

"Good morning Ted"

"Good morning Adam, I didn't see your stuff at your table, so I thought you were not in today."

"I have just stopped in for my porridge, and to do a few chores", Adam replied. As I quickly scanned the diner, I couldn't see his coat or his journal. I surmised that Adam must have left them in the back kitchen. He continued. "I am glad to bump into you. I am looking forward to our trip tomorrow. I hope you don't mind driving?"

"No problem Adam. It caught me a little by surprise, but I am up for it."

"Good, and thank you very much for driving Ted. I'll see you at 6 AM tomorrow." I thought he had finished, but he continued. "There is one thing I need to tell you, if you have a moment?" He was looking at my pen in hand with the journal and seemed worried that he had interrupted my writing.

"Sure, go ahead Adam, don't worry about interrupting me, I hope my new insight on how to achieve world peace will come to me again sometime."

He laughed. "I love your dry sense of humor Ted. It will make the long drive we will have tomorrow and Monday enjoyable."

"So the plan is to come back Monday then?"

"Oh yes, I guess I forgot to tell you that detail, sorry about that."

"No problem, good to know now, I will pack some more underwear." In my quick look at his face, and I could see he was extra glad he told me when we were coming back. Then he smiled sensing I was joking again.

"Ted, starting tomorrow I am going to be telling you a lot of my Life's work." He paused, and I didn't interrupt him with a flippant remark, which is my usual practice in a moment of silence. "I need to emphasize one of the points I made the other day. I want you to keep an open mind about everything you hear or see with me. Try not to judge anything. Being judgmental is a mistake too many people make. A quick decision or conclusion is made and then the person shuts down any possibility of future benefit in seeing new opportunities." I was nodding in agreement as he continued. "I am asking you or telling you that if you encounter anything that seems truly outlandish or 'way out there' for your current mind-set, to say to yourself two things. First, have a little fun – tell yourself – weird is good. Second, tell yourself it is okay to not have a clue what this new experience is about. You are going to stay open about it. Sometime later you will decide to either investigate the idea in more detail, or decide the idea does not feel right to you right now. If it doesn't feel right don't dismiss it, decide to let it be and focus on other things." Adam paused and needed to check my feedback. "Does this make any sense to you Ted?"

For some reason I had a flashback to the old TV show Kung-Fu, and Caine, as the young boy was talking to his wise mentor Master Po, "Yes Master, I will stay open to all possibilities."

Adam looked at me a little sideways, but he was smiling again. "Another thing Ted. Our relationship will not be a Master-Student. I will learn some things from you as you will from me, and we will learn together when we get to Gary and Lynette's farm this weekend. What I can tell you right now, if do you need a Master or a Supreme Guide for support, there is one is with you right now, and it isn't me." I glanced around the restaurant quickly; I was sort of hoping that Melissa would be looking at me, but the place was empty. Adam continued speaking. "The guide is within you, a quiet voice, and I am sure you have heard the voice before or at least experienced hunches or intuition."

"Yes I have Adam. Sorry about my Kung Fu moment a second ago." Adam toggled into his laugh mode. "Ah yes Grasshopper, I remember now, what a fantastic show. I'll have to watch some of it again if it is on DVD. There were some wonderful lessons in that show." Adam stood up and walked behind me patting my shoulder as he walked away "See you tomorrow Ted." He walked back into the kitchen area, and he had a big smile on his face, maybe he was recalling some Master Po – Caine (Grasshopper) moments from Kung Fu. I finished my second cup of coffee and left for the office.

By 8 AM, I had most of the files I wanted for my home office packed. Greg had said there was no hurry in making the move, but I got a start on it anyway. Thursday was a staff meeting in the morning, and Greg went through a bunch of items and mentioned I was setting up in a Home Office. The group didn't really take that as a Big deal because three other brokers had the same arrangement which I didn't know about until the staff meeting. Greg had picked up the vibe that he had forgotten to tell me about the other brokers that worked on straight-commission contracts. After the meeting, he dropped into my half-empty office to tell me, that he had hired me to be a Big Player as a staff member – Institutional accounts etc. and it didn't occur to him to mention the other compensation plan he had for investment brokers. He also emphasized that we could switch back to the original salary plus commission arrangement at any time. I was really appreciative of his offer.

Thursdays after work the staff always had a get together at a local pub/eatery. I went along but didn't stay too late. It was opportune for me because I met two of the "work at home" guys and they gave me some tips on setting up my home office. They also told me they felt like they were still part of Greg's team even though they didn't come into the main office every day.

When I got home, I packed two bags. One was for clothes and the other smaller one for notebooks, hand-held tape recorder, books, CDS, and some snacks. As I packed my clothes, I patted myself on the back for having over fifty under-shorts. However, forty of the fifty were rammed in my dirty clothes hamper, with all my other dirty clothes. I guess I should do some laundry soon. Good thing I have once per week dry-cleaning for my dress shirts and suits.

My car was full of gas, and I was really looking forward to my next great adventure, off to rustic rural Michigan.

As I drifted off to sleep, I could hear the voice of my dear departed mother speaking to me "Early to Bed and Early to Rise makes a man healthy, wealthy and wise."

CHAPTER EIGHT

THE SECRET ROOMS

It was approaching 6 AM Friday morning and I was driving my car down to diner. As I drove past the parking garage on Bishop I started looking for the spot to turn left and go down the alley behind the diner. I made the turn and as I slowly drove down the alley I noticed a lovely garden plot behind the building that was beside the diner. The garden was protected with a wrought-iron fence, which I assumed was to keep out two-legged or four-legged pests. I could see some very bushy shrubs and trellises and couldn't help thinking that the garden must look lovely in the summer. I also saw two basement windows in the diner that faced the garden. There was a light on in the basement.

During the car ride to the diner I was rehearsing my "Weird is good, I am open for anything" line to use on Adam if the opportunity ever arose. There were a couple of parking spots behind the diner, and I pulled into one. I started to wonder if I was supposed to knock on the back door of the diner or take the last part of my walking route from Bishop and up to Lester to go in the front door. I decided to knock on the back door. Just as I got out of the car the back door opened and I saw Adam smiling and waving me to come in. I smiled at the thought of Adam making porridge. As Adam escorted me through the rear entrance, I could see the kitchen straight ahead, and to my right was a stairway down into the basement. We exchanged pleasant good mornings. Being a conservationist and concerned about wasting electricity, Imentioned to Adam that he should tell the folks in the diner that someone had accidentally left the lights on downstairs.

"Oh yes, I know Ted. I turned them on; I am doing some work done there. Come on down, or would you like a coffee first?"

"No, thanks but I'll skip the coffee this morning Adam. Geez, you run around here like you own the place."

He quickly answered in a matter of fact voice, "I do Ted. Or I guess I own the place indirectly. I own a company that owns the building. I more or less own half the diner business as well. The employees own the other half."

I was surprised when I shouldn't have been surprised, but I managed to deliver one of my silly one-liners. "Oh... well I guess that explains your attachment to this place and why it is open 24 hours, so you can get your porridge at any time of the day or night."I had a big silly grin on my face. Adam was shaking his head, but he was smiling.

"Come on downstairs Ted, I want to show you something."

As we were walking down the stairs, a question came to mind, an inconsistency with something Adam said early in the week. "I thought you were a free spirit Adam, everything in two suitcases living out of hotels."

"I am."

He said no more as we walked downstairs into the basement. I was surprised at how high the ceiling was in the basement, about eight to nine feet. I was expecting to duck my head when I got to the bottom of the stairs. Adam was quickly walking through the first section of the basement where it looked like they kept all the supplies for the diner. I could also see some freezers, refrigerators and an old cooking range. We walked to a doorway which opened into a larger room, and Adam turned on the light. I was casually wondering where the light I saw outside was located. This room had a table and chairs and shelves all around with an assortment of who knows what on them, stuff most people would keep in basements of their houses. I saw some camping gear and some tools on a small bench. In my quick look around, I saw no windows. I could remember vividly seeing windows facing the garden on the outside, but they weren't in this room. The south wall of the basement was solid.

"Where are the windows?" I asked somewhat incredulously.

"In the other room."

"But I didn't see any windows coming through the other part of the basement, and I could swear that there are windows on the end wall and corner wall of the basement of the diner."

"There are."

My logical brain that likes to solve puzzles was taking over my Consciousness. "Perhaps you get into that area by coming down other stairs from the upstairs, or maybe from the antique shop next door to the diner?"

"No"

I pointed to the end wall. "I am baffled Adam. That wall looks like the end wall of the basement...but there are no windows to the outside?" I was suddenly hit with an idea, the benefit or the curse of someone who watches a lot of movies. "Maybe this is like the movie Panic Room where Jodie Foster figures out there is a secret room built by the old guy who owned the house before her." My ego was smirking at its brilliance, and my voice and demeanor carried boyish enthusiasm.

"Good deductions Dr. Holmes", Adam smiled, he was enjoying this little game. "I guess I could make you guess how to open up the secret passage way, but we have a long drive ahead of us today, so I am not going to take time do that. Ted, I have always liked all those movies with the secret passageways and the hidden rooms, you know the ones where you tip a book on a shelf and the fireplace swings around to show an opening. There are lots and lots of those movies, but at this moment I can't remember the name of one. Anyway, I had this dream of making my own secret room, and I did that. Follow me."

"This is really cool Adam." I was genuinely enjoying myself; I had the same fantasy and liked those movies with the secret rooms and passageways, especially in castles or large old mansions.

Adam walked over to a floor to ceiling set of shelves in the middle of the end wall, pushed one side of the shelving unit and the shelves and middle section rotated ninety degrees, leaving 2 foot gaps on either side. It was dark on the other side of the shelves. Adam stepped through first and turned on a light. First thing I noticed that this small room had no windows and it was weirdly shaped, with six sides, like a honeycomb cell. The far three short walls each had a wood door. I looked around in amazement. One door to my right, one straight ahead and one to my left. On a fourth angled wall to my right was a small oak roll-top desk and chair. At the fifth angled wall section on my left was a small table, with a three-ringed ornament of some kind on it. The sixth wall was behind us, the turning bookcase, and the way we came in. When Adam pushed the rotating shelves back to their normal position, I saw a strange looking painting on the wall section. A six-walled room, this was really incredible. Still no windows, I was now guessing the windows were behind door number three, but Adam was full of surprises, and I wasn't going to bet my paycheck on that speculation.

"Ted do you remember anything I told you yesterday morning in the diner."

"I sure do Adam. Weird is Good. I am completely open-minded. I will not be judgmental. Boy, I would like to see where this is going." I was excited, this was fun. Adam was smiling, he was happy to see me enjoying myself.

"Well I am glad you are completely open. This area of the basement is my metaphor on my Life's work in Metaphysics. I have brought you here to give you a powerful overview of the three areas I have dedicated 80% of my time for the last fifty years. We won't come here again until **I feel** you are ready. If you get freaked out and decide to leave and not come back, you are open to do so at any time." He glanced at me to gauge my reaction. I maintained my smile and nodded for him to continue. I did have a quick thought on the possibility of Adam being an axe murderer, but quickly discarded it. "Okay Ted, let me start the tour. The room we are standing in I call my Borromean Rings Room. It is the room where everything comes together for me. My Life's work is focused on learning all I can about physical form, the mind and the etheric. We will discuss this more in the car, but my theory of All includes the three facets I just mentioned working in harmony. At the joining point where all three elements work together is a node of the powerful force that can manifest any or all desires. I call this nodal point Quintessence. As we turn to face the three doors, I will tell you that door one leads to my exploration of Mind and Consciousness. Door two leads to my exploration of all things physical – Matter, the Earth, the Cosmos and our own human bodies. Door three leads to my exploration of all things Spiritual, etheric or mystical. Do you want to take a peak at any of these rooms?"

I was completely confused. I was not sure what to think, but my curiosity was peaking. It was also time for one of my patented one-liners. "I sure do Adam, but first can you tell me if there are any dead bodies or body parts in the room where you explore the human body?" I was visualizing scenes from the movie *Young Frankenstein* starring Gene Wilder.

Adam broke out into a smiling laugh, "No Ted, no body parts behind door number two. I should probably modify my introduction to the rooms. You are the second person to ask me that same question."

I stood looking at the three closed doors, trying to think of the name of the old TV game show where the contestant found out their prize by selecting Door number one, two or three. I felt goose-bumps of excitement and couldn't wait to proceed.

CHAPTER NINE

THE FIRST ROOM

Adam ended the suspense for me and opened the wooden door to our left. Just inside he flicked on the light switch and I was overwhelmed with amazement in what my eyes were taking in all at once. In looking around Room One, it felt like I was in a library combined with the huge office of an eccentric professor. There were shelves and shelves of books. On the right hand side of the room, there was a library aisle, books on shelves floor to ceiling on each side of the aisle. Against the east wall were four desks. I assumed that Lester Street was on the outside and the front street-side of the diner was directly upstairs. Each desk had a chair. Each desktop was meticulous with only one folder sitting on each desk-top, plus a small holder for pens and pencils, and a small desk lamp on each desk. At the end south wall was a table and a computer with two printers. There were a couple of whiteboards with drawings and printing on them, much like classroom black-boards. The room was huge and there was very little unused space. I also saw a TV monitor and both a DVD and Video player. Close by there was a wood stand with hundreds of CD's/DVD's, videocassettes and audiocassettes.

"There is not much room in here for conducting classes Adam."

"I don't have classes."

"How many people help you with research?"

"None."

"I was looking at the four desks and the whiteboard and could not help but think that you have people coming in to use them for study, research or work."

"No Ted, those are my desks." He saw my bewildered look and continued. "This room is my study area. There is so much material to explore in my various interests that I help organize myself and bring order to some of the chaos of my thought stream by having four desks. When I am researching History/Philosophy/Religion I sit in the first desk. For the study of all areas of Science, I use the second desk. If I am exploring material on the Human Psyche or Consciousness I use the third desk. The fourth desk is for everything else. In each folder, I keep my notes on my last work efforts and have listed questions that require further exploration."

"Wow. I have never seen anything like this. How many people have been in here?"

"You are the seventh person that has been here in the last twenty years. Most people are not ready to talk to me about my work. I feel that you are."

I had this huge urge and impulse to explore everything in the room, but I was containing myself. I was not sure whether it was politeness, respect for Adam or the fact I didn't want to become immersed in this room and create a delay in leaving on our trip. Adam sensed my dilemma.

"Ted, we may come back here another day, I don't know when at this point. If we do, I will allow you to ramble around here to your heart's content."

"Thanks Adam. This room is incredulous. I know we don't have much time, but can I ask you a couple of questions?"

"Sure Ted. We have time. We will be driving in the opposite direction of the rush-hour traffic coming into the city."

"The first thing that strikes me is on your white board. You have a big drawing of a matrix or quadrant. There are lots of written notes and arrows. Right beside it on the board is a diagram of three inter-locking circles. Each circle is a different color. What does it mean?"

Adam glanced at the whiteboard I was looking at and smiled. "It means everything Ted." He paused before continuing.

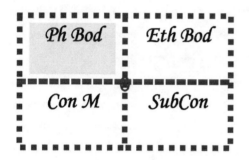

Diagram One
Adam's Quadrant

"Ted, take a look at the Quadrant first. There are five parts of the diagram, four boxes and a little gold circle in the center. These five parts make up all that is you or me or for that matter any human form. I use this diagram when I am contemplating how I can make transformations in myself or the events or circumstances that make up my daily reality. You are not ready at this stage to hear the process I use to orchestrate transformation and manifestation, but let me at least tell you what makes up the five components. Easy part first, take a look at the two boxes on the left. Many people feel these two boxes represent the only aspects that make up a human being. The top box on the left represents the Physical Body. The lower box on the left represents the Conscious Mind. These two boxes together represent our *physical form and reality.* If you are happy with your lot in life, and the circumstances we have in the world today we can stop here. If you are not happy with the current reality but don't want to get involved with changing the circumstances that make up your present reality, we can stop here. If you want to improve yourself, and your reality, and even on a grander scale the state of our world, we need to look at the other three pieces of our diagram." Adam looked at me to see if I was following his description. I nodded my head and smiled for him to continue, even though I was completely puzzled as to how little old insignificant me could ever change the world. I was anxious however to hear any advice whatever on how my personal circumstances could be improved.

"Just as the two boxes on the left represent the Physical, the two matching boxes on the right represent the **Metaphysical.** The lower right box represents the Subconscious Mind. I can speak for days about the power of the Subconscious Mind, but let me tell you the one thing you need to know in the present moment. The Subconscious Mind goes far beyond being a sub-set of the human mind, and being the part of your brain that quietly runs the physiological systems of your body and feeds images known as dreams to you while you sleep. The Subconscious Mind connects to All. The top right box represents your Etheric Body. Let's just at this moment describe it in two ways. First, it is Life force. It is that invisible field of energy that brings life to your Physical Body, Eastern religions will call it Prana or Chi. Second, the Etheric Body has a subtle physical form making it a 'body', it is comprised of a field of sub-atomic particles that match every atom, molecule and cell in your physical body. It is a template for your physical body, it has electromagnetic energy, but it is so light that its form is floating. The Etheric body extends beyond your Physical body, and it can also move away from your physical body. Just by looking at your face Ted I know I am starting to lose you in these descriptions, but I promise to come back to them later in our journey. The Quintessential little circle that sits at the intersection point of the four boxes has a host of names, but essentially it is a Divine presence, a spark of God that resides within you. Most of the time I call the Divine Presence my 'Higher Self'.

He stopped for a moment when he saw my face shift into a deeper stage of bewilderment. "Now I see that I have reached your saturation point of understanding for the present. So we will come back to this later as well."

Adam was right, I was over-whelmed and confused. Good advise to come back to this later.

"I am dazzled at this point, so I hesitate to ask for another explanation of one of your diagrams. But what is the three circle diagram?"

Adam picked up a marker and printed some letters on the circles.

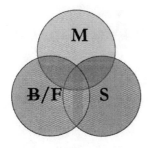

Diagram Two
Adam's Rings

"Hey Adam, I think I get this one. I have seen enough advertising on this stuff from Yoga classes to Health Clubs. Body, Mind, Spirit. But, you have crossed out the 'B' and put an F in its place for some reason.. Am I right about the Body, Mind, and Spirit?"

"Yes Ted, I put the B for Body on the diagram so you could contemplate the inter connections of Body, Mind and Spirit. Understanding inter-connections is mandatory to help me use this metaphor to explain the transformational powers of metaphysical energy. The letter M represents Mind but more appropriately Consciousness, the letter S represents Spirit, and the letter F represents Form. Form can be Body, if you are talking about a person. If you are talking about Physics it can represent matter. If you are talking about atoms it can be the proton, neutron, electron or even a subatomic particle – quark, meson, boson, whatever, including a photon observed in a particle state versus its dual existence as a waveform.

When we study a specific individual, we intuitively know the three circles of the individual's Body, Mind, and Spirit, are inter-connected and exist together. However, what we don't realize is that each one of the three spheres has dominance over one of the other spheres, and the domination tendency is circular. The best way for me to explain this, is that circular domination is like the game of rock, paper, scissors that two people can play with their hands. Have you played this before?"

"Ahhh, yes I have. You want to play now?"

It seemed like a weird way to change the topic, but I love games. In any case, Adam's explanation was confusing the hell out of me, and it would be nice to have a distraction. Rock, paper, scissors. I hadn't played this game in years, but I at least caught on to the circular domination analogy – position one, clenched fist (imitating a rock) dominates hand position two, a separated fore-finger & middle finger imitating scissors. The domination theory here is that rock can smash the scissors to pieces. Position three, the completely open hand (paper) dominates the clenched fist (rock); the theory being the paper can cover the rock and make it unseen. But paper is subject to domination by the scissors, as the scissors can cut it to pieces. The circular domination, each hand position dominates one other, but also is subservient to one other hand position.

Adam stood close and faced me. "I am only using the game analogy to make a point about the important relation-ship between body, mind and spirit. But yes, let's play now. Are you ready? Okay, count to three and see what position we leave our hand.....Here we go - one, two three."

We counted together – "one, two, three" as we waved our forearms up and down with clenched fists. On the count of three I left my fist clenched. Adam's hand was open.

He spoke "I win and dominate - I am paper, I cover your rock, this is Spirit dominating Body. Spirit dominates body because Spirit is eternal and Body is temporal. Ready to go again? One, two, three."

This time I extended my hand fully in an open position, Adam had an open hand with a gap between the forefinger and middle finger, geez, scissors, he wins again.

Adam continued with his Body, Mind, and Spirit analogy. "I win and dominate – I am scissors, I cut your paper. This is Mind dominating Spirit. Mind can dominate Spirit because only the conscious mind can make the decision or choice to ignore the existence or presence of Creator/God. Since the thoughts of the Mind can completely ignore Spirit, hence the domination. Let's go again, one two, three."

I can't believe that I was dopey and made a scissors configuration with my fingers, and Adam sure enough had his fist clenched representing rock.

He spoke again, calmly and gently, which is not my style in a fierce competition. I like the 'in your face' trash talking to my opponent when I am winning a game and I really hate it when I lose.

"I win and dominate. Rock is Body, dominating Mind. Body has various ways to dominate Mind. As an example body hormones are released to create urges that take over the mind– such as hunger, anger, fear or even the need for sex. Another example, a tired Body can shut-down the Mind for sleep. Or the best example, a sick Body will cause the Mind's thoughts to become pre-occupied with the illness. Body tends to dominate Mind."

I stopped for a second, and put my right hand on my head, maybe a sign of an on-coming headache.

"I am sorry Adam, I understand your analogy of slight dominance Body over Mind, Mind over Spirit and Spirit over Body and the rock, paper, scissors circular domination theme is useful to illustrate it. But so what? What does it mean? I can't see any big picture or purpose for the explanation." I felt myself on the borderline of getting angry, probably because of the emotional sting of getting my ass kicked at rock, paper, scissors.

Adam was smiling. "You still have some lessons to go through before you understand the big picture. But let me show you the amazing secret as it relates to humans and making meaningful changes in their lives. But we have to play the game again. Are you up for it?"

I started to smile, I don't know if everybody in their heart of hearts likes to play games, but I sure do. "Okay Adam, lets do it again." I raised my arm to get ready for the three-count.

"One, two, three." My fingers were in the scissors position and Adam's hand was a fist for the rock symbol. This was not a good start for my highly competitive self. Adam looked at our hands for a moment before he began to speak, "When we desire real change, we will not let rock dominate scissors. Body will not dominate Mind. The Mind is in place to help keep the body healthy or to heal the Body. Mind with its thoughts, provides direction for Body to heal itself, Mind through conscious prayer, enlists Spirit to also help Body heal itself. Mind refuses to be dominated with the carnal urges of Body. You win Ted, let's try again." Before, I could protest that Adam had made a mistake on the rules; Adam raised his hand to start another three-count. "One, two, three"

My hand was open, Adam had the scissor position. My instantaneous thought was about losing again. "Your open hand is Paper which represents Spirit and is freely open for the domination by the human's Mind represented by scissors. Mind has the power of free will giving it the opportunity to ignore Spirit. However, we can also use our free will to let Mind make the choice of surrendering to Spirit. Mind recognizes and accepts that Spirit is the Source of all that is good in our life and in our world. The Mind recognizes that Consciousness is not separate from Spirit but is in fact a part of Spirit. You win again Ted, even though you thought you lost." He raised his arm to begin the next three count.

"One, two, three." My competitive urge was to go with Scissors again because I was sure that Adam was going with an open hand. Sure enough, Adam had his hand open, but mine was clenched in a fist. How did that happen? In the pure context of the game, I had lost another three in a row. But Adam was making me feel like a winner.

"Ted, my open hand represents eternal Spirit that has the Power of All, but it smiles on the temporary existence of Body, a temporary form and an idea to be explored by the Divine Consciousness Mind. Spirit has no desire whatever to dominate Body. Spirit silently yet lovingly and compassionately observes the feelings of Body and records the memories of feelings and emotions as Body goes through a time cycle of experiences called *Life*. There you go Ted; you win three in a row."

As a Rock, Scissors, Paper professional, I knew in fact that I had played six games and lost six games. Adam just played his Body, Mind, Spirit analogy with two different versions of domination. I was trying to sort out my lesson learned, if there was a lesson to be learned when …

Adam shocked me with a quick change of topic. "Do you want to see the other rooms, or should we getting going on our trip?"

There was no way I was going to miss out on this chance to see what was behind the closed doors. I had no idea how long our drive to Michigan was going to take, but I had to see the other rooms.

"I would love to see the other rooms Adam. Forget the Body, Mind, Spirit analogy, do you always win the rock, paper, scissors game?"

Adam was laughing and he always seemed to pick up my vibes. He surprised me and threw me into a small howl of laugher with "Oh… I perceive in your ideal world the victor always rubs it in – so, let me try my trash-talk routine on you,. Yeah sucka, I'll beat ya every time…..no matter what the game, bring it on baby, let's see what ya got…."

I couldn't believe this guy was eighty-seven years old.

CHAPTER TEN

THE SECOND ROOM

Adam was still chuckling when he shut off the light in Room One and we boogied back into the six walled Borromean Room to open the wooden door for Room Number Two. We stepped into Room Two, the Room representing Matter and Body. He turned on the light and two words hit my Consciousness immediately. They are precious words and I rarely use them, but this was a special occasion. The impact of the room was so dramatic I said the two words out loud.

"Holy Shit!"

Adam had heard this expression before I am sure; he just smiled as I surveyed the room. The first room – Mind and Consciousness – was almost predictable – books, books and you guessed it, more books. But this Room! There was too much to take in all at once.Fortunately, no dead bodies or Frankenstein like monsters lying on a table which was my first mental image when Adam was giving his earlier description of the room for the study of the body. I have always found that when dealing with complexity, the best approach is to take the whole and slice it into small pieces for assessment, call it the "salami technique".

I surveyed the back left corner first; it looked like a mini-health club, treadmill, Nautilus equipment, and some free weights. I saw a big cushy chair with a small table, ideal in my case, for helping to recuperate after killing myself in the mini-gym. Beside the chair was a huge contraption on a stand. I couldn't figure it out, it looked a little bit like a hair dryer stand you would see in a fancy hair dressing salon, (not that I have seen one personally, every hair place I go to uses hand dryers), but a salon you would see in old movies, the movies that have scenes with ladies hair in curlers sitting and reading magazines or chatting with each other. The machine wasn't for drying hair; it had loose wires and probes hanging from it. My eyes continued to survey the room. I saw a counter with all kinds of plants growing in pots and cartons, fluorescent lights over top of them. I had a second look at the plants to see if there was potential trouble here. Maybe this was a secret "grow-op". Fortunately, no trouble, most of the small green vegetation under the lights looked like lawn grass. In the next segment of my visual scan, I focused on the small kitchenette with a juicer on the counter. I couldn't help but wonder why this was necessary, as Adam could easier go upstairs to the diner for food. The back wall had all kinds of charts and maps and cork bulletin boards. A world map, a diagram of stars and constellations, an anatomy chart, another picture of a human body with what looked like different colored lights on selected areas of the body and another detailed body picture with lines all over it. The bulletin board looked like one found in a chemistry lab, pictures of atomic structures, a periodic table and all kinds of diagrams. The far right corner of the room looked like an actual Chemistry laboratory. There was a lab bench with a Bunsen burner, glass tubing, some kind of oven, filters, test tubes, beakers and all that stuff. Along the wall to my right was a long bench with all kinds of wires and small motors, and circuit boards and electronic apparatus. In the middle of the room was a wood table with a couple of wood kitchen chairs. On the table was this metal container with wires and metal struts and colored little rocks or gemstones in different parts of the apparatus. The machine was about the size of a microwave oven. My first thought was, I won't be able to fit into it if it was Adam's time machine.

Adam spoke as soon as he saw my eyes complete their second full survey of the room, "I am guessing by your exclamation that you are somewhat surprised in looking at my research projects on energy."

"Yes, a little surprised Adam. There is a lot to take in when you enter this room. Energy? I thought this room was dedicated to Matter, Body, Planets and all things Physical?"

"All Matter is Energy Ted. Matter is only a dense form of Energy. Remember Einstein's $E=Mc^2$? This equation offers one of the first scientific postulations that Matter and Energy are inter-changeable, although the ancient Greek philosophers already knew that.Come over and have a look at my Alchemy corner."

"Alchemy?" I was puzzled once again.

"Yeah, I had a hobby a few years ago with exploring ways of converting different forms of matter into other forms of matter. You know the old story of the Alchemist who could turn lead into gold. I played around with it, but all the fumes made me nervous, so I don't bother with it much anymore. My primary interest these days is non-physical energy."

"Non-physical energy?"

"Again, I can't go into a lot of explanation here and now, I have studied non-physical energy for decades when I studied far-eastern mysticism, but I have had renewed interest since many of the world's best and brightest physicists have started publishing research efforts on sub atomic particles, string theories and such. I think science is finally catching up to the lessons taught 3,000 years ago by Eastern Mystics. We'll talk more this week-end on non-physical energy. You will learn some stuff from Lyncttc."

"I didn't know you had a degree in Science Adam."

"I don't."

"What is your education?"

"By education, do you mean schooling or my Life studies?"

"School."

"Hmmm....I left school in the equivalent of Grade nine. I had to. Fortunately, the lack of schooling opened up new doors for educating myself. However, I would never recommend to any young person to leave school early like I did. I had no choice in 1930, I had to help bring in money to support my mother." Adam was playing with a hunk of metal that was lying on his bench in the lab area. "Hold this Ted."

"Geez, it is heavy for its size, what is it?"

Adam reached into a drawer and pulled out another piece of metal, roughly the same size but shiny and golden. I had the dull metal piece in my right hand and he placed the golden piece in my left hand. "You have an atomic structure that has formed molecules that have been aggregated into a piece of lead in your right hand. In your left hand is the same matter but the atomic structure has been adjusted ever so slightly, making the piece in your left hand a metal we call gold."

My eyes were popping out, "But it weighs about a pound, it must be worth a small fortune!"

Adam calmly took the metal pieces back from me and threw them casually into the drawer.

"Value is relative", is all he said.

"You have the ability to turn lead into gold?" I was astounded, this was approaching the level of unbelievable. He looked at me calmly, "I have been blessed with obtaining the knowledge and developing the skills to facilitate the transformation of matter into its true highest value. My biggest project in this regard, is myself, as it will be for you, if and when you adopt the teachings I will guide you to."

"Well Adam this room is incredible, a combination of personal fitness center, NASA laboratory plus three times the number of electronic components that you would find in any Radio Shack. I guess I am only seeing a small part of your research, if most of your work these days is with invisible energy."

I knew the last comment would brighten Adam's smile. It did.

He put his hand on my left shoulder. "Well Ted, so you want to see what is behind Door number three? This must remind you of that game-show, *Let's make a Deal*, with your game-show host, Monty Hall"

We both laughed as we left the room.

CHAPTER ELEVEN

THE THIRD ROOM

We left Room Number two, I was now thinking of it as the Energy Room, and we moved on to the third wooden door. One thing I noticed in all the downstairs area, and it struck me as being unusual, was there was no evidence of a phone. I had a hunch we would not find a phone in the Spiritual Room unless it was a direct connection line to the Almighty, upstairs. And I wasn't thinking of Gerry in the kitchen. There was no need to turn on a light when we entered the room. There was a strange looking apparatus in the far right corner emitting light and there was some natural light now coming in through the windows, two windows on the back wall and one on the side-wall to my right back in the corner.I could see the bushes and shrubs in the outside garden, but what was amazing to me was the garden inside the third room. The lighting apparatus was providing a form of gentle soft light to the garden inside. There were rocks and soil. A small stone retaining wall kept the earth and water from spilling onto the main floor. There was a very beautiful Persian carpet in the center of the room. The floor was hardwood; I found this to be very unusual for a basement floor in an old building. In the opposite corner to the garden on the back wall was a wood cabinet that looked like an altar. The altar had candles and an incense holder on top, plus some ornaments. To my immediate left was a big cushy chair facing the back wall garden area. A sofa was on the wall area next to the chair. The sofa didn't look cushy, it looked to be made of leather, and I could visualize myself lying on it, eyes closed, speaking to my psychiatrist. On the right wall was floor to ceiling oak bookcases. There were only a few books, most of the shelves had an assortment of different colored stones, hundreds of them all shapes and sizes and colors including several clear ones.I saw a small stereo near the oak shelves, and as I glanced back at the garden I could see a waterfall in the garden, the flowers looked like orchids. Very cool. What struck me most about the room was the quiet atmosphere. In the other rooms, I was excited and energized at what I was viewing in the rooms. However, in this room, the dominant energy was a feeling of calmness and peace.

Adam wasn't looking at me as I surveyed the room. When I turned to speak to him, I saw him standing head bowed, eyes closed, hands together in front of a very nice painting. There were some other paintings and artifacts on the wall that was opposite the oak shelves. I was looking at some of the pretty stones when Adam spoke to me.

"Do you like my crystal collection Ted?"

"Oh, I haven't seen it, where is it?" I was visualizing some very cool Waterford glasses, goblets and maybe a tea set.

"You are looking at it."

"What, these pretty stones?"

"Yes. Those pretty stones are crystallized treasures made with loving care by Mother Earth."

"Yeah they are very nice. You have quite a variety here."

"It is a life long passion of mine. Let me show you the very first crystal I found when I was a young boy, probably eight years old."He walked down to the end of the oak shelves and picked up a large hexagonal clear stone.

"That looks like glass", I remarked.

"It is clear quartz crystal. It is a treasure from my birth-place."

That was an opening for me to learn another tidbit about this very interesting man."Where were you born Adam?"

"I was born in a small village on the northwest coast of Madagascar." He was smiling and his eyes turned as he probably was visualizing his old home.

Now, I felt I was whacked with another surprise. If Adam had told me to sit me down five minutes ago on that nice sofa and asked me to guess which country he was born in circa 1917, I could have guessed probably fifty different names of countries, but Madagascar would not be one of them.

I really didn't know what to say next, not that my mind was a blank, it was the opposite. I had over one hundred questions I wanted to ask, my conscious mind couldn't pick which question to ask first. I looked at Adam. "I guess we won't have any trouble finding stuff to talk about in the car ride to Michigan."

Adam smiled, "Thanks for the reminder. We better get going. My bags are on the other side of the secret passage way."

We turned in silence, closed the door to Room Three, walked through the Borromean Room, re-opened our secret entrance, and squeezed through the two foot opening. Adam picked up two leather bags in the storage area, and we headed up the stairs.

I knew this was going to be a really interesting trip.

CHAPTER TWELVE

ADAM'S LIFE STORY

By the time we packed the car, had bio breaks and grabbed a coffee for me and a tea for Adam, it was 7:45 AM. Not bad. We made small talk in the car for a few minutes and when I managed to get the car into an express lane, my city driving nerves had settled down.Adam didn't say much, he was actively gazing at the passing city scenery. He held a small journal with notes in it, and mentioned he had directions to Gary and Lynette's farm in it and their phone number. I had a chance to run a Mapquest travel directions for as far as Saginaw, because that was the closest city I knew in the vague outline that Adam had given as to where we were going. Adam told me that I was responsible for finding my way to Saginaw and then he would give me directions for the balance of the journey.

I didn't need to get my travel bearings, but I was longing to get bearings on my interesting travel companion. "Well Adam, living in Toronto sure is a long way from Madagascar."

"I don't live in Toronto Ted."

"Well I guess with that lay-out in the basement at the diner, I was assuming Toronto was your home."

"The diner is a nice port for me in my worldly travels. A place to keep a lot of my possessions, and a place to re-orient myself before taking off on another great adventure. I have spent lots of time there in the past doing research. But it has recently occurred to me that perhaps I should spend more time in active investigation of the secrets I have found. Now, at eighty-seven years of age, I probably only have another active thirty years, and then I will have to slow down a little." A smile was creeping on to Adam's face. "At least one Life Amazing Secret, on how to live a long, youthful life is working for me."

"It sure is Adam. You are definitely younger than your chronological age. Adam, if you don't mind, could you tell me about yourself, where you grew up, a short synopsis of what you've done and a little detail on events leading up to the present moment?"

"Are you going to write my biography Ted?" he turned to me with a smile.

"Well Adam I used to enjoy writing short stories years and years ago. But I don't think I have the time or inclination to write your biography, I am just interested in hearing Your Story."

"Well give me a moment to gather my thoughts together, do you want the five to ten minute version or the six to eight hour version?" he was still smiling.

"While I know you are a master Adam, and you have probably lived your Life to the fullest. I would love to see your Mastery in giving me the five to ten minute story." my turn to smile, but I was regretting my choice, I probably would really enjoy the six to eight hour version.

"Do you promise not to interrupt with questions?" he was getting to know me very well.

"I promise."

"Okay, the best way to tell a story is to begin at the beginning, now I must decide which beginning to select. My Mother and Father never told me on what night and where they had intercourse resulting in my conception as one of the outcomes. Hmmm...I will start this Life Story with some family history. My father's father was from Italy and he was a stone mason. He moved his family to Switzerland and then to France as he worked on jobs building Cathedrals. My grandfather had some exceptional stone masonry skills which were valuable in the construction of Cathedrals. My father attempted to learn the trade but was not as gifted as grandfather. My father met my mother in Lyon France. My Mother's family were shopkeepers. My father was twenty and my mother seventeen when they married. At that time, my father was frustrated in his endeavors to become a skilled stone mason. A life event point came when the group of workers led by my grandfather were building a Cathedral in Nice. One of the major benefactors who gave money to the Church to build the Cathedral in his city was touring the site and had casually asked the workers if any of them would be interested in working on a plantation he owned in Madagascar. My father signed up over the objections of his father. In 1912, my parents traveled afar to the plantation which was near the town of Majunga on the Northwest coast of Madagascar. This was a sisal plantation. Sisal is a jute like plant with long fibers and was ideal for making rope; it is also used for making rugs. There were about ten families from France who lived on the plantation, and there were over 100 Malagasy native workers, mostly Sakalava aboriginals. Madagascar was a colony of France and the French army maintained a small garrison in Majunga. My sister Helene was born in 1914 and I was born on January 28, 1917.

I can't remember much from my early years. I do remember Dr. Lavoie who lived on the plantation with us. Dr. Lavoie was a cousin of the plantation owner. He was a medical doctor but his passions were botany and geology. He had no family, and his primary reason for being there was to explore the unique animal habitats and vegetation of Madagascar. He would often take trips in the summer, after the monsoon season, and be gone for months. I do remember wandering around the plantation a lot, going to the beach on my own, and exploring. My mother and father did not seem to mind me doing this; I was eight years old when I started wandering. My mother warned me to not go in the jungle, there are tigers (not true), and don't go in the water, there are sharks (also not true). There was no school, my mother would spend some time teaching us how to read and write, and that was all. I spent a lot of time at Dr. Lavoie's little house. He had all kinds of books and I used to enjoy looking at the big books with pictures of plants and animals. Dr. Lavoie seemed to enjoy my visits and he told me all kinds of stories. I remember a day in the summer of 1925 when I had hiked off to play near a river that was probably eight kilometers from the plantation. There had been heavy monsoon rains months earlier and lot of flooding. The flood waters had resided but there was a lot of sediment deposited on the river banks. It was here I found pocketfuls of clear quartz crystals. I liked their clarity and their shape. I remember showing them to my sister, mother and father and they didn't seem to care, and then showing them later to Dr. Lavoie who was more enthusiastic about them. Dr. Lavoie asked me to take him to the spot I found them, and we journeyed there the next day. We found some more, including some different kinds of crystals, and Dr. Lavoie was very excited. Back at his home, Dr. Lavoie told me stories about all the beautiful gemstones that Madagascar had, and that people from all over the world had come to find sapphires and other precious gems. He told me that the natives used to kill foreigners who would try to take special gems away with them. The following year, in 1926, Dr. Lavoie returned to France. In 1927 disaster struck our family. Both my father and sister and several other people living at the plantation died of some malaria like disease. My mother was ill but survived. I remember laying up at night listening to the groans and wailing throughout the plantation village. I huddled in my bed grasping my clear quartz crystal praying to God to not let me get sick and to protect my mother.

My mother and I returned to Europe on a ship that was taking sisal to Belgium. None of our family in Europe knew what had happened. The Ship's Captain had wired my mother's brother in Nice. We stayed with a crew member's family in Antwerp and received some more bad news by mail. All of our family in Nice was no longer there, everyone had moved. My mother was in great despair.She was still ill and was having trouble traveling. One day after the bad news letter came, we were overjoyed when Dr. Lavoie came to get us. He took us by train to Nice and cared for my Mother at his home. My mother recovered and we found out that her brother had emigrated to Montreal Canada. Dr. Lavoie helped us with writing letters to find my uncle and even generously paid for our voyage to Montreal. We arrived in the summer of 1929 when I was twelve years old. My uncle welcomed us with open arms, and we lived at his apartment. My uncle helped us with getting Canadian citizenship, and was our sponsor. My mother did not have a job, but my uncle told her not to worry, he would look after her and me. My uncle was a salesman. He would be home for weeks and then gone for a week, and home again for a few weeks. I found out later that my uncle was actually in a whiskey smuggling operation. He and his partners would buy whiskey from Seagram Distillery in Montreal and smuggle it into the USA which was in the days of Prohibition.

I had started to go to school in Montreal, and this was very hard for me, as I had never been to school in my whole life. Fortunately, the lessons of my mother and the teachings of Dr. Lavoie had helped me, and I was not far behind the others of my age. My mother could not seem to do much of anything. She spent most days sitting in a chair by a window. I was very much a loner, and I did not make many friends. My most interesting memory of the time was the lady who lived in the basement apartment of our building. The neighbors called her the gypsy woman, but she was always very pleasant to me. She would give tarot card readings and crystal ball readings to a variety of people who visited her. I was surprised to see that both little old ladies visit her as well as distinguished looking gentlemen in nice business suits. Her name was Madame Comtois. She was originally from Hungary, and had married a French Canadian sailor and moved to Montreal. Her husband died during World War One, and she had to make a living from her tarot card readings. Every day after school I would visit her, but only if she had no clients. My mother sat in her chair, and barely spoke to me or anyone else.

Madame Comtois would tell me wonderful stories about her home country and her work. She looked into my palm and told me I would live a fantastic long life. Her clear crystal ball amazed me and one day I decided to show her my clear quartz crystals that I brought with me from Madagascar.. When she saw them and held them, I remember her gasping for air. She was terribly excited. She repeated over and over – Lemuria, Lemuria, Lemuria. I was amazed she knew they were from Madagascar, because I thought she was referring to the lemurs, a creature that is unique to Madagascar. When I said Madagascar, not Lemuria, she had no idea where Madagascar was. She began to tell me stories about an ancient land called Lemuria; I'll save some of those for the eight-hour story of my Life. I gave Madame Comtois one of my crystals, and it was as if I gave her a million dollars, she was so grateful.

One day in January 1930, the police visited us and told us my uncle was killed in New York. I immediately quit school to find a job. It was very difficult to find work, because it was the depression. Madame Comtois referred me to a business-man client who gave me a job working at one of his warehouses at the Port. He told me that Madame Comtois helped make him a millionaire and helped him stay wealthy when he heeded her warnings to sell his stocks before the October 1929 Stock market crash. Madame Comtois had never before asked him for a favor and he wasn't going to refuse her this favor, especially since it was so easy for him to accommodate it. I worked in the office doing odd jobs for Mr. Mackenzie the

Warehouse Manager. Mr. Mackenzie was a great fellow, but he had a horrible addiction to whiskey. The best thing about my six months there was I learned to speak and write English. Mr. Mackenzie would spend a portion of every morning teaching me English, he appreciated it when I could do his paperwork for him especially by late afternoon every day when he was too drunk to write anything, coherently at least.

I came home from work late one day in December 1930, a few days before Christmas and found my mother dead sitting in her chair. Madame Comtois helped me overcome the grief of my loss. Her businessman client answered her favor number two by paying for my mother's funeral.He then told me that good luck comes in three's and asked me what he could do for me to fulfill favor number three. I couldn't fathom my mother's death and funeral as having anything to do with good luck, but I managed enough boldness to ask the gentleman, if I could work on one of his steamships so I could travel the world.

For the next eight years, until 1939, I worked as a Ship's Engineer helper on different steamships owned by the businessman. I got to see many, many different places and got the best education in the world from my crusty old boss, Angus McLellan, a dour old Scotsman who was a Boiler Engineer. In the first few months of working for Angus he was really tough on me, but then he got to liking me when he noticed me looking at one of his books written by James Clerk Maxwell. His words still ring in my ear – 'do ya know anything about Physics laddie? If ya don't, ya cannee do any better than reading the work of James Clerk Maxwell, the most brilliant man in history, and I am proud to say, a Scotsman.' Angus loved

Physics, Mathematics and technology. Once I learned to sing the praises of any Scottish scientist or inventor, he would open the doors of Knowledge to me. He thought I was Italian with my last name, and confided in me that he quietly respected Italian Scientists especially da Vinci and Galileo. Angus was absolutely brilliant, he was self-taught and had uncanny technical skills as well as being an inventor. We worked together for over eight years on ships and on shore leaves we would go to Museums or Libraries together.I have met many PhD. physicists in my travels, and I swear Angus could teach every one of them something.A brilliant man and I was blessed to have him as a teacher. In 1939, Angus retired and decided to live in Sydney, Nova Scotia. I was 22, and had saved up all kinds of money. Angus also taught me the thrift of a Scotsman. He told me if I was going to invest my money, I should put it into stocks of Bell Telephone. A great invention, the telephone, he said, and invented by a Scotsman too. Ironically, I have never personally had a phone. I put all my money into Bell Telephone stocks and then enlisted with the Canadian Navy. I spent the War in the North Atlantic. While in the Navy, I became great friends with a fellow named Simon Sparling whose father had made millions in mining. Simon had a Masters degree in Archeology.

During the war Simon's father passed away and left him a large inheritance. After the war, Simon decided to explore Peru and look for the lost city of El Dorado, discussed in Inca legend. He asked me to be his working travel companion. We spent close to three years in Peru. We never found El Dorado but we learned much about the fabulous ancient Civilization of the Inca. Simon returned home in 1950, but I spent another five years in South America on my own working for mining companies or working on my own as a prospector in Bolivia, Colombia and Brazil. My quest was gemstones and I made a small fortune in emeralds. I was looking for clear quartz crystals and kept finding purest of green, high-quality emeralds. The value of clear quartz was next to nothing, but the emeralds I found had tremendous value. In 1955 I returned to Canada. Simon was living in Toronto. He had gotten married and he and his wife, Ester, had started their family, they had a little girl, now a grown up and a beautiful lady named Sarah.

I met Simon for lunch at George's Diner on Lester Street, my first time there. That is when I fell 'in-like' with Deborah and Sandy. I say 'fell-in-like' because both of them were happily married. Deborah was my favorite waitress and Sandy was her eighteen-year-old daughter who was also a waitress in the restaurant. Deborah is Melissa's Great Grandmother and Sandy is her Grandmother. Melissa's mother, Debbie, is a homemaker. I was staying in a near-by hotel and ended up having the majority of my breakfasts or lunches at the diner. Deborah and Sandy were my teachers about extroverts and 'Joie de vivre'. Me, a loner/introvert, had encountered the two most out-going people in the world. They taught me a lot. I met their husbands, Bill and Frank, and both are outstanding guys. Christmas of 1955, when Deborah found out I had no family, and was going to hang out alone at a hotel, she absolutely insisted I come to her house for Christmas Day. I tried my absolute hardest to avoid this commitment, but it was impossible. It turned out to be one of the best days of my life. It was one of those Christmas Carol stories, although I was never as miserly as Ebenezer Scrooge.

I spent most of 1956 traveling in the United States, I found some really fantastic clear quartz crystals near Little Rock Arkansas, and I spent over three months in New Mexico studying Native cultures – the Navaho and Toltec ways of life. I returned to Toronto in March of 1957 to visit Simon and his family, and of course had to stop into George's Diner. March 3, 1957 was the only day I ever personally saw Deborah without a smile on her face. As I was eating my breakfast she stopped off to confide in me that George Kotsiopoulos, the owner was going to have to sell the diner to pay off a gambling debt. He was having trouble finding someone to buy the place and pay him what he wanted, the employees had grouped together to make an offer and were rejected by the bank. The auction was going to be Saturday, first the property and then all the diner equipment and fixtures were going to be auctioned off.

At the end of the week I found myself the owner of a building and a business. George was running an illegal Casino downstairs. It was a nice big area, and I liked the idea for storing all my possessions there. I had stuff in storage in Montreal, Little Rock and Lima Peru.I hired Deborah's husband Bill to do renovations to the upstairs and downstairs. My three rooms project wasn't done until 1990.

From 1957 to now, I have roamed the world, six continents, seventy different countries. I am a Mystic and a Scientist, a teacher and a student."

Adam finally paused. I was enthralled and wished he would continue. He looked reflective, and turned to me. I had a sense that he was going to say something profound and important. He didn't disappoint me.

"There is a Service Centre coming up shortly, can you stop so I can take a leak."

CHAPTER THIRTEEN

QUESTIONS, QUESTIONS, QUESTIONS

We each bought a plastic bottle of water from a vending machine at the rest stop. I made a call on my cell phone to the office to check on things and to make sure they had my number if they needed me. We got back in the car and resumed our journey. Adam had a small notebook and pen with him in the car.

"Ted, I would like to map out some possible lessons for you. Before doing that, I would like you to ask me some questions, any questions, and I will make some notes on the questions you ask. The questions you ask will tell me something about you. Is this okay?"

"Sure Adam. I am dying to ask you all kinds of questions."

"Okay Ted, take a few moments as you are driving to think of three to five questions you really need to ask me. I only mention this, because once you ask the first question, my answer may trigger new questions, and you will forget some of the questions you originally wanted to ask me. I also want to mention, my natural inclination is to answer a question with one word or one sentence. If I go past a one-sentence answer, I might talk for an hour. If I don't say enough, tell me. If I ramble too much in my discussion, interrupt me with another question. When ever you are comfortable, ask away."

I thought for a few moments. I have trouble keeping more than three thoughts at a time together in my mind at once, there was a lot I wanted to ask, where to begin? My head was still swirling from this morning's experience with the three rooms. "Adam, perhaps you have already answered this question, but it is not clear to me, but can you explain again the significance of the three rooms, I think of them as Body, Mind, and Spirit?

"Well, I have been ambitiously trying to distill my decades of research into a short summary. Let me try my best to give you an overview. First, understand that the universe we live in has two concurrent and inter-connected planes of existence. The first plane is our physical world. Everything that contains matter-energy, with a scope on the micro side being atoms and their basic components and on the macro side the Cosmos, which includes all the galaxies of our Universe as we know it. The second plane of existence is interwoven with the first plane, this is the non-physical world. It contains energy, but not matter, the energy in this realm is in its purest form, which is vibration. How am I doing so far?"

"Good Adam, I've got it at this point, am I right in assuming that the non-physical energy vibration you mentioned is the stuff of Quantum Physics, and all the work being done on string theory?"

"Partially Ted. The Science around finding the theory of everything, with a focus on string theory is stagnated at this point, because, I feel, that there are non-energy elements left out of the equation.Einstein when he was a patent clerk in Switzerland, in his twenties managed to get published his three brilliant theories in 1905. He spent the next fifty years trying to discover the theory of everything, the one physical and mathematical explanation and equation that explains how all physical phenomena work together. I often wondered if he finally discovered the answer before he died. On his death bed, just before he died, he quietly made a lengthy statement before he passed on. Unfortunately the only person who heard it was a nurse, and she didn't understand German."

"What do you think the missing elements are Adam?"

"Yes, back to my not so concise summary, I was distracted once again by thoughts about that brilliant man Einstein. Summary statement one, We have two inter-connected planes of existence, the physical and the non-physical realms, now for me to understand things, I need to divide this interconnected complexity into segments. There are three co-existing components that operate in both the physical and non-physical realms. The first component we have already mentioned, because it is used in my definition of what is physical and non-physical and that is Energy. The second is Consciousness and the third is Spirit. These three elements co-exist and are, most important, inter-connected, on both the physical and non-physical planes. On the physical plane, energy takes on the full gamut from the electro-magnetic spectrum to all things comprised of matter. I have spent lots of time studying that special matter that has the precious additional complexity we call life. Consciousness doesn't include physical energy, but is all awareness, knowledge, perceptions and choices. When it comes to human beings, consciousness studies expand to understanding societies and group behaviors. Sorry, need to digress a little. When you look at an individual bee, or an ant or even a termite, they are really quite unintelligent. But a group of bees, ants or termites can achieve remarkable things as a group. Unfortunately, humans, in general, are the opposite, with evidence being both wars and our apparent group death wish to destroy our biosphere which is the life support system on our planet. Back on track, the third element is Spirit, which exists on both planes. How do you Ted define Spirit?

"Oh my God."

"Good start to the definition."

"No, sorry Adam, I was just startled with your question. A bit deep for me. When I hear the word Spirit, things that come into my head are God, Angels, Ghosts, boisterous enthusiasm a la 'team spirit', and booze."

"Booze?"

"Yes, hard liquor is sometimes called spirits."

"Well Ted, that is an interesting string of definitions. For me, spirit is one thing which is Divine. Call it God-force if you like. It is supreme intelligence which is focused on fulfilling purpose, it is also all things embodied in the emotions of joy and compassion, and most important, it is love. Well Ted, I will make a note to discuss this topic of Body, Mind, and Spirit further with you, especially the concept I call the Quantum Trio". Adam wrote a note in his journal.

"Adam, have you ever been in love."

"Yes."

He stopped there. I looked over at him, with a 'come-on tell me more' look, if there is such a thing, but I knew immediately that Adam was jerking my chain.

"Ah, your second question Ted, and you are not satisfied with my one word answer. First, let me mark this in my journal. Question two, love. Okay. This gives me a hint that this might be an issue in your life Ted. Well, nothing easy to start with, love is the most complicated subject to talk about in a rational manner. Love transcends logic. Love is an almost indescribable feeling, and words cannot capture the essence of the feeling, many poets and songwriters have tried, some with success. There are different kinds of love, but there is only one special true love feeling, the one you share with a soul mate. I have been blessed to experience that kind of love. In my case, I experienced true love in 1959. I can't remember all the details, on how I found myself there, but I was in Paris at a Neurosciences Conference. I was there with a young friend of mine who was a Ph.D. student at McGill University. He didn't have the money to pay for the trip to this international Conference, so I funded the trip, providing he could get me registered to attend the conference sessions. Carl Jung was a speaker at the Conference and I really wanted to hear him speak. Jung was well into his 80's, and his work was mesmerizing for me, I had to see him, money no object. Back to the main topic, at the Conference I met this lady from Shanghai. She was a Neuroscientist. The Communist Party had allowed her to travel to the Paris Conference. She didn't speak English very well, but she spoke French, which is a wonderful language for those in love. Her name was Li Wu.

I spent the most wonderful three days of my life in Paris in October of 1959. I'll stop the answer there, because I can go on in glorious detail, the memories are etched in my mind."

"You can go on Adam. At least tell me what happened with Li Wu"

"After the Conference, we managed to share some correspondence. I mailed her at least ten letters; I have three from her. But we lost touch. I am blessed to have had her in my life for even this short time. I know both the bliss of true love, and the pain of lost love."

"Thank you for sharing Adam. I will change topics altogether. Back in your Matter Energy room, there was a strange contraption on a table. Something with rocks and wires and metal. What was that?"

Adam jotted a short note in his book as he started talking again, "Question three, Radionics machine. I will start by mentioning that the rocks and stones you mention, are crystals. Crystals are captured energy vibrations which are created by Mother Earth. The contraption is a Radionics device, and the specific crystals are quartz crystals. The Radionics machine was a project of mine from a few years ago. The machine doesn't work, I need Lynette to give me some help with it, if I can ever convince her to come and look at it. I don't want to go through the hassle of sending it across the border. Radionics is a metaphysical science of diagnosing and potentially treating disease using energy vibrations.

A new question popped into my head, "What is Metaphysics?"

"Question four, Metaphysics. Well we can go back to Aristotle. He spent some time describing his limited view of the Sciences and called this Physics, then he started describing phenomena that didn't have rational explanations, and called that Beyond Physics or Metaphysics. Aristotle's definition still applies. Metaphysics is a broad area. For me, Metaphysics is a Science and a Philosophy. It is the study of all existence, consciousness and the phase of our existence that we call reality. I love Science and the ability to explain certain phenomena using rational scientific explanations. But Science can't explain everything. For those profound questions that have no explanation at present, some people resort to the answer that has been used for thousands of years, by every culture of humankind. The unexplainable happens because it is the Will of the Gods, or in most of today's civilization it is now unified to the Will of God, or the Creator, or any other name you would like to call the Divine. Metaphysics is a broad middle ground of study between established science and Religion. Maybe, unfortunately, Metaphysics is too broad, and all kinds of esoteric, paranormal subjects are all grouped together under the Metaphysics banner. I am open to everything, but I carefully select those topics I would like to investigate further. You saw that in my three rooms. The study of Mind and Consciousness, the study of Energy and Forms of Matter and the connection to Spirit. Beyond that, is the special study of transformation, both in a physical sense, which is mostly science and a non-physical sense which is both using the power of thought and metaphysical concepts." Adam sat back in his seat, and looked over at me, seeking another question.

There seemed to be so much to learn and understand. "Adam, I don't understand, how do you sort through broad subjects, and strange concepts, and determine those that merit further discussion or study?"

Adam maintained his routine; he jotted a note in his book. "Everybody is different in this, but I admire those people who have what at first glance might seem to be weird or unconventional ideas and theories and then they spend lots of their time trying to find the facts to prove them. That's why we know the Earth is round, and it orbits the Sun, and so on and so on. Science is based on hypothesis and proving or disproving the idea of the hypothesis."

I had to interject, "What did you write in your journal?"

Adam looked down, "Question five, the Bullshit test."

I had a broad grin. "Sorry for interrupting Adam."

"No problem Ted." He was smiling as well. "I have an insatiable curiosity as I think you know by now, but I really get side-tracked a lot when I hear new or different ideas. If the idea comes from a source I don't recognize or appreciate. I stay open to the idea, but I learn more about it quickly, when my first thought or challenge is that of a skeptic and I run a small test for myself called – 'Bullshit, prove it.'

When somebody is talking to me about a metaphysical concept, particularly some of these New Age folks, you should see them jump when I calmly challenge them with 'that sounds like cow's manure, what proof do you have?". I am open to new thoughts and ideas, but my brain is bursting at the seams, and I don't have time for bullshit. I cut some slack for those people who I respect and admire, but it is still possible for even them to be spouting baloney. When I hear a new idea, my initial mental process is to categorize. One, is the new idea substantiated by fact or testing? Two, if no facts or testing, is the idea based on logical reasoning? If so, I can categorize the idea as supported by intuitive deduction. The idea doesn't have to be supported by facts, we will find these later, but it does have to feel right and sit on platform supported by some form of logic. If there is no proof or resonation with my intuition, I categorize the idea as bullshit until I hear some proof, logic or substantiation. I challenge myself all the time with – 'Bullshit Adam, prove it'.

As Adam spoke, I was relating the "bullshit, prove it' method to my personal experience in the investment business. I have found with assessing investment opportunities, there can be major issues with the assumptions you are making on investments. What you sometimes assume is a fact about a certain company or situation, is in fact, really bullshit. Some really, really smart people in the investment business make mistakes because they make the wrong assumptions. The supposed facts prove later not to be so. My ex-father in law used to say – "Bullshit baffles brains". I made a mental note to talk to Adam more about intuitive deduction.

"Adam, I would like to know what process I am going through in my time with you. What steps do you see me taking? What stuff am I going to do?"

Adam started to jot the note, looked over at me, and smiled "Question six, what is the learning how to manifest desires program and agenda for Ted Gregory?" He stopped for a moment to collect his thoughts.

"This is more a question you should be asking yourself Ted. But let me address the starting point and some of the fundamentals of our project. Item one – you asked me if I could teach you about Manifestation and how to manifest your desires. Item two – I agreed to teach you what I know on this subject, if you would agree to the expedited method versus the evolutionary method, and you agreed. Item three – pretend this is a murder mystery and you jump ahead to the final chapter to find out 'whodunit'. If we do this, I will tell you the Final Answer to your question is readily available, but the answer resides in you, and I can't read the answer.Item Four, I will teach you about different ways for **you** to find the answer that dwells within you. For that matter there is a set way of finding the answers to any questions you might have, or problems you need to resolve. Item five, the answers will not have much value to you until you understand how to implement the Manifestation process. Item Six, the metaphysical process that I will show you, deals with non-physical Energy. You need special training. The energy is not electricity but it has the same beneficial and harmful attributes. Electricity is the essential power in our modern society, but you also know you have to be very careful when you are working with electrical sources or conduits. Only trained electricians should work on electrical systems. Likewise, metaphysical energies can cause harm, to yourself and others if you are not trained properly. Item Seven, the Stage we are at now for Ted Gregory is the First Stage which is the Assessment Stage. I am trying to figure out which lessons I need to teach you and in which order. We are fortunate in that I had a pre-planned trip to make to Michigan to see Lynette and Gary. It will be a chance for you to learn more, and a chance for me to learn more about how I will help you."

My cell phone rang. It was Mark our IT guy. He was a Type A personality, and was anxious to set-up my Home Computer to handle stock trades, setting up new configurations, system access passwords etc. As I spent a few moments talking to him about when he could come to my home office to work on stuff, I glanced at Adam and saw that he had his eyes closed. Was he sleeping, resting his eyes or meditating?

After I hung up with Mark, I decided to not disturb Adam and wait until he was alert. My mind wandered off to some practical matters on "to do" items for my home office.

CHAPTER FOURTEEN

THE RADIO METAPHOR

Adam really looked like he was sleeping, his mouth was slightly open, and fortunately, he wasn't snoring or drooling. I managed to turn the volume down on the radio and searched the FM band, finally settling for some nice Classical music. My mind was wandering, going through thoughts about all that was happening to me this past week. My time with Adam fascinated me. You could probably write books about what this man has done. Maybe I will someday, when I have the free time, and after getting all my other worries looked after. My stream of thoughts was broken.

"Do you like classical music Ted?" Adam was looking at me eyes alert and fresh.

"I hope I didn't wake you", I said. He continued to look at me, with his nice smile and then a quick glance to the radio and back to me. "Oh yes, I like Classical, but I guess I like many kinds of music. Rock, Hard Rock late 60's music. I even had stages in my life where I liked Country and Western. I could almost listen to anything other than Rap. You look refreshed after your sleep."

"I am sorry for dozing off on you Ted. When you took the call on your cell phone, I thought I would close my eyes and reflect, I guess my brain waves clicked into Delta level and I slipped into a dream state or a deep meditative state. Yes, I am refreshed. I don't sleep many hours in a day, so I enjoy my rest times and naps. I love the stories about Thomas Alva Edison, and how he took naps to help him solve little problems he was having with his inventions. I encountered a story recently that Thomas Edison used to sit in a rocking chair on the porch at his farm, eyes closed and holding a quartz crystal. Edison had a huge collection of crystals which he donated to Wayne State University. I have a number of stories about Edison, he is a great man. Looking at the radio and our discussion on music has given me an idea for a Ted Gregory Lesson. It just occurred to me now. A short lesson on Energy frequencies and matching your desired energy frequency to the frequencies made available to you in the Universe. Can I give this metaphor a test run with you as my guinea pig?

"You sure can Adam. I am all ears."

"Okay let me have a look at your car radio. Can you answer a few questions for me?"

"Sure."

"That button that says Band, what is that?"

"The Band button lets me select the range of Channels, I want to listen to. Press it once, we have AM stations, press it again, we have FM stations series number one, and press it a third time, we have FM stations series number two. Those buttons one to six, I can set to my favorite stations on all three bands. Most of my favorites are getting out of range, but a few with strong signals, I am still getting." I was playing around with the buttons, as I was explaining this to Adam, he obviously did not have much experience with car radios.

Adam focused intently on the radio. "Okay, I know the Power button, I know what seek and scan are and the volume, bass, treble buttons. Yes I think my metaphor will work. Let's try it. Are you ready Ted? Feel free to challenge me or ask questions on anything, I want to see if this metaphor stands up to your scrutiny."

"Sure, go ahead Adam." I had no clue what he was talking about, but I was sure it would be interesting.

"Let me first talk about the air-waves and the radio stations. Let each station simultaneously represent a set of personal circumstances and any person's set of desires and wants, which will be a sub-set of all possible personal circumstances. Assume there are an infinite number of radio stations representing almost all combinations and permutations of personal circumstances. Now, let's proceed with the application of the metaphor. It will be fair to assume that the majority of people have an existing set of circumstances in their life that is different from their desired set of circumstances. For the blessed, fortunate and for that matter the uncaring, their personal set of circumstances matches their personal set of desires and wants. They have set the button to and are listening to their favorite radio station. However, for the majority of people, their personal circumstances in life do not match their desires and wants for the life they want to live. They are listening to a station with a set of personal circumstances that doesn't match their desires and wants. Some people realize this, but others don't. Some people don't even realize that there is a perfect radio station for them, one that actually provides them their desired reality. If they are looking for it, they haven't found it yet, assuming they know how to scan and search for it. What do those numbers represent?" He was pointing to digital station number on the face of the radio.

"Those are all the station numbers. If I want the all news radio station, it is on AM at the number 680. All talk radio is at 640. Sports at 590." I flicked on the pre-set buttons on the AM band to illustrate the changes. Then I hit the band button to go back to the classical music station.

"Are not those numbers, frequencies?" He asked.

"Why yes, but don't ask me to explain frequencies." I had a sense I was going to get a lesson in electronics.

"Energy is fundamentally a vibration. Think of a pendulum, start at one extreme, swing through to the other extreme and return to the starting point. Call that little voyage a cycle. Radio is part of the electromagnetic spectrum. The frequency measuring time period is one second. One cycle in one second is a Hertz. Instead of a pendulum, the cycle is the full up and down ripple of a wave. Whoops, I am getting sidetracked. Back to the radio. Each station is assigned a frequency at which they are allowed to use in broadcasting their sounds. The AM stations, Station 680 is 680 kilohertz frequency. 680,000 cycles per second. The FM bands have higher frequencies. This one we are listening to is 96.5 Megahertz frequency; 96.5 million cycles per second, as mega means million. Now back to the metaphor. Your current circumstances – your career, your health, your love life, your financial circumstances may be set on an AM Station. You try changing and adjusting things, but you never feel satisfied that you are achieving your heart's set of desires and needs, because they are found at 96.5 on the FM band. Some people satisfy themselves by staying on the AM band, and live out their desires through fantasies or monitoring the lives of other people who they admire. Some people are put on the AM band through circumstances of the Universe, and their job is to find their favorite AM station, they may never get a chance in this lifetime to get on the FM band. In other words, their mission is to do the best they can in the situation they have. Others manage to get on to the FM band through favorable circumstances granted by the Universe, and decide themselves to switch to the lower frequency AM band, and not look for their ultimate channel on the FM band. The ultimate channel being living a life that meets or exceeds their highest expectations on desires and needs fulfillment. How am I doing with this metaphor Ted?"

"I understand it, I think. Let me throw a few curve balls at you."

"Okay."

"Let's say, I am on the FM band, sitting at Station 91.5 as my current circumstances. But my desired circumstance – good health, more money, finding my soul mate and having a life of bliss and harmony is at station 99.9, how do I turn the dial there?"

"First if you know what you want in life is at 99.9, you are ahead of 98% of the population. Most people haven't truly defined their ideal, concrete vision of themselves with all the itsy-bitsy details added up into one big picture or vision of themselves leading the life they desire to live. Do you truly know what you want in life Ted?

"I think so."

"The phrase 'I think so' really means 'No'. You haven't de-tailed the Vision of yourself leading the life you desire to lead."

"Not specifically, I have a general idea."

"A general idea is all the stations between 95 and 102 on your radio dial. You know what you get when you start searching every possibility in that range… a lot of static. Static is a painful noise, and you may have to endure some hardships getting to 99.9, but start the search at 98.5, so you don't get much static. Plus you might fall in love with that Country and Western station at 98.5 and never reach your ultimate station, hence missing out on something, and worse, not providing all the wonderful services you can to others in need. Your ultimate channel is always a place where you provide untold benefits to others."

"Can I throw something else at you?"

"Sure."

"What if one of my desires was to play golf as well as Tiger Woods. How do I reach that channel?"

"Well, you might be on the FM band, but golf playing abilities to the Tiger Woods level might be on those wavelength bands reserved for communications with space stations. On your radio, you have no chance of reaching Tiger's station number. Interesting point though, how to go from one bandwidth to another. I may need to work on my radio metaphor some more."

"Adam, it does help me though. I sense what we are talking about in this power to manifest your true desires, is learning the ability to push the button and go from lower AM frequencies to higher FM frequencies, and then once there, the mastery of manifestation allows me to go direct to my ultimate station. I have another question for you Adam. What is your ultimate station?"

"I don't know, but it has Beatles music 24 hours a day, 7 days a week."

We both laughed.

CHAPTER FIFTEEN

ADAM'S DEFINITION OF ENERGY

I set the radio at a Classical music channel. I looked over at Adam, I saw he had pulled out his journal again, and had written the number 7. He said nothing; he seemed to be listening to the music. I spoke first.

"I guess we should get back to the questions."

"If you would like to Ted."

"Do you often make little metaphors like the one with the radio, and channel frequencies?"

"Do you want that as your Question number seven Ted?" Adam looked over at me, he appeared serious.

"Sure, it doesn't matter, you indicated that this was a session where it was an open dialogue of questions, anything goes, did you not?"

"Alright, number seven is metaphors. But I won't write down question eight as your last question about open dialogue of questions." Now I could see he was smiling again.

He continued again, I marveled at how he pulled himself together to handle any question, Adam indeed was a wise man. "Language is an interesting topic. Humankind has evolved tremendously since ancient tribes started using words, then carving symbols that represented various words into rocks or tablets, then the invention of the alphabets in each language, and inventing new words, the invention of paper made it speedier to write the words than carve them, and so on and so on. We could talk a lot about language, but the real issue is communicating thoughts and sharing the same consciousness. In fact, I know it is not possible using language. Two people can get close to having the same understanding or the same consciousness when information is shared, but it will never be exactly the same understanding. Everybody interprets their experiences in their own way in their own consciousness using their own set of filters and explainers. The point is, it is difficult to communicate with language. The words I say now, and as I look over at you, I see you glancing my way, occasionally, which is nice, because I am glad you are spending most of your visual time looking at the road ahead, and the cars speeding along beside you, but as you look at me, I see you are hearing what I say, you appear interested, but I have no idea on what your inner voice is saying. Is your inner voice saying – 'interesting ideas', is it saying 'bullshit, prove it', is it saying 'donuts', like Homer in a Simpsons episode. I don't know. What I do know, is if I am going to explain something, and if it is a complicated topic, I am going to have to find some simple way of explaining it or find some way of relating it to experiences already logged into your memory banks. Therefore, I will use examples that will hopefully paint a picture in your mind, or I will use humor if I can. Politics aside, Ronald Reagan was one of the best communicators in conveying his ideas to others. He used both humor and metaphors to discuss complicated issues and concepts to better explain them to the general public. His body language conveyed both sincerity and approachability. Metaphors are elegant communication devices in language. Some people could listen to our discussion about the radio, and say – 'oh yeah, those channel numbers relate to radio frequency levels', others will think – 'I don't care, my favorite AM station plays the golden oldies and broadcasts the games of my favorite baseball team, I don't give a hoot about FM', and still others will see the analogy of tuning your personal vibration frequency to a frequency level established for you by the Universe. Language is marvelous, I am blessed at being fluent in three languages, and I can get by in conversations in three more, and I also can read some Sanskrit and ancient Hebrew." He paused waiting for me.

My mind was racing, I really didn't intend to turn an off-hand comment about the radio analogy into a question, but I was glad I did. I was now searching through the loose thoughts that were scattered through my brain like all the scattered notes, letters, print outs and unpaid bills lying on my desk at home. I had an important question I wanted to ask, where is it, ah yeah there it is. "Adam, I have to ask you to explain one word for me. I have my own personal sense of what the word means, but you use it all the time, your research work seems to focused on it, and I am finding it confusing. The word is energy."

Adam paused again, this was the first time I saw him squint his eyes before talking. He pulled out his notebook, and marked a small star. "Question 8, Energy. Well, I was wondering if and when you would ask me about Energy. Well, I am not going to be able to take you where you need to go with my answer. You need more exposure to concepts, and I need to give you some reading material. I can't remember if we covered anything when we were visiting the rooms in the basement at the diner. I will try to give you an overview statement, and in all probability I will accidentally leave some stuff out. Lesson One; everything in this Universe is either a form of energy or a void. Energy takes on many forms. As an example, we know that Matter is a dense form of energy. Thoughts are energy. If you could look inside your brain as you are thinking, you would find neurons with synapses firing for every one of your thoughts. Summary, everything can be categorized as energy or void. Lesson Two, Energy is categorized as either physical energy or non-physical metaphysical energy. After I did my 'baloney, prove it' assessment on the concept of non-physical energy, I bought into the concept and the existence of non-physical energy through intuitive deduction. But also on a fact basis, Eastern mystics have taught about non-physical energy for thousands of years. At least some very brilliant Physicists are now exploring this concept. Problem is that in science, all concepts and the Laws of Nature are based on Physical Energy. When you start talking about non-physical energy, you can't apply all the theories that are foundations of basic science. As an example, with non-physical energy the speed of light has no meaning. Non-physical energy can move across galaxies maybe across Universes instantaneously, with no time factor.Another example, you know from the simple science of magnetic energy or atomic structures, positive energy is attracted to negative energy. With non-physical energy this concept does not apply, in fact, when we talk later about using the Power of Intention as a way to increase your Manifestation skills, we find that positive attracts positive, and negative attracts more negative. Lesson Three, non-physical energy has many of the same attributes as electricity. Examples – it flows, it has degrees of power, it can be transformed, it can be blocked, it can encounter resistance as it flows, it can be described by the frequency of its vibration, it can be described by its polarity (positive or negative) or non-polarity (neutral or unified – with negative and positive co-existing), it might take the form of a particle or take the form of a wave, or have no form at all – just a blink in a space-time moment for a zillionth of a second. Lesson Four - all energy (physical and non-physical) can be classified as active or potential. A big rock sitting on that hill we see ahead of us, as it sits we know it has a lot of potential energy. When it starts moving for whatever reason we know that its potential energy can be a very powerful active force when it bashes into your car. Non-physical energy has unlimited potential, which is useful in creating something today, that didn't exist in any form of energy other than potential energy yesterday.

Lesson Five – for understanding energy transformation, it is important to note that all energy follows a prescribed set of rules. We call the most powerful rules Laws, and they apply to both physical and non-physical energy. As we learn more about the rules, we realize that we can make choices to use the rules or laws to work for our benefit." Adam paused. I thought he was going to continue, but realized he had finished his commentary.

"Hey Adam, we just passed the hill you pointed out earlier, no big rock realizing its potential by crashing into my car. For that matter I doubt there was a big rock on top of the hill. Can I call you a bullshitter?"

Adam started to smile broadly, "For that example on the big rock, yeah that was a form of creative license, which technically in this case, was cow manure thrown your way. But stay open on the rest of the stuff I talked about, or you won't even begin to learn how to manifest yourself out of a wet paper bag, let alone manifest the life of abundance and joy you were meant to live."

CHAPTER SIXTEEN

CARL JUNG CONCEPTS

Adam was glancing at is notebook, "Okay Ted, we have done eight questions. That is not enough for me to make my assessment on what Lesson Plan we draw up for you. Do you have some more questions?"

"Well Adam, there is so much I can ask. I have filed away a bunch of questions in my mind that I want to ask you, but darn thing is that I am having trouble remembering them."

"Don't worry my friend, approach it this way. Don't worry about the clutter in your mind and where you have filed away questions. The mind is a wonderful and mysterious friend. Let's agree to do it this way, the rule is, anything that pops into your mind, ask it. I will agree to answer the question, and not judge it as dopey, even if it is a dopey question. Oooops, sorry. No judgments allowed at this stage, it is like a brainstorming session, all ideas are allowed, we can't fire hose them, in other words be judgmental, and there are no dopey questions. First thing on your mind Ted?"

"I should be stopping for gas soon."

"Not a question Ted, but a very good practical consideration. Stop anytime for gas, I can be interrupted in the middle of answering questions."

"The study of the Mind. I have read some Psychology books in the past, and I read stuff in magazines, on the internet and in newspapers all the time. What lessons you can teach on the Mind and Consciousness?"

"Question Nine, the Mind, slash, Consciousness. Another good question that cannot be answered in a brief amount of time, but let me give some advice. Psychologist Carl Jung is one of my heroes. I buy into a lot of his ideas. Try reading some of the basic Jung concepts, I'll go over a few, but here is some good advice for you. Unless you want to, don't buy any of his books or read his articles. You will get bored out of your tree. I can't read his work, although I respect the people who can, because I read their articles and books. Jung and Freud overlap a little. Freud is more famous, but we have found that most people's problems may not go back to a troubled childhood, and problems with mother. Actually chemical imbalances in the brain might trigger some of the emotional or psychological afflictions that people experience. Jung theories marry into my metaphysical research findings, probably why his work resonates with me. Now, for an answer to your question, the order of the items that follow are not based on importance, but more on how they pop into my mind. Jung Lesson One – Meaningful coincidences. Jung called this **synchronicity**. I love the concept and have seen it happen for me, time and time again, as long as I keep my mind open. Example, I was playing scrabble once and one of the people that I was playing with used the word 'plethora', I am a worldly guy, but I was 40 years old at the time, and I had never heard the word 'plethora'. So we went through the challenge thing with a dictionary, and I learned that 'plethora' meant an over-abundance. Well for the next three days I must have encountered that word ten times or more, a friend says go to such and such a place they have a plethora of crystals for you to see, Deborah the waitress says 'my we have a plethora of blueberries on our pancakes this morning', and so on and so on. I never ever took the time to reflect on the meaning of plethora until that point in my life. As a result, I dedicated myself to reflect on abundance, and over-abundance. Example two – Henry Ford had invented his automobile, and it wasn't a commercial success in the early stages and he was wondering if he should change some design parameters. He was considering dropping the gas engine design and use a battery system for power, because there were barely any places in America that sold gasoline. Who should Ford run into at a restaurant, by accident, no less than the world's greatest inventor, Thomas Alva Edison. Ford's first thought, Edison being the genius he is with electricity is going to tell me drop the combustion engine and go with batteries. Edison who was making millions with Power Plants and battery companies springing up all over the place, listened intently to Ford as he described his car, and asked a whole bunch of questions. At the end, Edison slammed his hand on the table, and told Ford he had a wonderful idea, don't change anything. Ford said at that moment in time, in his words, a chance encounter, in my words, synchronicity, gave him the confidence to proceed full force with the gas combustion engine idea against the objections of some of his friends and financial backers.There are other stories about inventors struggling with blocks seeing the answer to their dilemma in an advertising sign on the side of a bus, and so on. Synchronicity, believe in it.

Jung Lesson Number Two – **Collective Unconscious**. First, the word unconscious doesn't mean knocked out or lying in a coma. Almost everyone has Consciousness, an awareness of the world around him or her and a free flow of thoughts in their mind in waking moments. Everyone also has an Unconscious part of mind. This unconscious part is an essential part of your mind, and an important part of your mind for the process of manifesting important changes in your life. We have purely defined Unconscious as not being Conscious or in plain speak you have no real idea on what goes on in your unconscious (or subconscious) mind. This wasn't Jung's idea, but he carried it one step further saying the Unconscious went beyond the individual. Everybody who exists and everybody who has ever existed on the planet has a portal or a channel into a collective unconscious mind which in other words is a pool of metaphysical energy. Some part of the collective unconscious, may actually be physically encoded in our DNA. Our sleeping dreams may come from the collective unconscious, and our inspirations may come from the collective unconscious. As an example, have you ever seen two people come up with the same new idea almost simultaneously? Jung Lesson Number Three – related to the collective unconscious is the fact our individual unconscious mind or call it subconscious if you like, doesn't pay great attention to language. The unconscious mind has its own language of symbols which is shared in the collective unconscious; Jung called some of these symbols **Archetypes**. You can get into this more in dream interpretations. What I will say, your dreams could have great meaning for you. I also believe you can consciously work with your unconscious by exposing your conscious mind to selected symbols, these symbols have no meaning to your conscious mind but your unconscious picks up on them, interprets them and acts on them helping to bring the positive or negative events that the symbol encourages into your life. This is a far-out idea, and I have just passed it through my own 'bullshit, prove it' assessment process, and I now believe it works. Your unconscious/ subconscious mind is a small part of the collective unconscious, whatever goes on in your conscious mind gets picked up by your unconscious mind, and therefore gets picked up in the collective of all unconscious minds. An integral part of your Unconscious is your personal Subconscious. The subconscious is the fabulous computer that performs all your actions now as you drive, so your conscious mind can listen to what I say, or as an alternative to listening to me, reflect on thoughts about pretty girls or donuts. Jung Lesson Four – the human psyche has different component parts making up the whole. Component one, The Ego, is the chatterbox in your head always focused on "me, me, me" – full of fears, full of wishes and wants, always trying to define you by comparing you to others, and so on. Component two is the persona – the mask you decide to wear every waking moment of your life. By mask, it is the behaviors you display to others, it is the Ted you want others to see expressed through your words, your behaviors and your deeds. Component three is the Shadow – a murky dark part of you that hides out in your Unconscious but comes bubbling up into your Conscious Mind at various times in the form of dark or negative thoughts, or worse in some people, with sudden evil impulses. Then there is Anima/Animus – if you are a male it is the feminine Anima, and the male Animus in a female. We will leave all conversations about getting in touch with your feminine side to another day.

All that is left over in your Psyche is your Authentic Self. A very nice spiritual guy, passive and observant, finding joy in almost everything. Too quiet most times because Ego and even Shadow can bully themselves into taking over many of your thoughts. Enough about Jung for now, but his work has been applied in Personality profiles and other research. I have tuned in on the ideas for unconscious because that is the area we need to work in to effect dramatic change, not only in you, but getting the flow of all good things to come to you when you need them."

"Adam, you are turning my mind to mush, but let us keep it going, first, I better stop and get some gas, and good news, we are at the border."

CHAPTER SEVENTEEN

THE POWER OF INTENTION

We had surprising little difficulty getting across the border. I was glad to see that Adam had a Canadian passport like me, but the border official asked us the customary questions of where we lived, where we are going and how long we would be there and didn't ask for identification. I was having worries about one hour into our trip that Adam had a Madagascar passport or even worse Colombian passport, or if the customs official asked him where he lived he would say the Universe or Planet Earth, something that would probably delay or prevent our crossing into Michigan.

"Well Adam, I was surprised, we didn't have a hassle crossing the border."

He looked at me with the little smile on his face that he had almost every time we talked.

"I knew there wouldn't be a problem."

"Is that some sort of psychic thing you have Adam?"

"No. When you told me we were close to the border, I started sending out signals, Conscious Mind to Unconscious Mind, to Collective Unconscious. The signal was - 'Please, we intend no harm, let us enter your beautiful country, thank you, bless you.' I repeated it over and over a few times until I felt we would be okay. I was using **Power of Intention**."

"Is this where I'm supposed to say, Bullshit, Prove It."

110

"You can if you like Ted, the proof is obvious, we got across the border with no problems. Our intent is pure, if we were smugglers or terrorists, the signal I sent out wouldn't work."

"Power of Intention?"

"Yes. You want to make that Question Ten?"

"Sure. I would love to learn more about Power of Intention."

Adam grabbed his journal, I noticed he grabbed a map and some written directions, I had the way to Saginaw on the Interstate memorized so that was not going to be a problem. I figured it was two hours away, but we would have to stop and get something to eat.

"Okay Ted, Question Ten, Power of Intention. I am going to make a few brief comments. Then, we are going to go 'live', and begin practicing using the Power when we pull off the highway to have a bite to eat. Actually, you are going to start practicing the power for some small activities. It will be fun. The Power of Intention deals with the nature of your thoughts. The key is, to be positive as much as you can in every situation of the day. It is tough, at first, you have to set up a security guard in your conscious mind, a little voice 'hey Ted, drop that negative thought, replace the thought with a positive thought now!' But like all things, with practice it becomes a natural way of doing things. The principle at play is the Law of Attraction, non-physical energy – positive attracts more positive. Eventually you have some physical energy evidence to demonstrate the benefits. Keep in mind, it works the other way as well. Negative attracts negative. There is some debate as to what can get categorized as positive or negative thoughts. The basics of using Power of Intention: Item one , we are talking about a future outcome that you intend to happen. Item two, form should be given to the intention. Form could be a clear statement that can be repeated silently in your mind, or verbally, or written out on a piece of paper. You should be able to see the desired outcome in your Mind's Eye. Visualize it, so to speak. Item three, your choice of intention should be positive, negative also works, but there is enough crud that happens to you as a course of natural events why would you want more. Item four, the greater the size or impact of the desired outcome, the higher the energy vibration that you must generate for your intention to become real. Also, the more skill you need in mastering the power. There is also some good advice for this power. Be careful for what you intend to happen, you just actually might get it. Other Laws come into bearing with any change, the Big One being the Law of Cause and Effect. Life is a series of events, a line of dominoes, every change event is a Cause that triggers other events to happen, call them Effects, when each Effect manifests it in turn becomes a Cause for a new Effect, and so on and so on. When we get a flow happening, we want it to be positive. Negative flows, or in other words, you are experiencing a series of what people would call bad luck, tough times, conflicts in relationships, trouble at work, ill health, depression, angriness and on and on. Every day there will be at least one thing, probably more, where it sucks to be you. When in a negative flow, a lot of energy and special practice is required to flip the negative into positive flows, more on that later. Okay that should be enough for the theory on Power of Intention. Let's move into the practical application. We are still in Port Huron, take the next exit."

All this was taking me by surprise, but I was going with the Flow. I was driving blindly, Adam was giving me directions, I didn't know if he had a clue what he was doing. We were traveling away from the Interstate, but on a major arterial road. Adam was looking around for something, I was not sure what, we had passed several restaurants and fast food places.

Suddenly he spoke. "Pull over here Ted into this plaza on the right." I pulled my car into what looked like a Shopping Plaza, a Big Food Store and a Wal-Mart were highly visible.

Adam was getting excited. "Stop here. I need to give you directions."

"Directions on where to go next Adam?"

"No Ted, bad choice of words on my part. I mean I need to give you some quick instructions. You are going to practice the power of intention."

"In a Wal-Mart parking lot?"

"A perfect place to start."

I was baffled, but hey, this guy is the Manifestation Master. Let me learn.

"Listen closely Ted, normally, you decide on your own what your intention is, but I am going to give you an intention, you are going to accept it as your own intention, you are going to give it form, and you are going to create your intended reality. Is this okay with you?"

I was getting excited, but I had no idea what we were going to create in a Wal-Mart Parking Lot. "I am ready Adam, tell me what I have to do." I was expecting a grand scheme or master plan, something out of a Raiders of the Lost Ark, or some other adventure movie.

"Ted, take a look over to the front of the Wal-Mart store, what do you see?"

I looked, but everything appeared very normal, obviously this was a very busy Wal-Mart store. A lot of early Friday afternoon shoppers, but I couldn't see much else. "Everything appears ordinary Adam. What am I looking for?"

"From your vantage point Ted, do you see any open parking spots close to the store?"

"No. Just some spots reserved for handicapped parking appear to be open."

"Okay, take a moment now, your power of intention is going to be driving in the parking lot closest to the front of the store and parking in an open spot, without a handicapped parking sign."

There is something about the excitement of an adventure in the anticipation of receiving your "Mission Impossible" assignment, but I was dumbfounded with the absurdity of Adam's suggestion. Once my head cleared I realized that this assignment might indeed be a "Mission Impossible" assignment.

"Uh, why Adam?"

"Practice. This intention is low energy vibration, but it does have a challenge element. Let's try it. Are you up for it?" He was getting excited, I couldn't believe it, you would think we were on a motor cycle going to pull an Evil Knievel jump over some buses or something.

"Ah yeah. Let's give it a shot."

"Do not move the car Ted, until you visualize what you intend, and see it happening, the challenge will be to park within 50 yards of the store front, in the first or second aisle. One other piece of advice. Don't think about the specifics of your actions, what aisle do I go down, where are those people walking to, etc. just go with the flow, and do what comes naturally. Your only thoughts might be, 'I'm coming to you my blessed open parking spot, don't worry' or something similar." Adam's voice was bubbling over with excitement. I was making a mental note, I wouldn't be telling the boys in the office about this adventure.

"Okay Adam. We're off." I put the car into gear and started driving to the front of the store. I turned on to the second aisle from the front of the store, as I was driving slowly, I noticed a car driving to the front of the store in the aisle that was perpendicular to mine. My little power of intention voice was saying "parking spot, parking spot". Surprisingly, a shopper at the end of the aisle almost twenty yards from the store front was pulling out of her spot, but my attention veered to my competitor to the left. I quickly put my signal light on, done, shopper one backs up in my direction, leaving the spot open for a second, as aggressive shopper number two quickly wheels into my spot. Adam looked at me with mild disappointment on his face.

"Drive back to the starting point Ted. Why did you do it?"

"Do what Adam?" I felt major disappointment, and for the life of me, couldn't understand why.

"What entered into your mind when you saw the other car?"

"Why my natural thought was, don't take my parking spot fool."

"This is a wonderful lesson Ted."

"What?"

"Your Power of Intention worked dramatically."

"Say What? I have no clue what you are talking about. I didn't get my visualized parking spot, some other clown stole it from me."

"Not a clown Ted, a shopper in a hurry, maybe on a lunch break or something."

"You are right Adam. Think positive Ted" I told my self out loud. "But explain the lesson Adam, I am not getting it."

"Okay, one thing I didn't mention. This wonderful web of non-physical energy we are playing in called the unconscious energy field doesn't understand negatives in Intentions. If you say 'Don't take my parking spot', what you are really saying is 'Take my parking spot', I am serious about this. That last thought of yours became your new powerful intention. It was powerful because your body was on high alert, some adrenaline was probably being released, your mind was highly alert and emotions were coming into play, and your Spirit self was focused on 'let's get Ted what he really, really wants which is to have the other car take the open parking spot'. Okay done.

It had to happen because you had the Quantum Trio (Body, Mind, Spirit) working in harmony, and in power mode, on a very specific intention."

We were back to the starting point.

I was dismayed. "Do I have to do this again teach?"

"No Ted, you learned your first lesson. Let's go across the road to that little restaurant and get something to eat."

"Hey Adam, you are not going to tell anyone we did this are you?"

"Sure I am. Let us tell Lynette. She will have a laughing spasm." Adam was smiling broadly. Good, because his smile is contagious and I was smiling again.

CHAPTER EIGHTEEN

RELIGION AND THE BIBLE

The restaurant was not that busy. I ordered a clubhouse sandwich, Adam had some mushroom soup and a bagel. He held his hands together and said a silent prayer before he started eating.

"Are you very religious Adam?"

"That is an interesting word – religious. When asked in a question, it usually means what religious discipline you follow. I believe in God although I don't always use that name for the Creator or Source. I believe that God is not a separate entity, but instead that God is a part of everything. Underline the word part. I don't know if this puts me in a pantheist category or not, I don't like categories for Spiritual matters. I believe in prayer, and prayer is meant to give blessings to God for all the wonderful things that we are blessed with, and prayer is also meant to pose questions to God, to ask for guidance and to ask for protection. Since God is a part of everything, prayers are always heard.Religions are a dilemma for me. The original intent of a religion, to worship God is wonderful. But then each Religion spoils the intent by establishing their unique set of rules to follow, and that is where I have to step back. Religious dogma, and groups of people saying their religion's dogma is right and other religious doctrines are not right, is a horrible problem. More people on this planet have been murdered because of religious dogma, than for any other reason.

Humankind has horribly insulted Creation for centuries and continues to do so. It saddens me. We will eventually get it, but I am not sure when. Any time now, an asteroid could hit our planet with no warning, and I mean no warning, and the small part of humankind that remains if anyone remains at all, will have a chance to start over again."

"Do you read the Bible Adam?"

"Yes, I have read portions of the Bible. It is a good book, the words in it are probably not exactly what the original authors intended, but it is still a good book. Think about it for a moment, for the Old Testament part of the Bible, someone wrote or more likely dictated their book about God and the events of the day. A lot of the good story tellers in ancient times didn't write, if they did it would take them a long time to write those fancy Aramaic scripts on to a sheep or goats skin. Item one – you have the author's interpretation of events. Item two – you have the original transcriber maybe making a few edits a long the way in transcribing the author's words. Item three- someone copied the original transcribers work on to another skin of some kind or maybe some heavy paper that they managed to get from Egypt, maybe a few edits a long the way, suggestions for improvements from a Priest. Item four – someone said no one reads Aramaic anymore, can anyone translate this work into Latin or Hebrew? So you get the translators interpretations of the story. Item five – the Roman Catholic Church wants to market their Religion to as many new markets as possible and realizes that the book should be translated into English, French, Portuguese, and Spanish. Result, with translations and there are even more interpretations of the words from original, with probabilities that the word meanings are changed. Item six – In the early days of the Church it would not be unusual to turn these translation sessions into opportunities to make some slight modifications to the script, leave a few things out, or add some emphasis here and there kind of thing. There you have a scenario, now we have that wonderful old story teller Timothy talking about Abraham and dictating his story to his personal scribe. Did Timothy's oral story, word for word make it into the King James edition of the Bible? I personally don't think so."

"What about the New Testament, and the story of Jesus?"

"Wonderful stories as well. There are a couple of things here. The stories themselves are probably fairly accurate, but I think there was some editing done by Church folks. I would love to see the juicy parts they cut-out. A bigger issue is the Books that didn't get put in the Bible. The Roman Emperor Constantine was really getting annoyed with all the bickering that was going on in the Christian Churches and they were dividing into all these different sects based on different interpretations in all these different books that were floating around. No one other than Priests were reading these books, because the publishing industry hadn't started yet. Most of the books in those days were made by Monks sitting in their Monasteries handwriting them. Constantine did a smart thing. In 325 AD he convened a Convention of all the Religious leaders that they could track down through-out the Roman Empire and paid their expenses to come to Nicea, in Turkey, not far from Constantine's home, so he could keep an eye on things. The Council was convened to straighten out all these different interpretations of scriptures. It was decided to put all these small books into one big book, which was later called the Bible.

The sub-committee set-up to handle this project went through all the books and decided to include some of the mini-books in the Bible and others didn't cut-it. Why didn't those books get included?"

Adam was doing a lot of talking but he managed to finish his lunch. We got back into the car, and re-convened our journey towards Saginaw. I saw him marking his notebook with three more questions – Religion, Bible, New Testament. He turned to me."Thirteen questions, good, do you want to talk a little about Lynette and Greg?" I nodded in agreement.

CHAPTER NINETEEN

MARCEL VOGEL AND LYNETTE

"Where to begin? Ted, why don't you ask me a question, to get the ball rolling?"

"Sure Adam, how long have you known Gary and Lynette?"

"Ah a good starting point. I actually have only met Gary once, and Lynette has only known Gary herself for two years. She says she keeps marrying him in every one of her lifetimes, but let's not go to the explanation for that, yet. I met Lynette for the first time, the same time I met you, sorry, we didn't actually meet formally, but when you started giving me your newspaper in 1988. We met at a conference convened by Marcel Vogel in California."

"Marcel Vogel?"

"Good side-track Ted. It warrants a short discussion here, and a longer one at some other time. Marcel Vogel's work is a very important part of my life. I have the highest admiration and respect for the man, and I try to emulate him. He was born in the same year I was, 1917, and he passed on in 1991. Marcel was a Research Scientist for the IBM operations in San Jose. He specialized in phosphors, luminescence and magnetic coatings. His name is on over 100 patents. He was a major developer of the magnetic coating on the 24" diameter hard-drives used in large computers. In the mid seventy's

Marcel started to research the special attributes of quartz crystals. We know the power of quartz in modern day technology. Quartz is silicon dioxide, the base material for many facets of electronics, again a pet topic of mine, but back on track with Marcel. Marcel developed a multitude of interests with quartz crystals outside of the world of technology. He got involved with using them to expedite healthy plant growth, to purify water, to age wine faster, and this was obviously, all kinds of things that IBM wasn't interested in, but he did this research as his hobby. He also became fascinated with the power of thought, as a non-physical energy that could with the proper channeling be used to adjust physical energy or matter into designed alignment. We call this healing. I love the story of Marcel carrying around a quartz crystal in his pocket, and one Monday morning chatting with a fellow IBM colleague about his weekend. The fellow had pulled some muscles skiing. Marcel, on intuition or for fun, asked him to sit in a chair, and he ran the crystal over the sore spots on the guy's back telling him he really wanted to make him better. Apparently, it worked or helped. It became a new area of interest for Marcel, the healing power of crystals. When Marcel retired from IBM in the mid 1980's he set up a new venture, Psychic Research Inc., and started doing all kinds of research with both crystals and thought energies. That is when I became aware of him. I was in San Francisco in 1986, and on an impulse picked up the phone and called him. And, an example of positive flow, I reached a busy man, quickly and directly, no telephone tag. I told him about my Madagascar quartz crystals that I had with me. Again, right in the positive flow and going with it, like a bolt of lightning, this busy man dropped everything, met me at my hotel and we spent almost twenty hours together over three days. What an incredible experience. I traveled a lot in the US in those days, and used to meet him on my trips to California. Marcel was a sponsor for a Psychic/Supernatural seminar in San Francisco and really wanted to attract experts in crystal energies and healing therapists. We were sitting together listening to some speaker talking about using crystals for healing ailments and Marcel nudged me and asked me to go outside the room with him. We quietly left the room and were standing at the back door and he pointed to a young lady sitting at the back of the room. 'We have to meet her', he said, 'My intuition is telling me she knows more about crystals than anyone sitting in this room does. She doesn't have any scientific background, but I know she knows.' I was surprised a little, because the young lady, in her early thirties was sitting quietly through all the speaker presentations, not saying a word, just intently listening. She only stood out in this crowd by being normal looking and quiet. This was an interesting group of people.

At a break, Marcel and I were chatting, and out of nowhere the young lady comes up to Marcel and tells him she got his thought message, about Marcel wanting to ask her something. They had a bit of small talk, and he offered her a job at his company, and asked her to name her salary. I didn't know what amazed me more, Marcel standing there with an almost a total stranger offering her a job working with him, at any salary she wanted or the young lady looking him square in the eye and saying 'Thank you Mr. Vogel, but no.' In the small talk we found out that she lived closed to Toronto. Marcel asked me to track her down, since she lived close to my semi-home base at George's Diner. I did, but there was no way she was moving to California, she lived with and cared for her ailing parents and had a young family. In any case, we became great friends. We meet once or twice a year, traded a few phone calls, and these days, emails."

Adam was looking over at me, to see if I had any more questions.

"Can I ask you what we will be doing this week-end?"

Adam put his hand to his chin for a second in the thinker pose, "Hmm, I'm not sure. What I do know is we will be doing a lot of story telling. Lynette is always working on metaphysical projects so we will share some ideas there, I am going to try to talk her in to coming back to Toronto to look at my Radionics machine, we are both going to Sedona in Arizona for a seminar in a couple of weeks, so we will make a few plans for that. You will learn lots and lots. Take some notes on questions to ask me in the car ride back. Lynette will gauge your personal energy field and let you and I know where you need some work. Who knows what we will end up doing. Gary and Lynette raise goats on their farm, maybe they will have us spend the week-end cleaning goat poop out of the barn." With that he started his laugh. I just shook my head.

CHAPTER TWENTY

GOOD HEALTH

I had to pull off the Interstate near Saginaw to make a call back to the office, I knew the call would take about ten minutes because I was checking on quotes and trading volumes for at least twenty different stocks. Adam said he could use the break to stretch his legs. He returned to the car just as I finished the call. I grabbed a coffee for the road and Adam refilled his bottled water container. We turned off on to Highway Ten heading toward Midland.

"Adam I have to tell you that I am amazed that you are eighty-seven years old, you look fantastic and you have all kinds of energy."

"Well thank you Ted, but we are not going to sleep in the same bed, okay."

"You have a very good sense of humor Adam"

"Well the sense of humor or having fun, laughing, smiling go together with the good health. The body is a fabulous organism, I have spent a lot of time studying physiology and biochemistry. There are several aspects of the body that relate to good health and postponement of the natural aging process. One of the critical processes is the body's ability to make its own polypeptides especially the ones you know as endorphins. Endorphins enhance the immune system, and they relieve pain, if you get a rush of them it is like taking the painkiller morphine, it gives a temporary high. Stress, anger, and depression deplete positive polypeptides, so it is critical that you avoid those emotions. The body produces endorphins in a variety of ways – rigorous exercise, laughing and sex are physical activities that create endorphins. Music, and for some interesting reason, both classical and rock music stimulate endorphin production in people. From a diet perspective, another diverse combination, chocolate and hot peppers. I pretty much have everything covered for endorphin production other than the sex thing, to compensate I'll just eat some more chocolate listening to Mozart. I was going to stop there, but I need to add one more piece of advice. Another bio-chemical process in the body that needs to be monitored by the Conscious Mind is the creation of free radicals. In the process of metabolism one of the negative by-products are free radicals. A free radical in simple terms is an Oxygen atom missing a few electrons. An Oxygen atom missing a few electrons is a nasty little beast, and inside a cell it will rob electrons from where ever it can, including the proteins that might interface with DNA/RNA in cell replication, causing potential mutations. Too many free radicals are detrimental to cell health. I was thinking that exercise is a good thing overall for health, and it is, but exercise produces a lot of free radicals. Antioxidants in the body are the friendly agents that will offer up and give up their electrons to allow the free radical to become a whole Oxygen atom again. Therefore, it is important that you eat fruits, vegetables and take supplements with antioxidants such as Vitamin E and Vitamin C."

Adam glanced down at his notes. "Take the next exit Ted, and stay to the right."

We proceeded north on a paved highway.

"Do you drive Adam?"

"No. I used to, but now I take public transportation, cabs in cities or con people into taking me places."

"Is this a con job on me?"

"Absolutely. I am going to **con**-vince you to make your best **con**-tribution to society." He had heavy emphasis on the '"con" syllables, and was smiling to help produce more endorphins.

"Can you recommend any books for me to read Adam?"

"Hmmm..there are a whole bunch. You are an initiate to this metaphysical project, I would recommend for a nice spirituality overview something by Deepak Chopra, Wayne Dyer or Stuart Wilde as a starter. You would also enjoy Steven Pressfield's *The Legend of Bagger Vance,* Scott Adam's *God's Debris',* *The Alchemist'* by Paulo Coelho, or one of James Redfield's books. Best advice is to tour a good bookstore something will shout out at you 'buy me, buy me' or fall off a shelf close to you. When we get to Lynette's tour her library, something in there will resonate with you."

Adam glanced at his notes again, "Okay turn left at this country road".

We drove down another paved road for about a mile, we were both admiring all the wilderness. "Turn right on this road ahead." After turning right, we drove down the road about another mile and Adam said "Okay, this is it, turn right into this lane way".

The mailbox at the road said 'Jones', I had never thought to ask about last names, it didn't seem important. As we drove up the lane, it was all bush on the left and a fenced grass field to the right.We pulled into a yard, were there was a pick-up truck, a van, and a small car. I scanned the scene - an old farm house on the right, an old barn with a fenced yard to keep some goats in to the left, and a brand new small building in front of us with a big satellite dish to the side of the building. As we got out of the car, a short lady walking briskly came out of the house and went straight up to Adam giving him a big hug. "Welcome, welcome", she said, "Come on in, we are so happy you could come."She took Adam's hand and we walked up to the house.

As we entered into the side door going into the kitchen, Lynette was smiling as she spoke "You want to make some gold this week-end Adam, or do you just want to talk?"

CHAPTER TWENTY ONE

MAKING GOLD IN THE KITCHEN

Lynette's comment threw me off a little. Was she serious could Adam really turn lead into gold like an ancient alchemist? Note to self - Keep an open mind. We went directly into a large country style kitchen. The first thing to strike me in my quick overview was a wonderful large wood table and chairs right in the center of the kitchen. We hung our coats on a tree rack and Lynette beckoned us to sit down at the table.

"Gary is working on something or another in his work-shop, he'll be here in a few minutes, can I make you some tea or would you like some water?"

"Tea for me Lynette", said Adam, he was stretching his arms out before he sat down. Coffee wasn't on this menu so I took another option, "I'll have some water please Lynette".

Lynette looked forty-something, short stature, grayish hair and full of energy. She put the kettle on, and grabbed a glass from the kitchen and walked over to a kitchen wall where there was a tap all by itself. "I have my still on the other side of this wall", she said, and the water was nice and clear as it came out of the tap "Gary keeps threatening to take my water distiller out and put in a cooler with a keg of beer, but he hasn't yet". Ah, my thoughts drifted to 'beer would be a nice option', after a long drive.

Lynette brought a glass of water over to me at the table and sat down. She had a nice smile and a sparkle in her eye. I could tell she and Adam would be sharing some laughs. She looked over at Adam and gave a slight glance in my direction. "You have some new meat here Adam, an Alchemist protégé or is there a dastardly fate in the works for this guy?"

"Oh Lynette, excuse me for my impoliteness, this is Ted, he is a friend of mine from the diner and we are working on a project together. He was very kind to drive me here for our visit."

Lynette held out her hand, "Nice to meet you Ted."

"Same here Lynette, I heard some nice things about you from Adam, I am looking forward to our visit." I shook her hand it was warm and soft. She held my hand for an extra moment it seemed, as if she was sensing something by holding it.

Lynette took over the conversation again, "Adam, you can sleep in the front room upstairs, and we'll put the rookie in the bunk house room in Gary's workshop, unless you want to sleep with the goats in the barn Ted?" She looked over at me to see how I was reacting to her humor. I hoped my late start at a smile would not destine me to the goat barn to find my sleeping spot.

I am not that quick on my feet, but I managed to make my contribution. "Adam was talking about wanting to sleep with the goats in the car ride here, maybe I can stay in the upstairs room?" Lynette was smiling, as was Adam.

Adam went with the flow, "Little Betsy, that nanny goat with the nice black spots is kind of cute, but I would still prefer the upstairs bed." As he was speaking Gary came into the kitchen.

"Looks like I got here in time to lay down the house rules about the goats", he chuckled.

Adam stood up quickly "Good to see you again Gary, I would like to introduce you to my friend Ted Gregory" they shook hands warmly and Adam pointed to me.

"Adam, great to see you again, and very nice to meet you Ted," he shook my hand with a nice firm grip and pulled up a chair at the table.

Lynette got up to prepare the tea and we shared some small talk about the trip and the drive. Lynette brought a tray over with the tea and some biscuits. Adam reached into a pocket and pulled out two small crystals, a small green gemstone and a hexagonal clear piece, probably one of the quartz crystals he talked about. "Before I forget Lynette, I have brought you two small presents." He handed her the two crystals.

"Why thank you so much Adam. What a lovely emerald, it has a beautiful dark green color and what else have we got here? Ah, a Vogel crystal, this is awesome." She was extremely excited about the clear crystal. If it were me, I would be fussing over the emerald. I am not a gemologist, but I was guessing the emerald was worth at least $500. She was feeling the Vogel crystal in the palm of her hand, "What a lovely energy transducer, I will enjoy using this for treatments. Thank you again Adam, you are so kind." She got up out of her chair and scurried over to Adam, giving him a big hug as he sat in his chair. He was obviously pleased with her delight.

I hadn't noticed it before but Adam had brought in a small leather satchel from the car. He reached into it and pulled out a small book, "Gary here is a book for you, I don't know if you've read it or not" and handed it over to Gary.

"No I haven't Adam, thank you so much." Adam continued to pull things out of his bag, this time it was two wirebound notepads and a pen. "Here Ted, something for you as well. These two blank journals and pen are for the homework assignments I will be giving you tonight."

"Ah, thank you Adam, I think." I must have had a dumb look on my face; Lynette,Gary, and Adam were all laughing.

"Ted what do you do for a living?" Lynette asked me.

"I am a stockbroker."

"Is Adam one of your big clients?"

"No, Adam is a friend, we don't have a business relationship."

Lynette continued "When I lived near Toronto, a Bay Street Stockbroker used to come to my house at 5 AM in the morning, to ask me questions about certain stocks and companies. He would come two or three days a week and stay a half hour to an hour. He paid me really well, so it was worth it for me to get up early."

This was peaking my interest, "That is really interesting. If you don't mind me asking, what advice was he seeking?"

"Oh I don't mind Ted, that was a long time ago. He was more or less getting Psychic readings, I was using my Divining gifts to tell him the feelings, and insights I was getting from the company names he gave me. I have no idea, what he did with the information I divined for him, but he kept coming back until he retired from the business."

"What town did you live in Lynette?"

"Peterborough. I still own a house there. The house has survived the years, and the visits from Adam."

I had no idea what she was talking about, and she sensed that she should give further explanation "Has Adam told you about the time we tried to make gold in my kitchen?"

My interest peaked again, and I started to smile in anticipation of a good story, "No he hasn't Lynette. I would love to hear the story."

"Well it was about seven or eight years ago, Adam was coming up to visit, I met him at the bus station and he was all excited, he had a book he wanted to show me." I glanced over at Adam, he was smiling broadly listening to Lynette as she continued "This book was very old, it was filled with all kinds of old writing, some in old English, some in Latin, but mostly symbols and glyphs all through the book. I recognized it as a notebook of an Alchemist. Years ago, alchemists used to invent their own language using symbols to record their experiments, so they could read them later, but they didn't want anyone else to be able to read them and learn their precious secrets. Adam had bought this book in some sort of antiquarian bookshop in England. He recognized the potential of the book because near the end there was some Latin words indicating that the Alchemist had some sort of success in one of his experiments.....a gold symbol with stars around it or something in the notes, I can't remember. Well anyway, Adam asked me if I could help him decipher the codes in the book, I had some familiarity with alchemy symbols working with runes and the like. Well we stayed up late poring through this old book and finally focusing on about three pages that dealt with an experiment the old alchemist had performed some time in the early 1700's. This was a very old journal and it had held up well, and the writer had dated each experiment. Adam was jumping out of his pants with excitement, and he wanted to try the experiment. Well it was late, and I said let's try it tomorrow. I get up on Saturday morning and find Adam working in the kitchen with my son who was fourteen at the time, setting up pots and pans on the stove, fortunately old ones that my son had fetched from the garage. Adam had brought along some sulphur and other stuff, and the kitchen was getting quite smelly, we opened a lot of windows, anyway, this concoction is brewing on a stove full blast and flames shoot up out of the pot, smoke everywhere, the smoke alarm goes off, my daughter who is sleeping wakes up screaming at the top of her lungs, the curtains over the window by the stove catch fire, I am running for the fire extinguisher, the neighbors see and hear the commotion and smoke and call 911, next thing you know there are two fire trucks outside and firemen with axes and hoses standing in my kitchen just as we finish getting the fire put out and everything cooled down. That's why I asked Adam when you were coming in the house if he wanted to make some gold this weekend. If he does, he better do it in Gary's workshop, not my kitchen."Every one was sharing a good laugh, Adam was almost falling out of his chair he was laughing so hard.

"That experiment didn't work very well, did it Adam?"

"Not that week-end. I forgot to put in the secret ingredient."

"Quintessence?", asked Lynette.

"Yes, in-deedy."

"You have some with you now?"

"I always have some. If I had a home, I would say, never leave home without it."

Back to laughter, and I was trying hard to remember the name of the Q word, why did it have to have so many syllables.

CHAPTER TWENTY TWO

THE HOUSE TOUR

Lynette enjoyed story telling and I expect there have been a lot of stories told around her kitchen table whether it be in rural Michigan, Peterborough or elsewhere. She looked over at Adam. "I guess we should make some dinner plans, Adam are you still a vegetarian?"

"Well mostly I am Lynette, I haven't eaten animals that come from farm factories for a long time – cattle, swine or poultry. All those synthetic hormones that are given to the animals to make them grow bigger quicker, are not good in the long run for those people consuming the flesh. But I do eat fish and other seafood on occasion. I feel that I am not getting enough nutrients and protein from a vegetarian diet. Even vegetables have expedited growth cycles in green houses and hydroponics centers. Most vegetables bought in food stores don't have all the nutrients your body needs. Supplements are a problem too, because most of the nutrients don't get broken down and just blast through your liver and kidneys and off to your urine. I really like my oatmeal, an old Scotsman boss of mine on a steamship got me in the habit of eating oatmeal every day, that was decades before I found it was good for me. I liked it back in the old days, because I had a full feeling that lasted to lunch time, it still does that, so I don't each too much every day. Now I also know, oats have some very good little molecules that are building blocks for proteins, and the beta-glucan in the oatmeal does a good job of catching and trapping those bad low density cholesterol globs and like a nightclub bouncer escorts them out of my intestinal nightclub."

"I guess you wouldn't be adverse to eating the deer that I hunt in the fall." Gary was starting to participate in the conversation.

"Well technically you have a point, I have enjoyed venison in the past. But I guess I don't want to disrupt my intestines by introducing red meat, and geez I love that Disney movie 'Bambi'."

Gary continued, "I was giving you the gears Adam, I am a hunter and a fisherman, I hope you won't hold that against me. I do have a salmon that we pulled out of the freezer earlier, I was planning to put that on the Bar-B-Q, is that okay for you."

"Sure Gary, I thought you were going to suggest goat meat tonight."

"No goat meat tonight, but a Greek salad with lots of feta cheese."

"Wonderful."

I was wondering if Gary and Lynette did eat their goats, but I thought I would try to change the topic if I could, I was getting hungry with all the talk about food, with the exception of Adam's references to his intestines. "Gary are you a fulltime farmer?"

"No Ted, I am in to a lot of different occupations and businesses. I have two hundred acres here, but it is mostly bush and wild grass meadows, I couldn't make a living farming here. The goats are more for saving me the time of cutting the grassland, and we make a few dollars breeding them and selling the youngsters. I am a building contractor, but I don't do much of that anymore. When the business was larger, I made my own web-site to promote it, and ended up doing that for other businesses. Now I own a small business that is an ISP provider and we also design and build web-sites. The business employs eight people, and I am just starting to make money with it after four years. It might be the time to sell it, and do something else. Adam, Lynette and I have been kicking around a few ideas on a new business venture. Could we get your inputs on that idea? Maybe tomorrow we could have a discussion about it, and Ted your input is welcome as well."

Adam looked over at Gary, "Well Gary I would be delighted to help if I can. That is my purpose in Life, the reason I am still roaming around this big hunk of rock that is orbiting the Sun. I look forward to encounters with people asking for a little bit of help."

"Thanks Adam, maybe tomorrow afternoon we will have a discussion on this. Well, I am going to put the salmon on the Bar-B-Q, and then I will go out to the shop to clean up the bunk area, so you have a spot to sleep Ted. Honey, you need any help with the salad?"

"No darling, everything is under control, we will see you in a bit", smiled Lynette.

Gary was a stocky, powerful looking man, in his mid-fifties, and full of energy. He jumped up off his chair, and was off to the outside porch.

Lynette got up from her chair, "Can I show you the house?" I had visions of this morning's adventure at the diner, with the secret rooms. Has this all taken place in one day? Wow! I wonder if Lynette and Gary have special rooms in the basement. We toured the upstairs and the main floor and I was impressed with this nice, lovely country house. There was one room off the kitchen we hadn't seen, and Lynette took us there last. I felt like I was entering the Garden of Eden, flowers and plants everywhere, big windows looking out on gardens and trees in the back of the house. Huge and small crystals were located on tables and shelves throughout the room. A small water fountain, nature sketches on the walls and what looked like a massage table in one corner of the room. "This is my healing center" she said. The room had a lovely warm relaxing feeling. I glanced quickly and didn't see any medical instruments or other stuff you would see in a medical practitioner's office.

"What is your specialty Lynette?" I asked.

She was smiling "What do you mean, my specialty?"

"What area of medicine to you focus on?"

"Oh, I am not a doctor, although I used to be a nurse once long ago. I work on the energy fields of people with physical diseases, stress or emotional traumas. I use crystals, my hands and my loving thoughts to channel non-physical energies to the physical energy points that need restructuring or balancing. I help introduce positive energy flow into the physical body and I help take away accumulated negative energies. Once the energies surrounding and enfolding the Mind, Body and Spirit are back in harmony, the body and mind become capable of self-healing."

Adam was nodding in agreement. I was trying to take it all in. It was getting to be too much for me to absorb. Time to change the subject.

"Hey Adam before dinner can you give me my homework assignments?"

"Sure Ted, lets go back to the kitchen table and review them."

CHAPTER TWENTY-THREE

.

JOURNALS

We sat back down at the kitchen table and I put the two empty notebooks and the pen in front of me.

Adam reached over and put he notebooks beside each other, I had them one on top of the other. "Ted, you are the type of person that gets exposure to a lot of ideas and different experiences. Your mind tries to process them and then it will run into information overload. Every one has a creative gift that they can share with the world – some people are singers, some are painters, sculptors or carvers, some are entertainers, athletes, story tellers, writers, cooks, gardeners, wood workers, poets, inventors and creative problem solvers. Every one is blessed with at least one gift, that if expressed, will positively impact another person or groups of people in a positive way. Julia Cameron is a writer and an artist and she has written a book called *The Artist's Way*, if you haven't seen it, I am sure Lynette has a copy of it in her library. There is a wonderful exercise that Julia describes in her book. It is called 'Morning Pages'. What it entails is every day writing three pages in a journal, preferably in the morning before you begin your day in earnest. The easy part and the hard part of this exercise is the same thing. It doesn't matter what you write in these three pages. Whatever is on your mind, write it down. You can be writing your solution on how to create world peace and if another thought hits your mind, like remember to buy a loaf of bread today, write it down. All your stream of consciousness should be written down even the thoughts like 'Gee I am only at page one, my mind is blank what should I write?' Write that thought down because it is your thought at that moment in time. The exercise clears the clutter in your consciousness and it opens up your Consciousness channels for creativity. I don't know how it works, but it works. I can attest to it. It does take some discipline, the first 21 days will be hard to do, you will have weak moments, but please try to do it. I believe you need to do this, if your manifestation project is going to work. Do you understand this exercise requirement?"

"Yes I do Adam." I was trying to clear my mind of its 'boy this sounds like a pain in the ass' thought.

"The second journal you can start on tonight or tomorrow. You can write anything you want in this journal, ideas you think of here, things you want to check out further, anything. But I have an assignment for you to write in this journal, and it relates to the manifestation of abundance desire if you still have this desire. It is a good project for anyone. Step one – write down as many goals, desires, wants that you can think of. Everything and anything that you want to have in your life or be able to do or see. Number each one and over the next few days, try to write down at least one hundred items. With at least one hundred items, phase two will be a little simpler, but I won't tell you about Phase two until you tell me when you have your list done. It is Friday evening now, have your list done for Monday morning before we leave, and I will give you the Phase two instructions. Is this okay with you?"

I liked the way Adam solicited commitments from me. He would be a good salesman. Maybe he is already. "Yes Adam. You have my buy-in."

"Wonderful"

Gary walked into the kitchen as Adam spoke, "You bet that salmon is wonderful, let's clear off the table, and get our meal served."

We had a fantastic dinner. Adam and I heard all the details on how Gary and Lynette met each other in a metaphysical chat room on the internet and how they made their connection, got married and all the details of making their life together until the present day.

I heard the word synchronicity used about ten times in the conversation, and marveled at the 'synchronicity' of hearing that word as coincidental with my learning of the word only this morning from Adam in the car ride to Michigan. I was also marveling at the fact that I didn't feel tired. A very long day, and driving usually makes me extra tired. I must be picking up the energy from my three dinner companions. After the dishes had been cleared away, rinsed and put in the dishwasher, Gary led us all out to the workshop. The building was less than two years old, but it was much more than a workshop inside. There was what I would call a workshop area with tools, table saw and some other carpentry stuff in one corner room of the shop, isolated so the sawdust wouldn't interfere with the rest of the studio like room. I saw an artist easel and a potter's wheel and lots of colored pens and crayons. A back room housed the famous Lynette library, the number of books rivaled and probably exceeded the number in Adam's Mind Energy Room.

The main room had a huge wood stove. Gary pointed to two doors to my left. "Ted that open door is the bunk room where you are sleeping this week-end. The closed door is a bathroom. No tub, just a shower. You want to grab your gear from the car and bring it in now, you can."

Adam followed me out to the car to get his bag as well.

"Well Adam, I am certainly finding this trip interesting, if not a little overwhelming. Gary and Lynette are wonderful people, I see why you enjoy them as friends."

"Lynette has been a great friend for fifteen years, and Gary is a terrific guy. They make a great couple, they are true soul mates. I will be interested to see if you write 'find a soul mate' on your list of 100 desires, wants and goals. We're reconvening in the kitchen I'll see you there after you drop your stuff off at the bunkhouse.

Soul Mate?The two words that make up one word and meaning struck some little used nerve in my chest cavity when Adam said them. I hadn't thought about it before he said it, now I wondered if I would get it out of my mind.

CHAPTER TWENTY FOUR

DISCIPLINE, RITUALS, AND BEHAVIORS

Everybody was sitting at the table when I got back to the house after dropping my bags off in the bunkhouse. I brought along a journal and a pen.

"Is that your Morning Pages Journal or your Notes and Ideas Journal?" Adam asked, but I knew he knew the answer.

"Well if I'm still sitting at this table past midnight, I'll make it the Morning Pages journal I quipped. Lynette, do you have that book Adam talked about, the one that suggests that Morning Pages is an excellent idea, I may need some convincing."

"Why yes I do. *The Artist's Way*, by Julia Cameron. I have done morning pages myself, off and on now for over ten years. I am in an 'off' cycle, I better get back to it, they are helpful, especially when I am seeking creative inspiration. I'll find the book for you tomorrow Ted."

Adam looked over at me, "I have been doing morning pages for 4,129 straight days."

The number rang a bell for me, "Why that is the number of days in a row that you have eaten porridge, what a weird combination. Can you tell us why?"

Adam continued. "In 1992 and I was in New York, going to some museums, attending a seminar, doing a business transaction and going to see a play . One of the speakers at the seminar was talking about the importance of self-discipline and using rituals every day to help cultivate self-discipline. I always thought I was self-disciplined, but maybe I was not as disciplined as I thought. I decided I wanted to develop a routine that would honor Spirit-Energy, Mind-Energy and Body-Energy. I decided almost immediately I would recite three prayers every day to honor Spirit-Energy. I thought for a while on Body, whether I should do specific exercises every day or drink 6 glasses of water or eat a special food every day. I finally decided to be a little different and eat one bowl of porridge every day, to honor Body-Energy and my old boss, teacher and friend Angus McLellan. Deciding on a Mind ritual was more difficult. I decided to seek guidance from the Universe, and developed my intention in the evening. The intention being that early the next day it would be clear to me what my Mind ritual would be. I woke up in the hotel, got showered and dressed, said my three prayers, went downstairs to the café, and ordered a bowl of porridge. At the table next to me, I saw a lady vigorously writing in a journal. While eating my porridge, I noticed she was continuing to write extremely fast, and I thought she had to rush off some where, but as she got to the end of the page she stopped writing at the very last line in her book, and let out a big sigh, and smiled to herself, and became very relaxed. She wasn't in a hurry to go anywhere. I politely had to ask her why she was writing in such a hurry. She was a very nice lady and told me about Morning Pages, and Julia Cameron, and how this helped stimulate her creativity. The Universe had answered my question on what was going to be my third ritual. I have been doing all three rituals every day for over eleven years."

Lynette spoke next, "I am not sure I have any porridge here."

"It's ok, I brought some. I never travel without porridge, my journals, one of my crystal friends and a small jar of peanut butter. I even have a small kettle to boil water."

Gary spoke up, "We have porridge honey, it is the back of one of the top cupboards. I should be heading to bed soon, I have to get up early and drive into town tomorrow, and go the office and do some work in the morning, I'll be back in the afternoon to talk about our new business concept with you guys. What is the overall plan for tomorrow, what do I need to bring for the afternoon meeting, in case I need to bring anything back from my office."

Adam looked over at Gary "What did you and Lynette have in mind for the meeting. What do you want to accomplish?"

Gary continued, "Well more or less we have all kinds of ideas for healing centers, web based businesses, and we have had trouble putting anything together for one solid idea for a future business. Lynette and I want to share a business together but we're coming at from all directions right now, and so if we had a round-table discussion on it with you, maybe we can reach consensus and start putting some concrete plans together."

Adam was nodding his head, "Ted, you are a fresh set of eyes, and have a MBA, did you want to participate in this discussion tomorrow?"

"Sure Adam, it sounds neat, I get pumped up with new business discussions."

"Okay Ted, how do you want to run the meeting tomorrow. How would a business conduct a strategic planning session, which sounds like what this will be?"

Before I could ask my clarifying questions, Gary enthusiastically spoke up, "That sounds great, let's pretend we are an existing company looking to launch into a new market opportunity. What do you think we should do tomorrow Ted?"

I didn't feel this was a Strategic Planning business situation, but I thought what the heck, it could be fun. "Well, I am going to treat this as a fresh overview, anything goes, brainstorming kind of session tomorrow. All we will need is some flipcharts, if you have three flip-charts (stands and paper pads) that would be helpful, maybe some colored Post-It notes, colored markers and masking tape."

"Masking tape?" queried Gary.

"Yeah so we can take some of the work done on the flip charts and if okay with you Lynette, put them up on the walls so everybody can look at them."

"Sure you're the boss Ted, I have all that stuff at the office, I'll throw them in the van, and bring them back for tomorrow afternoon. What else is happening for tomorrow?"

Everyone looked at Adam; it was funny how the three of us – Gary, Lynette and myself seemed to do that when we thought we needed direction. "I have an idea for tomorrow morning if it okay for you Lynette and Ted."

We both nodded, and looked at him as he gauged our reactions. "Lynette I would like the three of us to meet in the morning to discuss Energy Fields. Perhaps you can do a reading on Ted's chakras and see if he needs any Energy Healing."

I was biting my tongue from saying 'Say What' out loud. Lynette was smiling and nodding, "That would be great, no problem, I have been looking at your aura Ted and I think you have some blockages in some of your chakras but we'll do a more thorough assessment tomorrow."

I was suppressing another 'Say What'. Reminder to self, stay open. It was almost if Adam was reading my mind or my body language.

"Lynette, a lot of this Energy Fields and Energy Healing is completely new to Ted, but he is going to stay open to any or all new ideas."

Lynette was nodding again "I wasn't sure how much you knew about the work I do Ted, my special gifts, or all the different disciplines I study and practice. But don't worry, it will be fun and relaxing. Staying open and not closing any doors to new stuff is important Adam, but I find myself getting into too many things, perhaps closing a few doors now and then will help me focus better."

Adam was nodding, "I know your dilemma, it has been mine as well. Everyone who is raised in our Society begins to learn our own special tribe's belief system starting as a newborn. A newborn child is semi-helpless but has a complete and wonderful innocence, then the instructions on what to do and how to behave start. Don't get me wrong, developing good behavior is important, such as telling the truth, being polite and so on, but eventually we get into the belief training that may impose limitations on us, stories of the 'we are a poor family and only rich kids do that', etc. belief training is not good for young children who have an anything is possible attitude. Of course we need to adjust some aspects of the anything is possible attitude, we don't want our youngsters jumping off balconies thinking they are Spiderman, but we shouldn't impose limitations on their minds on what is possible or not possible for them. Or the 'we do things this way, other ways are bad' training that some children get. I am getting long-winded here and slightly off-track, but the point is we need to ignore limitations imposed by our tribal belief system, and we need to stay open to all possibilities, closing doors may limit our evolution and growth. Next, we can hold those ideas and make a decision on them – keep them as open ideas, hold them dear to us as a belief, or discount them as bullshit. The stage of idea evaluation should be a long and patient process. Another problem we have is making quick decisions on new ideas, either discarding them too quickly calling them poop, or vice versa adopting them as beliefs much too quickly. My final word for the evening to you Ted is have patience. Don't make up your mind too quickly one way or the other on what you see and hear."

Gary was good enough to leave the porch lights on as I found my way to the bunkhouse and turned on the light in the small room. When I turned the light on I happened to look at the night table beside the bed, on the table was a copy of the book *The Artist's Way*.

CHAPTER TWENTY FIVE

A PROCESS FOR TRANSFORMATION

I woke up at 6 AM, but rolled over and went back to sleep until my alarm went off at 7 AM. I got up, showered, shaved and got dressed. I was just about to walk over to the house, when I saw *The Artist's Way* book glaring at me and then I remembered. Morning pages. Okay let's give it a whirl. I really had a hard time writing three pages. Even using Adam's tips about jotting down nothing comments about having trouble thinking of things to write down, even the comment, 'okay here I am at one half page, just two and one half to go'. Geez, why didn't I use a smaller journal, this is a lot of writing. I wondered if I journal led in big letters and sloppily, maybe even at four words per line I could make it through this tedious assignment. It seemed to take forever, but I finished the three pages. I thumbed through the Julia Cameron book, lots of nice inspirational quotes, and some self-discipline advice. The book looked interesting, now to find the time to read it. I walked over to the house around 8 AM, Gary was just pulling out in the Van and waved at me, he had a great big smile on his face.

When I arrived at the kitchen, and Lynette was cleaning up dishes. She toasted a bagel for me and I had a bowl of cut-up melon. Lynette mentioned that Adam was upstairs meditating, he had been down early for his porridge and conversation with Gary before he left for his office in the near by town. Lynette also told me that she tried once to follow all the Julia Cameron recommended exercises for a daily routine, and didn't seem to have much time left to do anything else, but she still liked the book and the idea for the morning pages. Lynette had also filled her coffee maker and I was pleased to get my morning caffeine fix.

We were talking about the pleasantries and disadvantages of living in the country, as Adam walked into the kitchen. He was carrying his black journal but also had some loose pages with notes on them and a pen. "Good morning Ted, good morning again Lynette. Did you manage to get the morning pages done Ted?"

"I did Adam, but I am not sure it will be habit I can adopt."

"Maybe abundance is a habit you won't be able to adopt as well."

"Well, I can't see the connection."

"That is because there is no clear connection. The morning pages are a ritual to clear crud from the conscious mind and open up creativity channels. There are other habits or routines that can do the same thing as morning pages, but I suggest you find one, and get in a regular routine. It is your choice. I can only show you one or two doorways that can lead you where you want to go, you have to make the choices to open the doors and pass on through."

Adam put one of the sheets of paper in front of him. "I have been giving some thought this morning on what we are going to do. Ted, we have a great opportunity this morning to have a gifted spiritual healer assess your energy fields. I know Ted that you are a very practical person and this stuff must really sound like 'mumbo-jumbo' to you, so maybe we can take a few minutes for me to convey my thoughts on energy fields. Lynette, feel free to jump in at any time, my perspective is based on my logic, Lynette has very strong practical and intuitive knowledge of energy fields. She can teach us a lot we should know." Adam was pausing trying to pick the beginning spot to start the discussion.

"Ted, tell me what you know of alchemy?"

"Well, it is a practice where wackos, sorry did I say that out loud, I mean wizards, not wackos, apparently can transform low value metals like lead or tin, into high value metals like gold or silver."

Adam had a big grin on his face. "Well Ted, that is almost correct. If your reference is to my skills in alchemy, wacko is a good description for me. There really aren't any wizards, other than what you find in a Harry Potter book or movie, or something from the Canterbury Tales and stories about Merlin. Sir Isaac Newton was an Alchemist, and there were many others. Alchemy is a Science and an Art, although an ancient one, and the equipment and chemicals that the ancient alchemists had are no match for modern day chemistry labs. I played around with it, but did not have much luck, and I almost burned down Lynette's house. Alchemy has been a tremendous learning experience for me, and there is some basic alchemy principles that I think apply to my theory on energy. Step one – you start with a low value substance, use lead as an example. Step two – you break down the low value substance into a form where it can be reconstituted. For the lead example, heat energy (fire) and other substances that will initiate a chemical reaction are added to the cauldron. The molten lead blended with other substances creates a new concoction ready to fuse into a new form. Step three – cleanse the negative impurities from the concoction, so the atomic particles can properly realign themselves in a new configuration. Step four – add a very special substance to the molten concoction. In Alchemy this substance was called the Philosopher's stone, but, from a more practical overview in our example, we will call it a special spark of information energy. This spark of information is added to transmute the lead atoms into gold atoms and by-products. Step five- we have a cooling process and tempering process in isolation so that all chance of new impurities being introduced are minimized. The final product is a new reconstituted material, gold. We know in atomic science it will take a tremendous energy to break down a nucleus in an atom, and the risk in doing so could result in a devastating nuclear reaction, so how do we take an atom of lead with 82 protons and 125 neutrons in its nucleus and 125 electrons orbiting the nucleus in 6 different energy levels and transmute it into an atom of gold which has 79 protons and 118 neutrons in its nucleus and 79 electrons orbiting the nucleus? I have tried this for years and I still don't know the answer. But alchemy is my metaphor for a lot of things, and I have found that the five step process I just described can be used for energy reconfiguration and personal transformation."

"Step one – start with an initial substance, and specifically, let that substance be a person, and let us call that person Ted. Step two – break down the initial substance into constituent pieces. No Ted, we won't put you in a fire or a chemical bath, but we can keep the process going by improving our understanding the most fundamental elements that make up you, that being, the Conscious Mind, the Unconscious Mind, the physical energy body and the mysterious element of non-physical energy. Step three – after our understanding is enhanced, we know that the negative impurities need to be cleansed away. Perhaps these are negative thoughts, attitudes or habits. As well, the toxins in your body need to cleansed out of your body.Step four – the special information energy is added, I call this Quintessence. This energy helps realign all the energies of Ted, setting the stage for a new improved version of Ted and the life he leads. Step five - Ted patiently engages his new-found power and realigned energies so that external impurities or negative energies do not get a chance to spoil the final product."

Adam had been referring to his hand-written notes as he spoke. He looked over to me.

"What do you think Ted?"

"I don't know yet, I am trying to understand what you are saying. Step one, I'm here, and I want to learn more. Step two, I want to learn more about these energies that make up me. And step three, I am really, really glad that in my personal transformation, you have eliminated the alchemist steps that require that I get burned up in a fire or have a sulfuric acid bath."

CHAPTER TWENTY SIX

HUMAN ENERGY FIELDS

I was anxious to see where this energy discussion was going to go. Adam paused again to collect his thoughts.

"You know Ted and Lynette, I have spent many years on researching energy fields, and I don't know if I have found the final answers yet. I have theories that resonate with me, and maybe some day, hopefully soon, I can put it into a book or give the information to someone else to publish. I am looking forward to this project with you Ted, to see if Quintessence works for you and helps you receive the abundance of all good things that you are looking for. The following subject can be quite complicated, and I can tell Ted that you are getting overwhelmed, so at this stage all I plan to do is a simple overview and maybe use an analogy or two. Is that okay?"

Lynette and I both nodded in agreement.

"First some very simple definitions. Physical energy is defined as all the information that humankind has learned in the observation of all physicals forces and objects, this encompasses absolutely everything from the very large such as cosmic observations of the Universe to the very small, which is currently called particle atom physics and the theoretical and scientific study of the range of constituent components that make up atoms. Physical energy is comfortable for us, we know it exists even if we can't see the energy. For the unseen forces we can see outcomes of their existence. For example, we see that microwaves cook food, and we know that data travels through air, because we talk on cell phones. We believe the scientists when they talk about protons, neutrons and electrons and how they work in atomic structures. In that same field of play I just mentioned, co-exists an invisible, non-observed energy that I simply call non-physical energy. In fact, this energy has no boundaries. Some people do, but I don't, call this energy Life energy or Chi, Prana or the other terms. I believe this invisible non-physical energy is a divine energy, and it also includes the collective energy of humankind (we will use Jung's terminology of Collective Unconsciousness). This non-physical energy field, is like an eternal ocean, and like a physical ocean which is made up of drops of water, the non-physical energy ocean contains drops of energy which attach to physical forms. Some very special energy drops encompass and attach to both form and consciousness. Those drops can be entity specific, and there are probably a host of varieties here, but fundamentally they are souls. We can have a debate whether the non-physical energy is observable or not, I would say there are some individuals who can sense this energy with intuitive or psychic abilities, but Science has not come up with an objective observation method at this point in time."

"The next definition concerns Consciousness. Ted, I think you and I had a previous conversation on this, but simple definition is Consciousness is what you are aware of in your Mind, and Unconscious being all that you are not aware of. I believe you have a node in your Conscious where all your thoughts pass through, and this node has a virtual twin in your Unconscious where all the same thoughts in Conscious Mind also pass through the twin node which is a portal to the Unconscious Mind. And, note this, thoughts from the Unconscious can also transit from the Unconscious node to the Conscious node, becoming a new Conscious awareness. Each individual's Consciousness Mind is their own. Each individual's Unconscious Mind is both their own, usually all the activities of the Subconscious, but also is part of a great collective of all unconscious minds."

"The Unconscious node has tremendous power. It gets a steady flow of thoughts, up to 60,000 per day from the Conscious Mind, and files them away for interpretation, and some conscious thoughts are interpreted as orders requiring action. It sends signals to its twin conscious node that may become new thoughts, but it has hard to say, because some Conscious Minds have a huge amount of internal chatter, and the signals from the Unconscious might not be strong enough to overcome the chatter and be picked up as thoughts in the Conscious Node. I haven't figured out completely how Unconscious node selects which thoughts to send to Conscious node, but I believe they are generally selected because Unconscious Mind feels Conscious Mind has requested the information. The Unconscious Mind node also has a reciprocal relationship with the Collective Unconscious. The Jungian theory applies here. An individual's unconscious both sends out information that will get aggregated into the collective, and it receives information from the collective, which has the potential to become conscious thoughts. Unconscious speaks all or any languages, but its translation skills for words are limited. Instead of words or language, the Unconscious node loves visual images. A conscious mind that is skilled at creating and holding visual images in the conscious mind, is speaking powerfully to the unconscious. The most powerful thought any human can have is a visual image backed simultaneously by a conscious intention for the visual image to be created in the human's physical reality. These visualizations are often fulfilled, especially if they are repeated over and over."

"Three other things about the Collective Unconscious. The first is simple, think of the thought energy that makes up the Collective Unconscious as continually flowing with no geographic boundaries. The second point, regards the picking up of emotional thoughts from others. The Unconscious node in you is an active receptor of your conscious thought signals, but it is also the receptor for all emotional thought signals in its environment. In other words, it picks up the emotional thought signals of both the people physically surrounding you (a geographic or physical proximity requirement) and the people you have close relationships with (geography or physical proximity are not relevant). As an example of the case for physical proximity, I think you can see this, when you are in an audience for a theatrical performance. You can feel the collective energy of the group especially when it is an excellent performance because every one's Conscious Minds are thinking I enjoy this, there is a multi-sensory element, visual and sound, and the Unconscious node is reading it loud and clear and sending the signal to the collective. The second example regards family members who are emotionally close to each other. When one is experiencing emotional trauma, no matter the geography, the other will feel the trauma. The third point about the Collective, regards toxicity or negative elements.

Again, I can explain this better with an example. In the example, remember point one about flow, but also note that the Collective has a flow of Divine energy running through it, and this Divine Energy is the energy of Love and Compassion, and it is pure, pristine and clear. The Collective Unconscious also contains the flowing thoughts of all humankind from the inception of humankind to the present moment. In those thought inputs is a flow of hate, and even includes the desires to kill fellow humans. Those horribly negative flowing energies are dark toxins mixing with the pristine clear waters of the Divine energy. Therefore, when it comes to love and compassion in our world, the collective is not pure and pristine, but has a tainted color. All the Unconscious nodes of all living humans pick up this energy. The only way to clear the Collective Unconscious of its impurities is for all humankind to have lots of pure thoughts of love and compassion, sparking the Unconscious Mind nodes and sending the information to the Collective Unconscious. If done, all dark energies will eventually be diluted, and cleansed from the collective. I have seen this cleansing process happen in my lifetime when it comes to the darkness of bigotry. When I was younger, it was horrible to see the rampant bigotry versus people who did not have white skin. It was in the Collective Unconscious, generations of inputs. In my lifetime, our society has purified the Collective Consciousness. In regards to racial injustice, the collective is certainly not pristine for this element, but we have come a long way from what it used to be. The Divine energy of love and compassion still has a red tinge in the Collective with all the inputs that it is okay to kill others as punishment or in war. I am afraid it will stay take a few generations to dilute this toxicity, and, unfortunately in recent years, the level has been going up instead of down."

Adam paused for a moment. "I wish I didn't have to talk about the negative energies emitted by the Collective Unconscious, but they are real and must be dealt with by individuals."

"So far I have covered the four main components of Human Energy Fields. Physical and Non-Physical energies, Conscious and Unconscious Minds."

"I want to take a few moments to focus on the Unconscious Mind node. In the previous descriptions I might have left the impression that the Unconscious Mind node is a **passive** sender, receiver or retriever of non-physical information energy and it is to a major extent. But for personal major transformation, you need to know that the Unconscious Mind node is also an **active** sender, receiver or retriever of non-physical information energy that is attached or embedded in physical energy realities. Stop and think about this. By active, we mean it has goals to accomplish and it is working on the process of accomplishing these goals. The goals for the Unconscious Mind node are set by the Conscious Mind. There is a node in your physical body that is working 24 hours a day, 7 days a week, dispatching non-physical energy signals and attracting non-physical energies to yourself. The Unconscious Mind node is actively in pursuit of the goals set by its Consciousness twin. It is hard at work in the great field of non-physical energy creating a series of events which will make the goals a reality.Powerful stuff. Too bad most humans are unwittingly giving their Unconscious Mind nodes crappy goals."

"The Unconscious Mind node has a future state reality screen that it works with. It is a mumbo-jumbo of images of possible future events and realities with assigned probabilities. Even if it was possible to do so, the Conscious Mind can't read the imaginary screen because it moves too quick for Consciousness to comprehend and if it has audio, it is not in your native tongue. Your future state screen is in the Unconscious Mind language of visuals. Again, multiple images, and constant inputs being actively sought or passively received from the Collective Unconscious. I suppose if any human's Conscious Mind could actually see or hear his/her Unconscious Mind, they would experience insanity. There is no need to go there."

"One of the goals in using the life amazing secret of Quintessence is to help our individual Unconscious Mind node be clearly aware of our conscious desires and goals. We also want to help our unconscious mind node push up the probability ratings for good things to happen for us in the future, and lower the probabilities for bad things. "

"Our bodies are comprised of physical energy. Residing with the physical energy is the field or fields of non-physical energy. In all physical bodies, the most important field of non-physical energy is the field of information or intelligence that provides instructions to the atoms, molecules and cells of your body. Some of this energy clearly tells the atoms, molecules and cells to take on forms that result in good things happening in your body. Some of this non-physical information energy may not be properly aligned or be negatively misinformed and as a result is telling atoms, molecules and cells to take forms that end up being detrimental to your physical body. Outside physical energies can help or hurt your body – nutrients, chemicals, radiation etc. But it is also possible for non-physical energies to be channeled or redirected to help or heal your body. If the non-physical energies are attached with positive intentions, only good can be done. This is where I am going to turn over the Ted program to Lynette."

Adam sat back and drank from a glass of water, this little lecture had drained some energy from him.

"Well Adam, you continue to amaze me. What you are saying is profound and challenges me at the moment to properly understand what you have said, but it does resonate with me. I am really looking forward to the next stage". I thought about making a joke to see if I could get a laugh out of Adam but I had the feeling he was reflecting on the toxins in Our Collective Unconscious. No jokes right now.

CHAPTER TWENTY SEVEN

LYNETTE'S LESSONS

Lynette picked up where Ted left off. "I understand what Adam is saying about the non-physical energy field being a combination of amazing powers; the Divine Energy of love and compassion, the energy of Universal Consciousness, humanity's Collective Unconscious, and the mysterious existence of a great programming code, the information field that instructs atomic particles, telling them what they should be doing at any given nanosecond.And, all of these energies have two things in common – they are non-physical and they possess information. The Divine Energy is a supreme energy that contains all, and I believe it is a pristine energy that really doesn't get tainted by negative energies released by human consciousness or the unconscious mind node that Adam tells us about in his theory. I don't know what it is about Free Will that humans possess but every time a choice is made that contributes to the good of self and others, a positive energy spark goes into the Universe and a every time a choice is made that hurts self or others, a negative spark is released into the Universe. Those sparks are 'causes' for subsequent 'effects' to happen as events in the world. The positive sparks consciously or unconsciously become new causes creating additional positive effects and the same process happens for the negative sparks. Lots of movies have been made about the sequence of events that follow good deeds or bad deeds. My favorite is 'It's a Wonderful Life'. The Law of Cause and Effect works as part of the Law of Attraction. Do you know about these Laws Ted?"

"Yes Lynette, Adam told me about them. Unlike magnetic forces, in the realm of non-physical energies, positive attracts positive, negative attracts negative. Our best actions are to think positive thoughts and do positive deeds as much as we can. Unless of course our goal is to be in shitty situations all the time, then we should continue with negative thought patterns and do nasty deeds."

Lynette smiled, Adam was shaking his head but he started to smile too. Lynette went on to her next point. "I am having trouble putting into words what I know is true, and there is no handy reference manual on non-physical energies. This is an esoteric subject with hundreds of philosophical, religious and metaphysical interpretations. Now, even Scientists are getting involved as Physicists investigate Unified Field theories, coming up with propositions that subatomic particles are energy but can't be observed." I could sense some of her slight frustration, this was a difficult subject.

Adam spoke up "Lynette, why don't you talk to Ted about body energies and healing."

"Sure. But before I do that I want I want to mention that in talking about Divine Energy we get caught up in talking about all those Jesus-like qualities – Love, Compassion, Forgiveness, etc. but there is a quality of Divine Energy that is essential for healing, that quality is Order. Our Creator is very structured. Everything has a time and a place and a way it **should** be. But the Creator doesn't get in a tizzy when things aren't the way they should be. The Creator made a game, called it Consciousness, and put it in living organisms, miniscule amounts in bacteria and a lot more in humans, and to make the game interesting, the Creator gave humans the recognition of free will. Decisions, decisions, decisions, and will humans make the right ones. And in the Mind of Creator, if the right decisions are made or not, no big whoop, this is an eternal universe, and eventually a species will evolve to make God-like decisions, do the right thing, and make things as they should be. I mention order because in energy healing, the practitioner uses non-physical divine energies to tell the cells of the physical body what they should be doing, and instruct them to go to their proper place at this moment in time. However, the cells answer to their internal master seated somewhere in the Unconscious and will make a change in their function or alignment only with their specific head-office approval, so to speak. I use the term cells very loosely, but cells make up all aspects of our body, our organs, our bones, our tissues, our nervous system, our bio-chemistry, our vascular system, everything is comprised of cells. Now we are going to switch gears a little, into new territory for you Ted and talk about chakras."

"Ah that was on my list of questions to ask. A strange word."

"Chakra is Sanskrit for wheel. Your body has a constant flow of non-physical energy passing through you. There are numerous portals in the energy fields associated with your specific body, and we like to focus on seven main ones, and we call them chakras. The non-physical energy whirls as it passes through portals, and mucks around with the electromagnetic radiation in your body's physical energy fields, creating an image of wheel. Hence the name. We don't have a lot of time here to teach you about chakras but let me mention a logical context as to why they are important. When we are talking about anything with energy, flow is important. First, you want a flow to take place, and you want that flow to be positive energy. Second, for the flow to occur in your specific locations of your physical body you need to focus on the specific interfaces, call them portals or openings, or chakras, that exist between your physical body and non-physical energy. Sometimes theses openings may have blockages or the opening closes itself down because there is no flow, or your subconscious mind is protecting your physical body from flows of negative energy.The healing practitioner focuses on calling for a positive energy flow and works on opening all the channels (Chakras) into your personal physical energy body. Then we look at any specific ailment located in your physical body or if it is emotional stress of some kind, it will be associated with a specific Chakra location.Does this logic make sense to you Ted."

"Sort of. But his energy stuff is really confusing to me. I suppose it will be less confusing, the more I learn. But let me get this clear, say I have a physical ailment, like a sore shoulder, you are going to treat that with this energy flow thing?"

"Possibly. It depends on the injury or trauma. I would say the most common treatments are to release negative blockages from your energy fields, and to attack those negative energies that have metabolized in your body and are presenting themselves as physical ailments."

"Attack negative energy?"

"I guess a better choice of words would be to release it and send it to Mother Earth where it can't do any harm."

"I guess this will all take me some time to catch on. I have to go back to what we are talking about again, non-physical energy, and don't get me wrong, I am open to new ideas, but I am at the open stage looking for more information before I decide, yeah I believe it, or no, this is baloney. Explain the logic again of how this energy heals me, assuming, of course, that I have an ailment that needs healing."

"I am glad we are going over this Ted, because I know it is really confusing to understand, especially in a short time period. I like your approach by the way. Stay open, get information, ask challenging questions. Most of my students either enthusiastically accept what I say as gospel truth, which makes life easy for me, but it is not good for the student because they won't be able to support their beliefs other than say this is what Lynette has told them. And I have others who attend one session and don't come back because they have decided that I am a wacko or what I am saying is bullshit. Spending more time with me they will indeed find out that yes I am a wacko, but I also know quite a bit about Life's mysteries and they will genuinely learn things that will help them improve their lives and the lives of others."

"I am really comfortable working with wackos, as evidenced by the time I have spent with Adam this week. But I need you to go back to my original question, explain how this non-physical energy heals." I glanced out of the corner of eye at Adam and he was smiling.

"It doesn't heal. Your body heals itself. Let me create an analogy from the business world. The non-physical energy is a business consultant that has been hired by your head-office to come into your business to help you improve things. Your natural reaction is two-fold. First, if you are like most people, you may be quietly resentful that a consultant is coming in to maybe tell you how to do your job and you don't like that, and some people are fearful of the consequences of a consultant's report. Two, you know you have to co-operate by at least talking to and providing information to the consultant, because head office will definitely give you the gears if you don't do this. Overall, you know in your heart, the intention of everyone is to make things better, so you are open to proceed. While the consultant is doing their study, they identify the problem areas, and generally if you are open, you will show them the potential problem areas. At the end of the project you get a report on how things should be organized or handled and a list of changes that should be made or at least some options for changes to be made where other criteria like costs are involved. The Consultant doesn't make the changes. Either you make the changes or you don't, it is your decision in communications with your head office. Head Office might decide to not make the changes as suggested, and the situation remains status-quo."

"I like the consultant analogy Lynette. I have a 'been there, done that' in my business career in working with consultants. There is one flaw in the analogy, how do I consciously interface with the non-physical energy and get their report on what changes to make?"

"Your Conscious Mind doesn't decide. Let's put some more detail in the analogy using Adam's theory on the Unconscious twin node that works with the Conscious Mind node, shall we?"

"Sure, I want to see how you handle this."

"Say your Conscious Mind is the CEO of the large corporation, a company so big that it needs a separate Chief Operating Officer who is given the mandate to implement the plans and programs decided by the Management Committee chaired by the CEO. The management Committee is dealing with some unpleasant issues or feels that the company is not performing at its peak operational efficiency, so they decide that a Consultant needs to be brought in. The plan is turned over to the Chief Operating Officer (COO). In our analogy, the CEO is the Conscious Mind node, and the COO is the twin Unconscious Mind node. The COO will oversee the hiring of a consulting group, and selects the Non-Physical Energy Consulting Group, to visit the corporation's subsidiary company, which is having lots of problems, call the subsidiary, the I Always Get Migraines company. The COO is highly capable and understands Consultant-speak and agrees what they have recommended needs to be done. Recommendations are one thing, implementation is a separate matter. First, if it is minor tasks and programs that can be done to fix a problem, the COO goes ahead on his own in implementation. However, if it is major recommendation that that needs financial resources, human resources or a corporate cultural shift, such as changes in existing behaviors and attitudes, the COO knows that has got to go back to the CEO for a decision and he files his report and recommendations. The CEO is a busy person, he/she is dealing with many diverse sometimes conflicting department heads, he/she has major shareholders to deal with, board members and external public relations and government relations matters. In other words, he/she has a lot of chatter, and time demands. Will this CEO take the proper time to assess the proposal for change and make the decision to commit to the change, or will the CEO decide that there are more pressing issues and the company will focus on other priorities?"

"Wow Lynette, I didn't know you knew so much about business."

"I don't."

"Well that was a very well thought out analogy. How did you come up with it so quickly, and clearly articulate it for me?"

"Let us say my Conscious Mind node asked twin Unconscious Mind node to give her a business analogy to explain a concept to Ted. Unconscious Mind node says, hey where I am I going to get the right analogy in a hurry, ah, I know, I have a direct line to Mr. Ted's Unconscious Mind node, can you help, yes, wonderful, well shoot that analogy over to me so I can feed it to my Conscious Mind node. Ted, I had no idea what I was saying, I was channeling those words from another source"

I sat there blank-faced with a 'what the hell was that' look on my face, until I saw Adam who had gone from broad smile to laughing out loud.

CHAPTER TWENTY EIGHT

CELLS OF THE BODY

Adam had enjoyed Lynette's business analogy. I was still slightly confused with the whole concept of non-physical energy, and I realized the information was being given to me in measured doses because I had no experience or understanding at all of metaphysics.

Adam sat back in his chair. "You know Lynette, I enjoyed that talk you just gave, although my friend Ted still looks like he would like to learn more. I think you should probably take Ted into your Healing Room and do an energy fields assessment on him, but before doing that, can I make a couple of comments on cells?" Adam looked for our acknowledgement; Lynette and I were nodding our assent. "I find cells amazing, especially those cells in the human body. We are talking about how bits of matter exist in a living form. I don't have my research notes here, but I recall that there are 216 different kinds of cells in the human body, the cells that make up bones are different than neuron cells or cells that make up your eyes, and so on. They do have some common characteristics, almost all cells have a nucleus that is the home of that magical memory bank and programming code we call DNA. Cells have a watery body that is made up of millions of molecules. Lets overview this miracle of life, and you can understand why so many natural scientists – chemists, physicists

172

and biologists become spiritual. Ted, if you don't mind, let me use you as an example. Ted, your physical body probably has something like 93 trillion cells. We are not going to count them, or find out how many cells you have in each of the 216 categories. And, we are not going to get into a discussion as to whether some of the bacteria that are born and die within your body should have their cells count in the total. I will put on my biologist's hat, and decide to really closely examine one of your 93 trillion cells, so many options, this is like trying to make a decision in a Starbucks Coffee shop, okay, I am going to look at one cell from the billions in your heart muscle. If I take this one cell and put in under an electron microscope, I am going to see a myriad of different structures and clusters, and the best way to review this picture is to now put on my chemist's hat, or more exactly my bio-chemist's hat, and decide that the first way to examine this cell, is to find out how many molecules are found in the cell. A molecule is a combination of atoms, example, a water molecule is H_2O – two hydrogen atoms and one oxygen. How many molecules are in this single cell from the 93 trillion choices? I can't really put an exact number on this, but there are billions of molecules in this single cell. Now, each molecule is made up of atoms. Let us jump ahead to amazing coincidence. How many atoms are in a cell? Ted, the average number of atoms in each of your 93 trillion cells, is 93 trillion atoms. From a different perspective, there are more atoms in one of your cells than there are stars in the entire Milky Way galaxy. Now, I am going to put on my physicist's hat over the top of my chemist's hat and grab a single atom from the 93 trillion atoms, by numbers in your body, hydrogen will the most abundant, by weight, oxygen will be the most abundant. Let's pick oxygen. And assuming we pick out a perfect oxygen atom, and break it down, it has 8 protons, 8 neutrons and 8 electrons. Now as a physicist, I want to break these components into their constituents and I will call them particles, and to be precise, sub-atomic particles. The electron in itself is a particle, but let's look at a proton. Here we go into wierdsville. I don't want to make this confusing, let's say there are variety of different sub-atomic particles with weird names – such as bosons, muons and quarks. Side note, I really like the name quark. But, what makes up a quark? Physicists tell us there are six different types of quarks. But if it was possible to see what 'stuff' makes up a quark, what would that stuff be? The answer? **There is nothing physical left.** We can theorize that there must be energy there, and there must be some form of information that tells the energy that at this moment this energy packet will become physical as one of the six types of quarks, which will assemble into a proton, which will cluster with eight other protons, and meet up with eight neutrons to make the nucleus of an oxygen atom as long as eight electrons can link in, and this oxygen atom finds itself bonded with a single hydrogen atom to make up a hydroxide, which finds itself carbon and nitrogen atoms to make up an amino acid, which binds with other amino acids to make up a protein, which is directed to be bonded in a special sequence of proteins that make a DNA molecule which is the memory and the master of the cell which I have taken from the heart muscle of Ted Gregory. What is this non-physical energy and information that underlies, over-rides and makes up all things physical? That is were I take off my three hats of the scientist, because, we mystics don't like to wear hats."

I thought to myself, that was a terrific interruption. Yes, there is continual amazement to be found in this thing we call Life. Adam and Lynette stood up from the table, Lynette took my hand beckoning me to come with her.

"Come on into our Healing Room, I want to check out your chakras."

I was thinking 'Chakra' what a word, how am I going to remember that. I was thinking about the singer Chaka Khan, maybe one of her songs would trigger the memory bank for the word Chakra, just add an "r" to chaka. Hmmm, songs, 'I'm every woman', nahh that doesn't work for me. I better not worry about it. On to the magic room and let Lynette ream out my chakras or whatever she has to do to open them up.

CHAPTER TWENTY NINE

THE HEALING ROOM

As Lynette was guiding me into Healing Room, she looked over at Adam "Are you coming St. Germain?"

"I sure am Lynette, I want to see how you check out the rookie."

I looked over at Lynette "St. Germain?"

"Oh that is a pet name I have for Adam, I really don't believe that story about him being born in 1917 in Madagascar. He reminds me of St. Germain, you will probably read about him some day. I think Adam is really St. Germain"

"I vaguely recall the name St. Germain, a myth of about a guy, someone who had discovered the fountain of youth, or was eternal, and who lived forever through history, taking on different names and important roles."

"No he is real, some people say he has adopted a variety of disguises over the years. But everything about Adam reminds me of St. Germain. When are you going to come clean and admit the truth Monsieur St. Germain?" She was directing her question at Adam, I was trying to figure out if Lynette was joking or serious. Adam wasn't saying anything, he was laughing about it.

"Well Monsieur St. Germain, I was going to ask you if you wanted a chakra reading, but I am looking at your aura now, and I see a nice white glow around you and I know that a reading won't be necessary."

I looked at Adam – aura, glow, white light, what the blazes is Lynette talking about.

Lynette asked me to lie on her large massage table, and look at the ceiling. She had put on some nice Nature sound music and I began to contemplate having a little nap. Lynette went over to a set of drawers and began pulling out several small colored rocks, probably crystals. She put a white sheet over me. I decided then I would forgo the nap, and see what she was up to. Out of the corner of my eye, I was glancing to see if there were any large, sharp knives in the room.

"Hey Lynette, there isn't any dissection involved with this procedure is there?"

"No Ted, just relax, I am trying to hear what crystals I need to use."

"Hear?"

"My inner voice tells me what to use and where."

She continued. "Now the first thing we need to do is to check the openings on the chakras."

I needed to see which instrument did this. I was surprised when she brought over a silver chain with a large clear quartz crystal on the end of it. The crystal had a sharp point at the bottom. "What's that Lynette?"

"A pendulum. Now be quiet and watch if you like, you can ask questions when we are done."

I glanced over at Adam, he was sitting on a stool, watching and smiling. Lynette began to hang the pendulum over various parts of my body. I was slightly nervous when she was hanging it over my forehead, because of the sharp point. The pendulum moved slightly at the top of my head and my forehead, did a full circle over my throat. The pendulum didn't move at all over my chest and stomach, and I got nervous again when I saw her hanging it over my private parts. What non-physical energy was hanging around there? I was never planning on being a father but having the sharp pointed rock hanging over that region made me more nervous than the forehead area. While Lynette was going from spot to spot with the pendulum she was saying something under her breath. Again, I was wondering what quiet words she was saying while hanging the sharp rock over my privates.

At the end of this bizarre exercise, she quietly made an announcement 'Well Ted, all your Chakra's with the exception of the throat chakra seem to be closed. This may take a few sessions but I would like to conduct a session now and see how we do."

I had no idea what to say other than "Sure". If she was going to put those colored crystals on me, I was curious about which ones get placed near the gonads.

She put some small pieces of metal around me on the table. "This is hematite, it will help protect you from negative energy. I am going to use clear quartz crystals, and various pieces of malachite, lapis lazuli, rose quartz, garnet, kyanite, amethyst and obsidian." She might have been speaking Sanskrit for all I knew, I was guessing those were the names of the crystals, I was glad she started with the clear quartz, that one I knew.

She proceeded to put crystals on different parts of my body and around me on the table.

Lynette fiddled with the crystals a little, changing them around, I only felt the one on my forehead. I could smell some incense burning. She leaned over to me "Relax Ted, close your eyes and think of a pleasant vision". I decided to delete the initial pleasant vision in my mind of Pamela Anderson, and go with a new one of lying on a white sandy beach. My eyes were closed, the nice aroma, the soft relaxing music, I almost dozed off. I could hear Lynette again, "Okay Ted, we're done."

When I opened my eyes, Lynette was pulling off the white sheet. Adam was sitting on the stool smiling. "Well Ted, we managed to get them all open. But they are not used to being open, so I expect we will have to repeat this treatment. You can ask your questions now."

Lynette was placing all the crystals she used in a glass bowl.

"You are not going to put the crystals back in the drawer?"

"No I am going to cleanse them."

"How can they get dirty on a white sheet?"

"Cleansing is a figure of speech. The crystals have absorbed negative energy, and I cleanse the crystals of the negative energy and I re-program them before putting them away."

"How do you cleanse them?"

"There are various ways, I usually smudge them with burning sage, then make a recitation for the Universe to take the negative energy away, and another recitation to program the crystal with loving light and energy and instructions to help perform the greatest and highest good in their next use."

"Smudge?"

"The sage is burning, and a very nice smoke comes from it, I put the crystal in the smoke to cleanse it. Sometimes when Gary gets home from work, and I have been cleansing crystals, he thinks the sage smell is wacky tabaccy. I have to set him straight."

"Why did you dangle that clear stone on a chain over various parts of my body?"

"I put it over each chakra – your crown, your brow, your throat, your heart, your navel, your sacral, and your root area. The pendulum tells me which chakras are open. When it circles clockwise with this pendulum, others might be different, the chakra is open."

"Are my crown jewels in the root or sacral?"

"Sacral, the root is the base of your spine."

"Is there….I'll hold that question for another day, I was going to ask about potential areas of concern in the ah – sacral area…but no need to answer that now. But tell me what the crystals do?"

"They have a variety of uses depending on the chakra. The primary logic is that each crystal has a special energy frequency, I try to match the energy frequency of the chakra area with the energy frequency of the crystal. When I get harmonious matches, the chakra will open up. Some crystals I use to help absorb negative energies form the chakra. I can sign you up for one of my courses if you like?"

"No Lynette, that is it for questions. I quite frankly still don't understand this stuff, but I am still open."

Lynette smiled, "At least for the time being your chakras are open as well"

CHAPTER THIRTY

THE BUSINESS PLANNING SESSION

We had finished our "healing" session, although I had no idea on what had been healed in me.

Gary called and said he would be back at 1:30 PM. We decided to have soup. Adam said he wanted to do some research and Lynette had some household chores to do. I decided to go back to the bunkhouse to make a few notes on the Strategic Planning session we were going to have in the afternoon.I remembered as I looked at Adam before I left the house, that I had to write out my list of desires, goals, wants, needs, wishes (my word, Adam doesn't like it). It was almost like Adam sent me a Psychic transmission when I looked at him, he said nothing, but in my mind I heard his voice "Ted, don't forget your list".

I got busy with the list, and managed to get fifteen things down on the list, quickly, twelve more a little slowly, and another fifteen items struggling before I stopped. Forty-two items, and I thought I could write the list of one hundred in a breeze. I guess this will take a little more work than I thought. I had no idea what to do with the strategic planning session, if anything it would be a good chance to find out what Gary and Lynette's plans were for the future.

Sure enough Gary pulled in around 1:30. He always moved in a hurry. Such energy and a smile on his face every time he saw someone. He pulled three flipchart stands and pads out of the van, I started to rush out to help, but Gary was already in the living room area by the time I caught up. Gary and Lynette wanted to use their spacious living room area for the session. Lynette had made some coffee and tea. Gary started to tell us about some of the projects his website design and web hosting business was working on. The business was in a dilemma stage, if they were going to make money with it, it had to get bigger. Gary was noting that the software for making web-sites was so much better now, people could design their own web-sites, and the big web-hosting companies had so many options with standard templates for web designs that they offered in their service packages, it was getting difficult to sell web design services. A company in Chicago was interested in acquiring the client base, but they didn't want the equipment such as the servers. Gary liked the business but he wasn't happy at spending fifty to sixty hours a week working at it. Customer service is important in the business, and the business was staffed with technical support 24 hours, 7 days.

"This would make a great case study for my old Business School Gary", I remarked.

"Well, I don't think we have much time to study anymore, I need to make a decision."

The best way in any dilemma is to note what you would like to see happen, and then assess if there is any probability of that happening. As I mentioned that to the group my Conscious Mind flashed to my healing session on Lynette's table where she asked me to visualize something pleasant. Visualize a desired situation, then assign a probability factor for it happening. In nanoseconds, I assessed a probability rating of spending some nice time with Pamela Anderson at 0.00001%. Not impossible but probability potential was diminishing with time. Another visualization, me lying on a nice warm sandy beach, probability factor in the next three months, 20% with some upside potential depending on money flow.

Gary thought for a moment. "I need to look at everything in my life, or our life together. I am 56 and I want to spend time on my real interests. The web biz doesn't cost me cash right now, but it sucks up too much of my time, and that is happening even after hiring a General Manager for the business. I see Lynette and I starting some sort of Metaphysical learning center and healing center. I don't know much about the alternative healing modalities other than using music and sounds to facilitate relaxation, meditation and creative mind states, but Lynette has been and is into everything. She is tremendously gifted, and I have learned so much from her. To reach a wider audience for the healing center and learning center, I believe we need a web presence, and Lynette does as well. All my money is tied up in my business and our property, so we don't have much, if any, to invest in the healing center or metaphysical learning center ideas. So we have a current situation that is holding us back from where we want to go, and for that matter, we really haven't decided what we want to do specifically because there are so many options."

I felt like a classroom instructor, I was standing up, and had made a few bullet points on one of the flipcharts for a page title CURRENT SITUATION. I went to another flipchart and wrote the word VISION and made a few more bullet points"Lynette, is there anything you want to add"

"Gary is completely right on, I have some funds available for the new business, even though healing, teaching and creating are my passions, I feel we need to look at our shared dream as a new business. We need an income, and both of us will be spending all or most of our time in it. My personal dilemma is that I have so many metaphysical interests, and I don't want to sound like Forrest Gump, but it is like there is a big box of metaphysical chocolates and I have taken little bites out of each chocolate to taste them all, but I haven't decided which chocolates I want to eat, and now I have to eat them all or throw them out because I have eaten little pieces out of each one."

Gary chimed in for support, "Don't worry honey, I'll eat some of the chocolates, I don't mind your goobers."

We all had a laugh. I went over to third flipchart and marked it ISSUES and made two bullet points – one being focus, the other being investment dollars. I looked over at Adam. he was enjoying the discussion. "Our learned Monsieur St. Germain, aka Adam Almeida, do you see anything that we can add to our assessment of the Current Situation, Issues, or Vision."

"Lynette, I am going to cast a spell a spell on you for teasing me about St. Germain in front of my new friend Ted"

Lynette interrupted him "Exorcising harmful spells is one of my specialties St. Germain, bring it on baby, lets see what you got."

We had another group laugh. I can't remember if I had ever laughed in any other Strategic Planning session I have ever participated in., I guess there is always the first time. Adam picked up my question again, "Well Ted, I don't know where these initial thoughts of mine fit on your three lists, but let me throw them out while I am thinking of them. One - first thing that Gary and Lynette are going to have to do is make a final decision about future of the web business and implement it, that issue has implications for timing for the new venture, financial matters, and whether Gary will be involved with it at all. Two - I am interested in learning about Lynette's skills, knowledge and metaphysical interests. I have a general idea, but I would like to know in what areas she could help other people whether that is with teaching or healing. Three – I am not a business man in any great way, but if I was, I would want to know what market are we going after and, with that point, who will be the paying customers for the products and services? There are other points in my mind, but they are not as relevant as these three, and I see Ted writing them down on the issues page."

I was thinking of possible next steps, and the best choice in my mind wasn't one I wanted to raise, because it wouldn't include Lynette, as I finished the thought, Lynette spoke up.

"Why don't I take one of the flipcharts and write down all the areas I am interested in and for which I have teaching or healing skills. It will take some time, so why don't you Ted, Gary and Adam go into the kitchen and review some possible future options for Gary's web business. I don't mind not being involved in that talk, in fact, I prefer not to be, I don't want to influence Gary, in saying or doing what he feels he needs to say or do."

Geez, Lynette must have her Unconscious node monitoring my Unconscious node's phone line to my Conscious Mind node. She articulated my exact thought "Okay, that is an excellent plan".

The three guys moved into the kitchen. It was remarkable, all four of us had our own notepads. As we sat down at the table, I glanced back into the living room, and saw that Lynette had flipped over the first page on all three pads, I was wondering if she was going to fill them all.

High energy Gary jumped right in "I need to sell the business, get all my investment money back and a nice return for time and effort for the last few years. Everything paid to me in cash. End of story."

"Well this will be a quick meeting", I started and then hesitated, "Gary is that possible?"

"I don't know for sure, I haven't really tried to sell the business. I called one of my equipment suppliers and told him what I was thinking of doing. He was very little help at first, and seemed more concerned about whether I had money set aside to pay off the financing for the equipment he had placed with me. But, at the end of our chat, he gave me the name of a big company in Chicago, and the name of the President. I called the guy, we talked, but all he wants to do is buy the client list, he has more than enough equipment capacity he doesn't want to buy my physical assets. Besides the fact that the equipment is obsolete compared to what you can get in speed and storage today for less money."

"Gary, I really don't know the business you are in very well, but I do know it is a growth market. What concerns me is that I hear about companies going bankrupt all the time in this market segment, and I wouldn't advise any of my investment accounts to buy into one of these businesses unless the business had a strong cash position. And, none of the companies that I have seen have this area have strong cash positions, even after raising money with stock offerings. A big chunk of the investment money raised in the new stock issues goes to pay off banks and venture capitalists. I think it will be hard to sell the business, since your business prime competency and profit generator, web design, is under pressure. Can we take a few moments and explore other options?"

"No point. I guess I need to close down the business, there are no other options."

"Well, option one would be to shut down the business and option two is"

Gary pulled back into his chair, arms folded "I can't see any other options."

"Gary, we need to list the options first, no matter how silly they might seem, then decide how we are going to evaluate them, and then decide what is worth further investigation. Let's not jump to a decision without going through the process."

Adam was a quiet, passive, observer to our dialogue. I recognized that I was on my own here with Gary for the time being. I spoke again.

"Okay, let me list the options as I see them, then Gary you add yours, and Adam yours. One- Sell the business. There are probably a variety of sub-options for this we'll note them later. Two – Close down the business. Three – Invest in the business, make it bigger and stronger. Four – Modify the business. Again, more subsidiary options here such as scaling it down, or adding new or different products and services. Gary, anything to add?"

"I was biting my tongue on jumping to conclusions again, but no, those are good basic options."

I looked at Adam, he was shaking his head in a no motion. He had nothing to add.

"Okay, what is important for us to use as option evaluation points, we'll call them criteria?"

Gary started, "What are some of the business selling sub-options and sub-options for business modification?"

"Well first, let us note some of the important things for evaluation, the criteria, before we go back to the broader list of options."

"You are on a roll here Ted, why don't you put a few on the table."

"Okay, as I see it there are a couple of points and only you Gary know their importance in the big picture. One- financial, two- value of Gary's time, three –assessment of the true value of the business, is it asset value or is it cash-flow generation (now and in the future) for each option. I am not sure if employees are a consideration here."

Before Gary could answer, Adam spoke, "People are always the most important consideration Ted. I consider people as the most important assets of any business" I wasn't going to use my pure capitalist's viewpoint argument with him. It is Gary's choice.

I could see that Gary was torn, he had is own financial and time involvement interests, but I could also tell he cared for his staff. He spoke, "I have great staff, they are local people, friends and family of friends including my cousin's daughter. If I sold the business, I wonder if the new owner would shut it all down. A downside when the staff finds out that I am in the process of looking for a buyer, a couple of my highly skilled and creative employees could leave, in effect diminishing the value of the business and creating all kinds of new hassles for both myself and the remaining staff. And guys, my rationale mind is telling me that I won't find anyone with money to buy the business. Man, what am I going to do here?"

I looked over into the other room, Lynette was still patiently filling out the pages, now I was wondering if she was going to use more than three pages on the flipcharts. I turned back to the guys, "Well, let us look at the options again. Selling the business, still the ideal state if we get our price, and we keep all the operations alive in town and all the employees keep their jobs. Can we sell the business to the employees?"

"Yes, but I get no cash, they really have no money to invest, and it will be hard for a bank to finance the employee purchase, even with my solid equity in the business that I have now, I still get unbelievable hassles from the bank in making any changes to my line of credit. My biggest debt in the business is with the company that sold me the servers and the telecommunications lines. The only way for a sale to the employees could work would be to find a benevolent financier." I know why he looked at Adam when he said this, but Adam was focused on Lynette in the other room, he had no facial expression.

"Okay, let's change gears, and talk now about ways to modify the business. Is there anything you can think of that we can add to the business, or do things differently or pieces of it that we can sell off or shutdown?"

Gary thought quietly for a moment "There are a whole bunch of things I have thought about, but nothing that would give me the money I want. I have decided that I am not going to put anymore of my money into the business or borrow any more money from anywhere. In this case, I don't think there is anyone I convince to invest money in this business. But let me throw out some other possibilities. First, I haven't thought about this until Adam raised the point, I have now decided the employees are important to me personally, more important than money. But I can't go bankrupt to keep them all working.

Here are some mixed up possibilities One - sell off the retail client list, which is home based businesses, small stores and individuals because it is time consuming from a service standpoint. But we would maintain the commercial and industrial clients because we don't need to have 24/7 service staffing for these accounts, and the revenue per client is higher. Although in this business segment we don't have a lot of clients in our area of central Michigan. Two – two of my talented people have both said they would make more money on their own free-lancing because their skills can be used for other things such as developing new software programs or specialized applications. I could let them do their own thing and just pay them for project work. If I did this, I would cancel all my web marketing activities spent in seeking small new accounts. Then, I or someone else spends some time in sales efforts in the local area trying to expand our commercial and industrial client base. Lots to consider here, it might take me a little time to work this out into a plan, but I feel this plan has some potential"

I looked over to the other room; "Well it looks like Lynette is almost finished with her list. Gary, I know where you can get five new commercial accounts in a short period of time."

Gary perked up, "Where's that Ted?"

"Lynette. It looks like she has enough metaphysical interests to start up at least five separate web-based businesses."

We all laughed as we stood up to go to the other room.

CHAPTER THIRTY ONE

THE VISIONING EXERCISE

Lynette was staring at her fourth page on the flipcharts. "I know it looks like I am finished with my listing, but I have just stopped to see if there are any duplications and I wanted to count them. I have sixty-four items of the things I feel capable of teaching or doing. I know I can add another ten or more, but maybe we should stop here and see what we need to do next."

Gary sat down, but Adam and I both spent a few moments reviewing the notes. Strangely enough we both were making "hmm" sounds. Adam 'hmms' were because he was probably personally interested in the subject matter. My 'hmm's were related to wondering how I managed to live on this planet for over fifty years and I was seeing words I had never encountered before. I hadn't even considered that there were so many specific alternative or metaphysical areas that thousands, maybe millions of people, have in the past or are presently studying or practicing.

I wanted to move into a discussion on the specifics of the business and how to bring value to customers, but I had no idea of what the business would be like. I chose another path for this stage of the session, "Lynette, can you verbally describe, or help us paint a mental picture of your vision or your desired situation for us."

Lynette was glancing at her lists, "This was a tremendous exercise for me she said. I forgot to even put on the list my favorite two things which are writing and painting. I have been blessed to do so many things, and learn so many things in my life." She paused for a moment and closed her eyes. When she started talking again, I noticed that she had not opened her eyes. "I see our farm as it is now, the house, the barn and the workshop. The workshop has an extension with a large room upstairs that keeps our computers and where a small number of people work on the web-sites we have created for metaphysical teaching and counseling. We have a room of treasures, creations of the earth, crystal artwork, and pendants and healing tools. People buy these for pleasure or to help them in practical applications such as meditation and healing. There is an amazing pathway that runs behind the workshop and the beautiful gardens behind our house. This pathway veers into the woods and gently winds it way through Nature. You can walk on this path, or ride your bike or drive slowly along it because you will want to take in the wonderful gifts of trees, plants, rocks, birds and small animals that Mother Nature has blessed us with. The path will take you to a clearing and as you come out of the woods and into the meadow, you are struck with bright golden sunlight. The path cuts to the right and up a hill. The beautiful meadow is filled with tall grass and wild flowers. A stream runs through the meadow, and there is a pond. There are fish in the pond. After standing for a moment, to breathe in the wonderful smells of the meadow, we continue walking on the path. Looking ahead we see that the path climbs a hill into the edge of the woods, and we see a beautiful log cabin, on the hill with a vista of the large meadow below. The cabin has a large front porch. If you are driving you can park behind the cabin. When you go inside you see open spaces, and your first glimpse of a large stone fireplace. The modern kitchen is also open and there are many tables and chairs. Perhaps twenty people or more can sit down for meals or sit and turn to face a speaker who is giving a talk or lecture on some interesting subject that deals with healing our planet or ourselves. There are bedrooms at the back of the cabin for guests to stay in, there are quiet sitting areas at the back for meditating or healing sessions. You pause to once again to take in the meadow by viewing it through the large glass windows or you can go out to the front porch, and sit in a chair to gaze down at the sea of tall grass and flowers and listen to the babbling of the brook below. At night you can sit on the porch and look up at the clear night sky, view the constellations and a glorious silvery white moon. People come here to learn, they come here to teach, they come here to heal others, and they come here to be healed themselves. People can come here anytime they wish, because there will always be someone here to greet them with a warm and friendly smile. There is harmony, peace, love, simple order and joy in this setting." She stopped, her eyes were still closed. She was savoring the sight. Gary also had his eyes closed. Adam was sitting and smiling with me.

Almost every company has a vision statement. I have read or heard literally hundreds of them. I have spent untold hours working and even bickering with colleagues as we sat in our workshops creating new vision statements for our companies. This was probably the best vision statement I had ever experienced. I could Lynette's desired situation clearly and I felt like I was walking the pathway with her.

I closed my eyes. You can see great things more clearly with your eyes closed.

CHAPTER THIRTY TWO

BUSINESS COMPETENCY

When I opened my eyes, everyone was staring at me. I stood up, "Well that is a fantastic vision statement, now we have some practical matters to deal with here. Do Gary and Lynette act like Kevin Costner in *Field of Dreams*, where he takes all the family life savings, and money borrowed from a bank, and whacks down a big part of a corn field to make a baseball diamond with bleachers, and night lights etc. on a farm in the middle of no where? All this risk taken on the advise of a quiet voice coming from the corn field saying 'build it, they will come'"

Blank faces in my audience. I guess not everyone watches as many movies as I do.

"I know we have a wonderful vision here for a combination Metaphysical Learning Center and Healing Center. But I think you also want it to be a successful business. Am I correct Gary and Lynette?"

Lynette was nodding in agreement, Gary verbalized his nod, "Absolutely."

I continued with my short lecture on business competencies. "A lot of new businesses fail because they try to be all things to all people, and they can't pull it off. The research that has been done on successful businesses has found that successful businesses have many positive traits, but they all have a special mastery in only one of four areas of competence. This is called the Miller Heiman model. Competence area one- the business knows the wants and needs of their customers better than anyone else. And, the business devotes itself to delivering a range of products, and, more important, special services for their customers who will repeatedly buy from this company because they trust and value the company. Business Strategists call this competency area Customer Intimacy, and don't take the intimacy word literally. Competence area two – the successful business has products or services that are unique, that no other business has. These companies are generally found in the newer high technology or biotechnology sectors for both industrial and consumer goods and services. These companies have innovative products, or are building new markets. Competence Area three- the successful company is one that makes incredibly high quality products and/or offers excellent services that are hard to match. We call this competency product excellence. This excellence is valued by their customers who will pay more for it. Competence Area four – the successful company is set up to be super efficient in making its products or offering its services. When the company is so efficient and effective at the same time, they have the ability to provide good quality products and services at the lowest prices. Call this Operational Excellence." I picked a clean sheet of paper and wrote down the four competence areas – Customer Intimacy, Product Excellence, Innovative Products and Services, Operational Excellence. Then I went back into teacher mode."No more discussion on this, unless you have a point for clarification. Our goal is to make sure Gary and Lynette's dream project will be a successful business. Each of you with no consulting with the others, write on a sheet of paper what you think will be the one, foremost area of competence for the enterprise for it to be successful. I will also write a choice."

This was a tough case. I figured that this was a totally new market, with a barely known product or service. Any prospective customers would be the ones that would go for something totally new, so I selected Innovative Products and Services. Back to teacher mode, " Okay, let's go around the room, state your choice and why.

"Let's start with you Gary."

"Operational excellence, because it will only be Lynette and myself and a few others in the business, we will make our money by doing a good job, and not spending too much money"

"Lynette."

"Customer Intimacy, we really need to know what our clients need so we can do the right thing for them."

"Adam"

"Product Excellence. There are now thousands of books, hundreds of web-sites, hundreds of seminars and thousands of practitioners, in the areas that Gary and Lynette will be offering. To be successful, Gary and Lynette's Learning and Healing retreat must become a leader with excellent products and services."

I told the group my choice. "Well I must say I have never had four people pick four different answers. I guess they are all right in a way, but we must select one specific one. What is the drawback to my choice?"

Lynette spoke "The markets for alternative and holistic healing modalities are diverse and growing rapidly. More people are disillusioned by the drug dominated preferred method of treatment and the high cost of western medicine. People are now recognizing that age-old Eastern healing methods and North American Native healing traditions have merit. None of this is new or innovative."

I thought for a moment "Okay. I agree. But I don't know which of the three to switch too. I need to ask you, Gary and Lynette, whether this business will be small or large."

Lynette spoke again, "The Healing Center will be small, it will be more or less dedicated to training new practitioners, the web business will be larger because it will appeal to a mass market."

"A follow-up question, do you really think you can pull off mass marketing sixty-four or more specialties?"

Lynette stopped for a moment, "I think the sixty-four metaphysical subjects can be covered in the Metaphysical training sessions, but I agree there is no way we can handle mass market healing treatments on the web, it is more or less personal interface. There are some things we can do in marketing educational materials and energy tools like crystals, but even using staff, unless we have excellent healing practitioners with strong psychic gifts, healing treatments over the web will be a challenge."

"One more follow-up question, what areas or groupings of the sixty-four items will bring the most benefit to society?"

Lynette didn't pause, "Energy healing, and guidance in personal transformation"

"Gary, are you standing firm on your choice and want to challenge the other two options?"

"No Ted, I am switching to Product Excellence, I think if we narrow our focus to Energy Healing and guidance in personal transformation, we need to develop a top quality program, to draw people to us either on the web or to our learning center. The energy of the program, will create that positive power of attraction. We need excellence in products and services, first and foremost. I love customer intimacy, but having twenty customers that we know intimately, giving us $100 to $200 for the year will pay the hydro bill but nothing else."

Lynette was smiling, "I will settle with intimacy with my husband. I will also get to know my students really well, so I can help and guide them. I switch my vote to product excellence."

Before turning to Adam I spoke, "I think Product Excellence is the Competency area, if achieved, which will result with this business being successful. Product is defined as all services and products related to Energy Healing and Guidance in Personal Transformation including courses. Adam, our wise and learned friend, do you have anything to say which will lead us to a higher understanding of the world we live in? "

"Yes, two things. Both related to the body. I need to pee, and I'm also starved."

CHAPTER THIRTY THREE

THE CLEARING

We agreed to break for the day. Both Gary and Lynette thanked us for the help we gave them today and told us that they would decide the next steps of action on their own. I offered to continue helping them, all they had to do was call or email me. We had a spaghetti dinner with salad, and after cleaning the dishes, it looked like everyone wanted to go have their own quiet time. Lynette asked Adam and myself to be in the living room at 8 PM. She wanted us all to watch a 'Lesson' movie together. As I went back to my room, I managed to think of another four items for my goals, desires list. On the night stand was another book, *The Legend of Bagger Vance*, I remembered the movie with Will Smith and Matt Damon, but did not know the movie was based on a book. Where the blazes did the book come from? I don't remember seeing Gary, Lynette or Adam leave the house and come over to the bunk house. At eight o'clock I joined the others, and we watched *The Dark Crystal*, an animated Jim Henson movie. Lynette spoke briefly after the movie about the lessons in twin souls and polarities. I made mental notes to ask Adam about these lessons.

Before retiring for the evening, Gary and Lynette said they wanted to take us on a Nature hike in the morning. If we had boots with us, we should wear them. Adam had given me the warning to bring boots before we left, and I was prepared. Lynette said to come over for breakfast anytime in the morning, we would leave for the hike at 9 AM. I went back to my bunkroom, got ready for bed, and just before lying down on the bed, I noticed another book. *God's Debris* by Scott Adams, the Dilbert cartoon guy. Geez, is the book fairy leaving me these books to read? Choices, choices, *God's Debris* looked like the shortest book to read, so it became my bedtime reading choice for tonight.

I was up at 6:30 AM on Sunday morning. I got myself ready for the day, and sat down to write my morning pages. Before starting, I said to myself, I still need a few items for my big goals and desires list, hopefully a few ideas will come to me as I write these pages. Sure enough, I managed to get the three pages done, and pick up another eighteen items for my list. As I was copying them from one journal to the separate list, I thought of eleven more, I was now up to eighty-nine items for my list. I just needed eleven more to reach my goal of one hundred, I wonder if my project of writing a list of one hundred items for my goals and desires list can count as a goal or desire for the list? I'll hold it in reserve in case I need it.

I slipped over to the house at 8 AM. Gary and Lynette were having their breakfast, Adam had already been down and had his porridge, and he was now up in his room doing "Adam stuff". Lynette asked me if I wanted an omelet, it sounded pretty good to me, and the coffee was ready. We had a good chat about the sessions we had on Saturday. Lynette told me she wanted to check out my chakra openings after the walk. Gary had suggested that instead of walking, they could take the All Terrain Vehicles. They had two ATV's. Lynette said she would rather ride on a bike. Adam came bouncing into the kitchen. He had picked up on the conversation.

"Gary, you take one ATV, I'll take the other. Ted do you want to bike with Lynette or ride on the back of an ATV with either Gary or myself."

Not a hard decision there. "I'll bike along with Lynette."

There was a shed at the back of the barn, Gary unlocked the door and we saw the toys. Two ATV's, two snowmobiles, two mountain bikes. Adam found a helmet, and put it on.

"Where are we going?"

Gary spoke, "We'll take you down that path behind the workshop. It is rather narrow, and rocky, so we better be careful." Gary got his helmet and put it on, got on and started his machine. He looked over to see if Adam needed help, but he had already started the ATV. Gary took off slowly and started down the trail. Adam was following. Lynette and I took out the bikes and started biking down the trail. I looked ahead and saw that Adam had put his machine into full throttle, bounced off the path and raced past Gary. Adam had now bounced back on to path ahead of Gary and was pulling away. I could hear his distinctive laugh. Is this guy really eighty-seven years old?

Lynette sighed as she biked beside me. "Boys and their toys". It was a nice bike ride; I could still see pockets of snow nestled amongst the trees in the wooded area we biked through. We were by ourselves; Adam and Gary were long gone. I couldn't hear the engines. In another five minutes of biking, I could see we were approaching a clearing ahead. We were now at the edge of the wooded area. The sight looked familiar. We stopped biking. Adam and Gary were waiting for us. There, down the slope was the expansive and glorious meadow of Lynette's vision. Too early in the season for flowers. I could see a stream in the middle area of the meadow, but no pond. There wasn't a path to the right, but I saw a little clearing on the hill, my imagination kicked into full throttle like Adam on the ATV and I saw the most beautiful imaginary log cabin with an imaginary stone chimney and imaginary smoke coming from the burning wood in the imaginary fireplace. I felt great joy. That was a feeling I wasn't imagining. It was real.

CHAPTER THIRTY FOUR

BOOKS

We walked around to the spot where the cabin would be built. It was a wonderful view, just as I had imagined it when Lynette was reciting her vision yesterday. I could see it was all going to come together for Gary and Lynette.

Adam was standing on the crest of hill, hands on his hips taking deep breaths, filling his lungs with the nice, fresh country air. I walked over to him.

"Well Adam, I could see you living here. Nice little cabin in the woods. I could also see you living as monk in some Tibetan monastery. Meditating every day, and also teaching the young Buddhist Priests about enlightenment."

He looked over at me and smiled. "Yes those same ideas have tempted me in the past, but there are missing ingredients. Isolation is an excellent method to help with self-exploration, but on the other hand, you can find time every day for twenty to thirty minutes of silence and meditation, and that is all I need. Isolation in a cabin or a Monastery would be selfish of me, and I don't need it. I need to have contact with people every day, feel their problems and help them if I can. I need to stay in motion, and do things I have never done before to experience as many of Life's offerings that I can. Look at the ATV, that is the first time I have ever driven one. That was a lot of fun." He was smiling broadly.

"You are a maniac driver. You are not driving my car." I was smiling.

"Thanks for the compliment Ted. It has been awhile since I was last called a maniac. It sounds nice. Do you like it here?"

"It has been a wonderful trip Adam, I am really pleased to be here."

"I know."

Gary, the ex-contractor, went into great detail on how he was going to build the cabin. He was also going to build a dam to make a pond in the stream. He wanted to also put up a windmill at the top of the hill behind the cabin to generate electricity. We wandered through the woods for a while looking at different trees and plants that were starting to emerge from the thawed ground. When it was time to head back Lynette commandeered the two ATV's and helmets and ordered me to drive one, Adam and Gary would bike back. Lynette was leading the way back the path, at about the half way point, I looked ahead and saw a mountain bike come racing down a slight hill on our left, dodging two trees and scooting up on to the path ahead of Lynette. It was Adam. Gary was behind me on the path. I looked back at him and he was grinning from ear to ear.

Back at the house we had locks and bagels for lunch. Lynette wanted to take Adam into town to the bookstore, Gary wanted to show him his business. I knew they had some other items to talk about, so I asked if I could stay back at the farm and catch up on some reading.

I had a nice leisurely afternoon lying on my bed reading my book. I even managed to catch a snooze. I was most proud of the fact that I managed to reach my goal of finishing my list of one hundred goals and desires. When Adam, Gary and Lynette returned they brought with them some Chinese food for dinner. That evening the 8:00 PM Lesson movie was *The Matrix*.Lynette was commenting on the multitude of little lessons in the movie, how we impose limitations on ourselves, is the world we are living in real or an illusion, the importance of choice or free will, is reality a dream, your biggest quest is gaining self-knowledge, etc. I really liked the bad guys, especially Agent Smith.

Before heading back to my bunkhouse room, I mentioned that I was getting nice surprises for reading material and asked if I could borrow the books. Lynette told me I could keep *The Artist's Way*, it was her gift to me. Gary said I could keep *The Legend of Bagger Vance* it was his gift to me. Adam said I could borrow *God's Debris*, when I was done with it, I had to give it to someone else.

When I got back to the bunkhouse, and entered the bedroom, I saw another book on the night table. It was a larger book, *A Short History of Nearly Everything*. I could see some paper sticking out of the book, and I pulled it out. The note said "You can keep this book, it is excellent reference material, love (platonic only), Adam."

CHAPTER THIRTY FIVE

DREAMS

I was up at 5:00 AM, got my stuff packed, showered and ready for the day and sat down with my pen and journal and completed day three of the morning pages. I looked out the window and saw a light on in the kitchen, so I headed over to the house.

Adam was in the kitchen standing by the stove.

"You are going to have some this morning Ted."

"Have what Adam?"

"Some porridge. I saw the light on in the bunkhouse, knew you were up, so I decided to make double my normal amount this morning."

"Sure I'll have some? Did you sleep well Adam?"

"Oh yes. I always sleep well. I had a lot of REM last night."

"Isn't REM a band?"

"Oh yes, I should have said Rapid Eye Movement sleep. It is our dream state. I guess the eyes under your lids are darting all over the place when you are lucid dreaming. I had a dream where I was sitting on some large stone steps listening to a guy in a flowing gray robe talking about something philosophical. I don't know who it was, maybe Aristotle, Plato or Socrates. But as it is in a lot of dreams, the meaning is not always evident. This great philosopher was talking about techniques used in bird watching, and he had a pair of high-powered binoculars. I am not sure if they had those lectures in 360 BC. I'll pick a time in history when Plato and Aristotle both were around. Although Aristotle was a young kid in 360BC and in my dream was probably sitting on the steps with me listening to Plato describe how to sneak up on the Lost Bird of Paradise without startling him. How was your sleep Ted?"

"I slept very well, but I rarely remember dreams, so maybe I don't have REM sleep."

"Oh I think you do. You just need to get in the habit of making your first conscious thought of the day, 'what was that dream?' Before doing anything, including your morning wiz, give the dream a title, so you can remember it. 'Viewing the Lost Bird of Paradise by Plato' or whatever. Try it. I encourage you strongly to do this. Dreams can be important, especially the lucid ones because the node in the Unconscious Mind is creating a special Lessons movie with each dream. All lessons are important, and some of these lessons are very important for the Conscious Mind. The Unconscious Mind node is hoping Conscious Mind node gets a glimpse of these dream movies or maybe even watch and remember the whole thing. Conscious Mind node can't select the dream movie. Unconscious Mind node is like Lynette who picks the movie she thinks you should see. The Unconscious Mind node might pick a dream with an historic setting and time. Some analysts say this is a playback of scenes from a Past Life. Sometimes the Unconscious Mind node might play a dream of current events, but you might find yourself flying or getting killed or some other thing that hasn't happened. The Unconscious Mind node has its own language, it loves visuals instead of words, it loves symbols, such as using animals and birds instead of plain speak. There are lots of books out there on interpreting dreams, and analysts have made a lot of bucks asking their patients to tell them their dreams so they through dream interpretation uncover the cause of any neurosis. I do my own dream interpretations, but I will have to ponder this lost Bird of Paradise dream, and see if I can find my lesson. I will stay open today looking for a sign that will help me interpret the dream, and discover my lesson"

Adam had put the porridge on the table, I put some milk with it, but I couldn't find any sugar in the kitchen cupboards so I got some maple syrup from the refrigerator. This discussion on dreams was interesting. "Adam, you mentioned Past Lives, do you believe in reincarnation?"

Adam paused for a moment, "I think it is highly possible. I would say I am still in the open stage, I have been in this openness stage for sixty years. I haven't adopted reincarnation as a belief, but I haven't closed the door on it either. Reincarnation does fit with one of my beliefs. You are not a body with a Soul, you are an eternal Soul with a temporary body. After Death your Soul goes somewhere, maybe back to the Divine Source or maybe it floats in the vast array of non-physical energy. If it does the later, it becomes logical, at selected times, that the soul will take on an assignment to another body in another time. The prime theory on reincarnation is we have a number of lessons to learn, if we don't learn them in this Life, we come back in another life to learn them. I am open to the theory, but it is not a belief. There is also the Hindu belief system that you start out in a lower life, maybe an insect or an animal and your Soul if it is good in one life keeps going upward in status in future lives. I don't believe that. But if I did, the ultimate reincarnation is to come back as a pampered cat or dog."

"You sure emphasize the 'staying open' philosophy, if I never see you again Adam, I would say that is one way you have changed my Life."

"I am glad Ted, because that is a Prime Lesson for anyone with any dreams or desires of making something better, including themselves. Being open and aware. This state of mind keeps you adaptable for now moment and future positive changes. In seeking a Life of abundance, it means you stay open to the opportunities, and you enjoy yourself on a continual basis. Ultimately you will lead a blissful existence. I feel I am almost there myself. I have found that Life is not like watching a DVD or video, because you can't hit the pause button or rewind to a part and say let's play this over again. If you miss out on an important lesson, or miss a big opportunity for growth, the Creator is a good sport, another opportunity will come. You just have to keep that open mind and be alert for it. Plant those seeds of intention for the things you want or want to do, and take some daily actions in that direction. We talked about synchronicity, if a meaningful coincidence occurs, stop and think about it, because growth opportunity for you, either small or large, is in the vicinity."

I looked over at Adam "Daily practice to help build my mastery of Power of Intention, does that mean I go to Wal-Mart every day, to get a parking spot by the door?"

Adam laughed, "No Ted, just go on really busy days, you need to be challenged to develop your skills, and in mastering this specific skill, degree of difficulty practice is more important than daily repetition although both are necessary. No Wal-Mart stops today on our way home." He was laughing as he picked up my bowl and his to go back to the sink.

CHAPTER THIRTY SIX

THE TRIP HOME

We loaded up the car with our stuff, and headed back to the kitchen. I was trying to decide whether to find Lynette's coffee maker to brew a pot or not, but didn't have to worry about it when we got back, both Lynette and Gary were up and the coffee was brewing. I found out that Adam and Lynette were flying to Phoenix this upcoming Sunday, Lynette was flying from Chicago and would meet Adam there as he was going from Toronto to Chicago, Chicago to Phoenix. They had a mutual friend named Ray who was going to meet them in Phoenix and drive them to Sedona. Gary and I sat at the table drinking coffee listening to Adam and Lynette talk about vortexes, and travel between dimensions, and the stuff you might read in a SCI-FI novel, or glance at in the pages of a tabloid, alien abductions and that kind of stuff, waiting in line at a food store check-out counter. I could see that Adam was in his "I'm open" mode, while Lynette had a distinct set of beliefs.

While listening to them I was daydreaming of standing in a long hallway of experiences with open doors on the left being, "I have reviewed the idea and reject it"; once rejecting it that door closes. On the right hand side were open doors labeled "I have reviewed the idea and accept it as a belief", when the idea becomes a belief the door closes. The fascinating thing was once one door closed, the one opposite closed as well. As I walked a long this hallway, in my daydream, I walked around some ideas or experiences still sitting on the floor, doors open on either side. I obviously hadn't decided for myself whether this idea sitting on the floor should be rejected or accepted as a belief. For example, the reincarnation concept was lying on the floor of my hallway. I was thinking that most people didn't walk very far along their hallways, and if they did, when they looked back there would be a lot of closed doors. I had this image of Adam's hallway of being incredibly long and he was miles along the hallway, and if he looked back at the direction he had come from, most of the doors would be open.

When all the vortex discussions were completed, we knew it was time to go. We had our hugs and handshakes, Lynette was a "I hug, I don't shake hands person", and we were off on our next great adventure.

"Well Adam, I forgot to tell you, I finished my list of one hundred goals, dreams and desires. What do we do next, do you want to look at them in the car?"

"No Ted. I want you to look at them tonight or early tomorrow and whatever the number you have, pick ten percent of them as Prime Goals or Desires. Let me know at breakfast tomorrow at the diner."

"Are we going to make breakfast at the diner a regular routine when you are in the city?"

"No. But we will tomorrow, because you need to drive me to visit another friend." He immediately sensed my "Say What?" thought. "Don't worry Ted, this friend lives about thirty minutes by car from the diner, we can take the subway, cab or walk if you like. We are seeing him at 10 AM."

"Who are we going to meet?"

"My old friend and colleague, Simon Sparling."

"Simon, oh yeah, he was the guy from the Navy, and the guy you roamed around Peru with, looking for El Dorado."

"Yes"

"You want me to meet him?"

"Yes"

Adam had switched into his one word answer mode; I liked his one-hour to answer a question mode better. "I'd love to meet Simon Adam, the time with Gary and Lynette was a tremendous learning experience for me, and I am sure you have something similar in mind with Simon, maybe learning the Amazing secrets of the Incas or something like that."

"I actually don't have anything planned in our visit, it may be the last time we see Simon, he is very ill."

I had a dilemma in what to ask next, then Adam started talking again, "The last few years have not been kind to Simon. His health has deteriorated steadily for the past three years, since Ester passed away. Then there was the debacle with Terrence Brown."

"Terrence Brown, not the same guy who pretended he ran an investment fund and ripped off hundreds of people."

"The same"

"How would Simon get involved with a guy like that. I would guess that Simon is about the same age as you, he should have his retirement money in safe investments, not the get rich quick stuff that Brown was hooking people on."

"It was a family connection."

"My goodness. How unfortunate. Did Simon lose much money?"

"He lost everything and then more, because there were huge loans taken out to provide funds for the Brown schemes."

"Wow. How is Brown connected to Simon's family?"

"Terrence Brown is now the ex-husband of Sarah Sparling, Simon's daughter."

" Boy, this is tragic"

"Yes it is. It is not one of the lessons you want to have in Life, but it happened. But something that major, causing untold hardship on two great people, I have spent much contemplation time wondering why it happened."

"Most of the Brown pyramid investment schemes crashed about four years ago. Mrs. Sparling was still alive wasn't she?"

"Yes she was, she adored Terrence. He manipulated her to co-signing on some loans that Simon did not know about until later."

"Where is Brown now? He managed to elude the Police who were looking for him."

"I don't know if anything was published, but he didn't manage to avoid a distraught investor who had lost everything, but knew where to find him in the Cayman Islands. He took Mr. Brown on one final boat ride in the Caribbean. Four years later they still haven't figured out where all the money has gone. They found $100,000 or so, but over $30 million was embezzled."

"Where is Simon now?"

"He is in a nursing home."

"He lost everything?"

"No. He still has a keen mind, a wonderful daughter who loves him dearly and he loves her, he has great friends, and he has managed to hold on to about five or six artifacts of the thousands he collected over the years."

"Well I would be happy to go with you to meet him, but I am not certain on my purpose in this visit."

"Ted, I am not certain why you need to come. But you must come; my inner voice is telling me this. It took me a long time to smarten up and start doing what my True Self inner voice tells me to do, but I do now. The reason for your involvement will make itself clear in due course, to you and to me. I know it must be significant for me at least because it is a strong calling to me, telling me that you need to be involved. That is all I know."

Adam closed his eyes, I think he was going to have one of those inner conversations he has with his Inner Voice.

CHAPTER THIRTY SEVEN

NEXT STEPS FOR TED'S TRAINING

Adam didn't open his eyes until we got to the border crossing. We didn't have much trouble with the good folks at customs. I had stopped to grab another coffee for the road, and Adam wanted some water. Back on the highway, my mind was rolling over everything we had talked about in the last few days.

"Where is your little list of numbered questions Adam, perhaps I can ask you a few more?"

"I don't need the list anymore, I thought I might require it as a reference tool, to view what areas you need development in, but I have come to the conclusion that you are totally hopeless, so no need for the list." I learned enough about Adam to know when he was joking; he had a special little smile when he wanted to pull someone's leg.

"Seriously, no list anymore?"

"No need for it, I know the areas you need guidance."

"When are you going to share that with me?"

"I am always going to share it with you Ted, it is a continual adaptive process, some areas I can help you in, others I have to point a finger in the direction you need to go, it will your choice if you follow the guidance or not."

"What is my current development plan?"

"Well, there are a few action items. One- You need to get caught up with some reading. Only you know what you have to read, I can't tell you that. Two – you need to meet one or more other students of Life's Mysteries. I don't know who they will be for sure, or whether you interact with them when you meet them. But be open and aware for this opportunity, you need this interaction with my other students to facilitate your development. Three – develop your list of eight to ten desires. Four – practice the little things; power of intention, looking for synchronicity, remembering and thinking about your dreams, morning pages journalizing, using your ideas journal. Five – you need to find at least one prayer that you can say every day. Use your power of intention, you will find the right ones for you. I'll stop there."

"Thanks Adam."

"You're welcome Ted. There is another one. I forgot to make that Item One on a list of six action items."

"Huh?"

"Gratitude. Practice gratitude all day long, for little things and not so little things. Express thanks to any and all that surround you. Gratitude generates a positive flow of non-physical energy. Every time you express sincere and profound gratitude you connect with the Source."

"The Source?"

"Yes. The Source, the Creator, Universal Consciousness, God, Allah, the Great Spirit, or whatever name from hundreds to chose from."

"Saying thanks connects me to God?"

"If you sincerely express gratitude, which means not giving thanks in a token manner. Gratitude is your strong connection to Source, and the best clean and clear connection happens when you express sincere thanks after the poop hits the fan, and you are getting the full spray of the brown stuff. Or when you are in physical or emotional pain. Or when you feel you have absolutely nothing, find something to give thanks for. And, give thanks in advance for the great things that the Creator will bestow upon you in fulfilling your desires. That will speed up their manifestation."

"Adam, before you went into your quiet moment of contemplation a while back in the car, you were talking about listening to your Inner Voice. I know we have had conversations about this before, but I still have trouble with it, I find it hard to believe that my True Self Inner Voice told me fifteen minutes ago 'Ted, get a coffee', and then shortly after that little voice message, there were too more voices, one saying 'Ted get a donut too' and another saying 'You don't need a donut, it will be added to your already expanding waist line.'"

"Well, your Inner Voice was quiet through all that dialogue you had about the donut and coffee, your Inner Voice was actually sitting back in it's chair, slight smile on its face, listening to your Ego gang yakking."

"Huh?"

"Ted, I can take a few moments to talk about my Quantum Trio theory again. I love them dearly because when all act together in harmony they lead me to Quintessence."

"I really still don't know what Quintessence is, I thought it had to do with energy in a previous discussion."

"Yes it does that as well. Perhaps I'll start with my definition of Quintessence; it is my personal interpretation of a concept that has several different definitions and interpretations. Let me walk you through the different views and meanings. First, in pure terms, and in alchemy, it is the fifth element.

Earth, Air, Fire and Water are the other four. Some alchemists and metaphysicists used the theory that a mysterious fifth element existed to facilitate transmuting low value base material into high value material. For some, quintessence was synonymous with ether, an unseen inert gas that filled up the Cosmos, so you could say there was no void. For others, they call it the unseen force that holds the other four elements together. In a mystical sense, Quintessence is the call for a Cosmic unification, a joining of all forces to work towards a single goal. In the old alchemy books, some alchemists used a five-pointed star, or a pentagram to symbolize quintessence, others used a six-pointed star, like a Star of David symbol. In plain speak, essence is the purest ingredient of anything – material or non-material – and quintessence to some, is even a more pure form of a distilled essence. Area of use number two - we have a new group of astrophysicists using the name, Quintessence, as the name for a hypothetical dark energy in the Universe. Different scientists on different occasions have calculated the total mass of the universe – the sum of all the stars in all the galaxies and all the planets, asteroids and cosmic dust. This was done through cross-referencing the forces of gravity required to hold all this stuff in the pattern it is in now. They came to the same conclusion that there is a whole lot of matter missing, so there must be an undiscovered, unseen dark (it has to be dark because light is absorbed) energy, and one or more of these astrophysicists picked the word Quintessence for the name of this unseen, and as of yet, undiscovered energy, which keeps the Universe from flying apart. Now back to me and my definition of Quintessence."

Adam paused for a moment to gather his thoughts. "I call it the purest essence that you can and will discover on your own. It is the word I use to give meaning to the underlying connection of different forces, objects or phenomena. Remember, my talk about the human cell and the substance that makes up sub-atomic particles?"

"Yes ,sort of. You take a cell, break it into molecules, break the molecules into atoms, break down the atom down into electrons, protons and neutrons. Then you break these parts down into subatomic particles with a lot of weird names. Then, when you break the weird name stuff down into their constituents, you find nothing, but you know there is an energy that must be there, and there is intelligence that must be there for it all to come together."

"Yes. That non-physical energy and intelligence influences and controls both all matter and all life. For me to understand the workings of this divine non-physical energy and intelligence, I have created the Quantum Trio metaphor. There are three aspects of this non-physical energy and intelligence. I have taken the alchemist's definition of Quintessence and use it to describe the harmonious output of the Quantum Trio – the simultaneous and harmonious co-existence of consciousness (Mind), programmed form (Body, Physical energy forms) and Spirit (God force). That magical juncture exists simultaneously in the non-physical and physical world of energy. It is the point where the non-physical changes physical energy into a new form, action or creates an entirely new conscious thought. In my life it is the final summation of all parts of my life, and the point, perhaps at the very end, maybe sooner, where I will say, 'ah, that is what it all means', but that's me, and my use of Quintessence as a meaningful word for me."

CHAPTER THIRTY EIGHT

THE QUANTUM TRIO OF THE CONSCIOUS MIND

I was still trying to get a handle on Quintessence and its meaning, but I had a feeling I was going to see it in action, not today, but some time in the near future. Experience will give the term meaning, as words fall short. I will keep my awareness open for Quintessence in action.

I recited the key points of Adam's description to myself.

Three inter-related, yet separate and distinct items coming together. When the separate items work in harmony, the point of interaction reveals a special meaning to the viewer, a meaning where all is understood.

I turned to Adam, "I still need help in sorting out this Inner Voice thing. Describe the Quantum Trio again, and what is has to do with my Inner Voice."

"Okay Ted. This is my unique description of Inner Voice. It is a story I developed for myself to help me understand the source of my thoughts. I think I had the same frustration as you trying to isolate my intuition thoughts from all other conscious thoughts. I finally got some help in this, I discovered my intuitive thoughts had a strong feeling happen at the same time, I can't explain the feeling to you. You will have to discover your own special feeling that occurs when your intuitions occur."

"Thanks Adam, I am trying to remember what feeling I was experiencing when my inner voice was suggesting I buy a donut a while back. I will have to make my observations about my feelings at another time in a coffee shop."

"Ted, I run the risk of really confusing you in my next little lesson. I have several variations on the Quantum Trio, which I use to describe all things that make up me, and all things that happen to me. The Quantum Trio, sounds like the name of a folk group, you know back in the sixties, on the same flower child gigs as Peter, Paul and Mary or maybe a set-up group for the Kingston Trio. I am sidetracked again, sorry."

"It is okay Adam, I simultaneously think of Body, Mind, Spirit, when you use Quantum Trio. It helps me understand."

"Yes. Body, Mind, Spirit. But different versions of what constitutes Body, Mind or Spirit. In our discussions in the past few moments we have been talking about conscious thoughts, and trying to determine what thoughts are your inner voice speaking and what are not, etc. "

"Yes." My turn for a one word acknowledgement.

"For conscious thoughts, let me introduce the three members of the Quantum Trio; Personality Self (a version of Mind), Higher Self (a version of Spirit) and the Code-Master (a version of Body). The trio are like Borromean rings, they all need to be connected to function. One ring gets disconnected and the other two fall away. Someone has calculated that the average person has over 60,000 thoughts per day. I have no idea who did this study, or how it was done, I heard the number in a lecture. It made sense to me in my personal case, it works out as an average of 3 thoughts a minute for my wakened state. But I can't get into the heads of other people. Now back to the Inner Voice thing. Code-Master does not participate directly as a thought in your consciousness, the 60,000 thoughts are predominantly your personality self as chair of your consciousness committee. Code-Master's role is vital in two ways. First, as the record keeper and search engine. Second, as the liaison between Conscious Mind node and Unconscious Mind node. All of your 60,000 thoughts a day flow through the Conscious Mind node and Unconscious Mind node, Code-Master follows his programmed role in grabbing some of the 60,000 thoughts and filing them in the brain's conscious mind memory banks, for recall and utilization at other points in time. The second function of Code-Master is to work with the pre-programmed DNA codes for the human species and maintain a connection with the brain's receptors for the five main senses which monitor all experiences of the body. As an example, we have DNA codes that unconsciously help us to survive, call them survival instincts. This is a good thing because if something really bad is about to happen, and the five senses pick up on it, Code-Master will yell in tandem with the Unconscious Mind node 'hey Ted, look out a boulder is going to fall on your head, we have triggered the automatic survival instincts of jump out of the way if we can'."

"Thank you Code-Master which resides in me, Ted Gregory."

"Unconscious Mind node feeds a steady stream of objective events to Conscious Mind. The Unconscious Mind node works with the huge team of receptors, and feeds all the inputs basically unfiltered to the Conscious Mind node, it is up to the Code Master sitting at the interface of the Conscious Mind node and Unconscious Mind node, to filter all the inputs and make interpretations of the events or decisions. You can see the Unconscious Mind node saying 'My job is to feed CMN (acronym he uses for Conscious Mind Node) all the now moment pick-ups from both the five senses and all the gobblety gook I am getting from the Collective Unconscious, it is not my job to make choices or interpretations. Example- Sight sensor picks up a lady in a Red Dress walking on the sidewalk, I don't care what she looks like, my job is to send the data to CMN, and Code Master makes the decision, whether to feed the signal into Conscious Mind thoughts.

The Code-Master is the Strong and Silent guy; the other relatively quiet guy is the Higher Self. He rarely speaks, but he answers if spoken to. Like Code-Master he works 24/7. Higher Self has a clear mandate, he looks out for the best interests of Personality Self and he does not want Personality Self to hurt others in any way. But Higher Self recognizes that Personality Self has free will, and listens to Higher Self at various degrees depending on the stage of Life and depending on the degree of other activity in the arena of Consciousness where the Per- sonality Self resides. Higher Self has a little more say in the Conscious Mind of those people who meditate on a regular basis. These people have the ability to quiet their personality self, and generally they seek advice form Higher Self, so medi- tation makes Higher Self very happy. Higher Self also watches the sleeping state movies (i.e. dreams) that the Unconscious Mind node plays when the brain waves hit the REM level. Higher Self is always observant of everything that all parts of Self is thinking or doing, it has feelings of right and wrong, but opinions are expressed quietly and may get drowned out by the cries of Ego and other active participants in the Person- ality Self's consciousness arena. Higher Self listens to prayers, and will help Personality Self compose or recite the prayers if asked, and also helps send the thoughts out through the Unconscious node to the Collective Unconscious."

"I like both the Code-Master and Higher Self. If my body needed energy to help survive, Code-Master might have been the source of the thought to buy a donut. I doubt it was Higher Self, who would know the donut would overall be bad for me."

"No Ted, neither Code-Master or Higher Self are responsible for your donut thoughts. This is the wild and crazy world of Personality Self and the Consciousness Committee that he chairs."

"I think wild and crazy is a good description for this whole lesson."

"You are probably right Ted. But let me finish. The Personality Self works in the constant bedlam of the Conscious Mind, it would be overwhelming if he didn't set up some form of organization. A small baby doesn't have this organization set up in its early stages of life, but it has to have structure and rules in place once ego arrives on the scene. The baby's world is divided up into what's out there (curiosity about self and surroundings), sleep, feeling of comfort (smile, relax), feeling of discomfort (cry). Then behavior patterns start, and conscious decisions are made to get more of this comfort stuff, crying seems to work most the time.Now back to your question about Inner Voice, which in most people is the Personality Self mouthing the dominant thought from an array of possible thoughts coming at it. In its organization, Personality Self engages and deploys bodyguards, call them thought filters. First place to do this is at the data terminal/phone line coming in from the Unconscious node. Code-Master takes the lead on this. If the Conscious Mind can handle 60,000 thoughts a day, there is probably ten times that 600,000 or more potential thoughts streaming in from the unbiased, unfiltered UMN, acronym for the Unconscious Mind Node. The filters have assignments on what to watch for, the Conscious Mind doesn't know how to set-up the filters so the Code-Master interpretation of the signals that Personality Self has sent about it's desired protective filters. The Code Master interpretation may not be accurate or valid. The Conscious Mind is operating within a certain hierarchy of needs so the filters work from this. Personality Self and Code-Master work out a plan, consciously with thoughts of intention and programs that are created from experiences – the bring me more of this, and help me avoid this type of experiences. Standing behind the filters as they monitor the data flow coming in from the UMN, are the analytics, imagine them as quiet guys wearing white lab coats, pocket pen protectors, with glasses holding clipboards with notepads, some of them have calculators, when CMN is reviewing a problem, or reading something these guys elbow their way close to the data stream. CMN generally listens to them. Also hanging around the data stream are the emotives, one for every possible emotion, they shout when they see something that has meaning to them. Personality Self usually lets Code-Master know which emotives are allowed to view, or their positioning at the 600,000 plus signals data stream coming from UCM node to the CMN. He might send Envy to the back of the line, and let Joy have a better spot to watch the data stream as in my case. Anger is a very strong emotive, it is tough to move anger away, the best way to handle anger is tell a strong analytic like logic to hang by the anger emotive, if anger gets excited by an UCM signal that becomes or could become one of the 60,000 thoughts for the day, Code-Master asks logic to try to talk him down, if that is the predetermined program. In some human minds, Code-Master is programmed to let the negative emotives – such as Anger, and Fear to stand at the front of the viewing screen of the potential thoughts of the day, and have a free reign at bringing in their favorite thoughts into Consciousness. The strong emotive can take over a thought stream, not necessarily bad depending which emotives are programmed to be strong and the situation at hand. In most cases, you will benefit if the compassion emotive is programmed to be strong, and has ample say on what goes into the thought stream, at least I do, when I see someone in pain or hurting. I always think of Star Trek – Spock and Kirk. Spock Personality Self had his emotives either eliminated or banished to the recesses of his consciousness and the analytics given preferential seating around the data stream coming in from UMN. Kirk's Personality Self had his Code-Master let his emotives go where they pleased. Fortunately for him as Ship's Captain he found good spots for his analytics as well."

"You have made no mention of ego Adam."

"The most difficult area for Personality Self to deal with is ego. In a lot of people ego takes over the cushy chair by the Conscious Mind Node and controls the majority of thoughts going through the thought stream, at least the thoughts regarding choices. The ego may even put a couple of its own filters close by with instructions 'if you learn of anything that is either good for ego or bad for ego' pump it into the Consciousness thought stream as soon as possible. A dominant ego is ruthless with Higher Self, shouting him down. Ego concerns itself with the body part of self in every way, pleasure and protection dominate, elevating self-importance even at the cost of disparaging thoughts about others, to achieve supposed elevation of self. A lot of negative non-physical energy hangs out with ego and is protected because ego won't even consider the existence of non-physical energy as a possibility. All the emotives can hang out with ego, and one of the negative emotives called greed might try to convince ego to review this non-physical energy concept because it might bring in more of a wonderful substance called money. Use it for outrageous pleasure not to help self and others. The biggest job Personality Self has is making decisions on who he wants near him. He needs to tolerate ego and the negative emotives but they should be asked or told to move away from the CMN, so they don't occupy too much of the thought stream. Personality Self needs to clearly define desires and ask the Code-Master and Subconscious to help set-up the right filters to look for stuff in the data stream from UMN that will become thoughts related to the potential or real time fulfillment of desires. The choices that Personality Self makes and the messages that Personality Self sends out are critical for Self evolution."

Adam paused for a moment. "Ted does that answer your question on Quantum Trio?"

"It does for now Adam. Wish I had you on tape, so I could review this lesson again. Now tell me, is it an analytic, an emotive or just one of those ordinary filter guys, who cries over to the Personality Self 'hey, put his in the thought stream, I gotta go pee, and soon!'"

CHAPTER THIRTY NINE

FREE WILL OR PRE-DETERMINATION

We had a chance to pull off the highway, we had our rest break, got some bottled water and some fruit. I put some gas in the car and we resumed our trip home.

I still had some questions that were bugging me. "Adam I know this might be a deep philosophical question, but you have talked about making choices and free will. Some people say everything is predetermined. Some people say everything is a result of the choices you make as a part of Free Will. Some people say everything is random. As an example, is our recent trip and even what we are doing in this car, having this conversation, all part of the Big Plan, randomness or a result of choices we both made."

"The best way for me to answer that question is a quotation I heard a long time ago. Jawaharlal Nehru who was the Prime Minister of India when it became an independent country said 'Life is like a game of cards. The hand you are dealt is determinism; the way you play it is free will.' I think it is our job to play the hand the best we can, and because it is a game we should have some fun and enjoy it as well."

"It might be more fun to play the hand out when you are holding all the high trump cards, as opposed to the other way."

"Or maybe the Creator won't deal you a hand with all the high cards, because he feels you need the challenge. Do have

230

more fun with a killer hand cleaning up, or having a so-so hand and using your awareness on how the hand is playing out, to take a few tricks that you didn't think you would get in the beginning?"

"Both are fun for me, but the later is a little more fun."

"Me too."

"To carry the analogy a little further. Why does the Creator deal out some horrible hands to people? I think of those starving children in Africa, or people inflicted with horrible handicaps. I can see that some hardships and challenges builds your character and appreciation for the gifts you receive, but how can a loving Creator, create those other conditions that almost make free will meaningless?"

"A question that plaques every great Philosopher and Religious leader, and you send it my way. I don't have a direct answer. Those that believe in reincarnation believe every soul comes to Earth to learn lessons, and horrible suffering is a lesson to learn in one of your lifetimes. Your soul needs to have a personal lesson in experiencing horrible suffering, so that your soul can appreciate love and compassion. Perhaps it will be a lesson to realize that part of your mission in any lifetime is to help relieve the pain and suffering of others. Look at Mother Theresa as an inspiration for this. Groups of agnostics and atheists believe that everything that has happened since the beginning of the Universe has been one series of probabilities, from the creation of matter, to the creation of this Solar System, to the creation of life on this planet, and it follows the circumstances that every individual has a series of probability factors that determine that individual's life events or destiny. I am not sure what name you give my philosophy but I believe that a part of the Creator is in every living entity in existence. I am sure there are separate souls, and perhaps souls are involved in a reincarnation process, but maybe not. Sure, the laws of probability govern part of our existence, but we exist, and we have conscious minds to explore questions of existence and laws of probability, that must have come from somewhere and for some reason. My conclusion is to accept that all we experience came from a Creator. Now the hard question of starving children in Africa or other disadvantaged people. I feel tremendous compassion for the plight of the disadvantaged because part of me is a part of them. There is trouble and hardship everywhere. We can pull off this highway, in one of the most prosperous and advantaged countries on the globe and we can find an individual or a family in need of help. The dilemma is what can we do about it? The answer is do a little every day whenever the voice of the Higher Self tells you to do something. Pray every day, to build up the good and positive vibration level of the Collective Unconscious. If all six billion living humans on this planet can do this, eventually our evolution will bring us all Peace and Harmony."

"I am sorry I asked that question, I can see I have made you sad."

"It is alright Ted, I am just feeling that I have not done enough in my Life to help others in need. But I owe it to myself and others to not be gloomy, Life is Amazing and it is truly wonderful, I have been blessed and I am grateful. I should be happy and back to my cheerful self momentarily."

"Can I ask you another question Adam?"

Adam seemed to be perking up. "Sure Ted. I enjoy these moments. Maybe I like to hear to myself talk. Fire away with your question."

"On the ride down here, you talked about love and your experience in Paris in the 1950's. Did you ever see your true love again after that time, or try to find her again?"

"Ted, you are really doing a good job right now, of bringing me down. I feel like I have taken a solid one two punch to my chops, first starving children in Africa, and now lost love."

He looked over at me with a big frown. I zippered my lip. But as I glanced over him, I could see he was starting to smile again. " I was listening to a few lines from a song in my mind, you know the one Paul Anka wrote for Frank Sinatra – *I did it My Way* , the line that goes 'regrets, I've had a few' and you know we shouldn't regret anything. What is done, is done, take the positive of learning from it, and move on. It is tough to say, and it is really tough right now for me to believe it. I will answer your question, and you asked it out of the blue taking me by surprise. Therefore, there is something I can learn by answering your question. I can't remember specifically what we talked about in the car ride before, but I believe I told you I met my true love in Paris and I spent a total of three days with her. Imagine that. Three days. In 1959. And I have three letters from her, the last one was dated January 27, 1960. I think that letter managed to get out of the country because the government censors monitoring mail going in and out of China were celebrating the Chinese New Year. I have always cherished this letter, and this letter was also very informative. It was written in French which is my first language, as Li Wu did not know very much English. But I recall several things from the letter which is emblazoned in both my heart and my memory. First, Li Wu mentioned that government people had visited her, they had some of my letters that were not delivered to her, and they had some of her letters that were not sent to me. The government people had a hard time finding someone who could translate French from handwriting, so they really didn't know what the letters were about, they suspected they were love letters and not some form of espionage, as one of my mails contained a dry rose. They made it clear that she would be sent to a tribunal if she sent another letter to me. Yet she sent that one on January 27, 1960 knowing that she might be sent to prison if the letter was intercepted, and that the tribunal could decide to make an example of her. Second – she expressed her undying love for me in the letter. I have no idea why I made that point two in this conversation, it should be point one. Third – she told me things I did not know from her past. She was born into a privileged family, in the early 1920's, and she was an only child. She was a somewhat rebellious young girl challenging her own family's status as a wealthy family that kept money for its own good, while many people were poor. In the late 1930's her family had two fears, one being the rising strength of the populist movement of Communism, and the other was the Japanese invasion. When she was fifteen, her family had given her away to be married to an older man who was a businessman from the south of China. It was their hope that the man would marry and then take their fifteen year old daughter to the south where it was safer from both Communism and the Japanese. But Li Wu and her husband were unable to move. She told me she gave birth in

1940. The next few years were very hard on the family. She told me she heeded her internal call for justice and joined the Communist movement, and told me also of her guilt when the Communists took all the possessions of her mother and father. Her mother had given her a few precious heirlooms that were passed down through generations of her family. Her mother looked after her baby boy, when Li Wu was working in a hospital. In 1949, she came home from work and found that her husband had left and had taken their son, who was nine at the time. Her mother supported the departure, as she was uncomfortable with her daughter's Communist support. Her mother had told her that she gave her son-in-law the remaining family heirlooms and told her grandson to pass them on through to his children or it would be bad luck for the family. Li Wu told me that she decided to let them go and she also decided to devote her life to medicine. Four – she missed her son terribly and wanted to find him again. She had learned that her husband and son had managed to escape China and were living in the British colony of Hong Kong. Five – she asked that I remember those precious days in Paris, and perhaps in another Life we would fulfill our destiny of being together."

Adam paused for a few moments. "I did go to China in 1980. But my movements were restricted and I was unable to find Li Wu, I wasn't even sure if she was alive and if alive, where she was living. China is a huge country. There are some times were I almost decide to accept reincarnation as a belief, but it is not logic or a knowing feeling telling me to believe in reincarnation, it is a desire to find Li Wu again in another Lifetime. I know however, my connection will be made with her when it is decided to give up this body I am schlepping around with me now and my soul moves into a spiritual plane. One of us will be waiting for the other."

It was nice to see Adam smiling broadly again. He closed his eyes. I did not want to disturb that moment.

CHAPTER FORTY

BACK HOME

We made good time on the rest of trip. I decided to not ask Adam any more heavy questions. We talked a little about his adventures in South America, and his tough luck in not finding a large hexagonal clear as glass quartz crystal. I joked with him about his definition of tough luck by finding millions of dollars worth of emeralds instead of clear lumps of low commercial value metamorphic sand.

I dropped him off at his hotel and went home to get my laundry done. If Adam pulls another surprise trip on me, I would be in trouble, because I would be out of clean socks and underwear.

I got to the diner about 5:30 AM, I had made my check-in call with Jimmy Wong from my home office prior to leaving for the diner. And I spent twenty minutes writing my morning pages. The Universe had returned to a recognizable pattern. Adam was at his usual spot in the alcove.

"Good morning Ted, I feel bad because I didn't properly thank you for driving me down to Michigan this past weekend."

"No need to thank me Adam, I am the one who should be thanking you. That trip was an education for me."

"Nonetheless, I want to give you a small token of my appreciation." I was visualizing another book to add to the pile of unread books I had already. He handed me a small crystal. It was a small clear quartz crystal rod, hexagonal shape, with points on each end.

"Well thank you Adam. This is very nice. Now, what do I do with this?"

"Use it for moments of reflection. It has a crystallized energy that will help amplify the positive non-physical energy coming to you."

"I am still not sure what that means, but eventually I will. Thank you." I ordered a coffee and a muffin.

Adam picked up the conversation, "Have you picked your key desires yet?"

"Oh geez, I knew there was something I forgot to do. I am sorry Adam. But they are not done yet. I have my work folder with me, I have the list of one hundred goals and desires with me"

"No need to apologize to me. You have some time this morning, if you want to, why don't you review your big list and pick eight to ten items to call your Prime Desires. Then before we unleash the Power of Intention on the Prime Desires, I want you to look at each one, and write out a visualization of the desire."

"A visualization?"

"Yes. Two ways of doing this. One - is the Lynette way, a nice story that paints a picture of your desire, as if it already exists. Two - is make another list of descriptive points of the desire. As much detail as possible. You have to be very detailed because the both the Code-Master and the Unconscious Mind Node are not very good at understanding the language in the thought stream rushing through the Conscious Mind node. Even as you write the details of your Prime Desires, visualize them, run mental images in your consciousness apply the five senses, even if the exercise is imaginary. What does this desire look like, sound like, smell like, feel like and even taste like (if applicable). When you do this, you are giving reprogramming instructions to your Code-Master."

Adam stood up, "I am going down to my special rooms, you can stay here or you can use a desk in the Mind-Energy Room, your choice."

"Maybe I will come with you, if I finish my project early, I can browse through your library."

"Excellent idea". We went downstairs, and went through the secret passageway. Adam opened the door for me and told me he would be back later, he was going to meditate, water his garden plants and read some old journals. It took me over three hours to finish my assignment and I didn't feel happy about some of the descriptions I had written out. Adam came into the room around 9:00 AM.

"Do you want to check my work now Adam?"

"No I don't need to see it."

"It doesn't quite feel right to me, some of the stuff I have written here."

"Change it, and keep changing it until it does feel right."

"What do I do with these lists when I finish them?"

"I would recommend that you pick one, and read it in silence at least once a day. Three times a day or more would be better, but try to do the reading at least once a day. At the top of the list or description statement write a line that says 'My Intention is for this to happen by a selected date" and at the bottom of the list or description write a thank you statement to God the Creator, blessed Spirit, whoever, our Creator doesn't really care what the name is, it is the power of the thought that matters."

"I have eight desires with description lists, if I pick one, what about the other seven?"

"You said you had changes to make."

"When I am done the changes?"

"However you feel, you want to review them all go ahead. If you want to pick times to review them, go ahead. It is a matter of what feels right for you. Being new at the use of this Power, I suggest go slow at first, then pick it up as time goes on."

"And you don't want to see my list?"

"No. You should show the list to no one. It is for you."

"Not even you?"

"No one. Even if you had a Soul Mate, I wouldn't suggest you doing so. You could talk about the list or lists but don't share them."

"Why?"

"I would say it creates an influencing factor that might sway the intention."

"What do you mean?"

"Two ways. One - your confidant might not think you have all the right things on the list and suggest some changes to you. Then you might be swayed from your natural discovery process. Changes have to be suggested from inside yourself, not from others. Two – your confidant might love your descriptions and want to please you and help you so much that your confidant is influenced to change his/her descriptions on his/her lists if he/she had them. Your confidant must develop his/her own list of desired intentions if he/she is so inclined. They should not be influenced by your descriptions."

"Ted, pick one of your desires. Write down the desire in as much detail as you can. Important, as you write the details, visualize the existence of the desire in the here and now. Start the process as soon as you can. I have some stuff at the other desk I need to file away before we leave."

I sat down at the chair, and looked through my hand-written descriptions for the eight desires. I picked one and wrote an opening line in the top margin and a closing line at the bottom of the page. I read through it twice. It felt good to me. I don't know why I did this but I had picked "Find My Soul-Mate" as the first Intention I was going to work on.

CHAPTER FORTY ONE

BEAUTIFUL INTENTIONS

We left the diner at 9:30 AM; I knew the location of the Nursing home so I didn't need directions. I turned to look at Adam "This Power of Intention exercise will be interesting."

"Exercise? I call it Life Transformation, but we deal in semantics. You follow the disciplines of the so called exercise and believe it will happen, and then detach your self from the outcome, and then your Life will unfold in a way that will make all your desires come into reality."

"Detach yourself from the outcome?"

"Thinking about all the details on the process to reach the final desired outcome creates two energy consuming problems. One- you might limit yourself in the way you think the desired outcome should happen. There are many paths to the same desired outcome. Let the Universe worry about the details on how to get to your desired outcome. Two – a constant focus on the end of the journey distracts you from a more important activity, being, 'let's work on the step I need to do to get started', or if you have started the journey, 'let's work on the next step', focus on what is needed to be done now."

"Do these Intention Statements always have to be written?"

"No. But putting them in writing gives them form, and helps you maintain the regular discipline of reviewing them.

But writing them out is not necessary, only helpful. I love the 'rags to riches' stories of new people to our country with hardly any money in their pocket becoming wealthy and valuable contributors to our society. No intention statement written down, but their intentions are etched into their Consciousness. The incredible desire for a better life than the one they left, and the unshakable belief that fulfillment of their desires would happen in their new circumstances. The first step, get a job, any job, and work hard it to earn money for their families, buy a house, get an education for their children, and so on."

"Why did I have to write out over one hundred items, before picking eight?"

"Thinking. If you decided to write eight, who knows if you would pick the top eight desires that are in harmony with what you really, really want. Pick one hundred and then carefully select the five to ten desires you want to start with. The thought process generates positive non-physical energy."

" What is your experience, on how fast it takes to accomplish these desires."

"It depends Ted. A high-energy desire might require some alignment of the flows of non-physical energies. Your personal energy fields might have blockages that need to be removed. You may need to reinforce positive thoughts to generate positive energy flows. On the other hand, everything could already be in alignment, you just don't know it. Then the desired outcome will come quickly. Just be aware of meaningful coincidence, remember synchronicity?"

"Yes I do. Thank you for your advice. Here we are."

We arrived at the home, found out which room Simon was in and went up to his room on the third floor. We walked down a hallway with tall paned glass windows, the sun was shining brightly. It was a beautiful day.

We found his room and went in. Simon was lying in bed, head propped up and was half-asleep. When his drowsy eyes noticed Adam, it was like a jolt of energy went through his frail body. He had a huge smile on his face as we shook hands with the introductions and he warmly embraced Adam. Adam and Simon spent about ten minutes reminiscing about the good old days, especially the time they had together in Peru. I sensed that Simon wanted to discuss something in private with Adam, and I was wondering why Adam had such a strong feeling that I had to come and meet Simon. I was planning an excuse to leave the room for a while when I heard a shout from the door.

"ADAM!"

We all turned to face the door. The bright sun was shining through to the doorway, and it created a tremendous golden aura around the person standing in the doorway. She took one step forward from the doorway, and stretched her arms wide facing Adam in a "come here and hug me" pose.

Adam rushed over to hug her. "Sarah. It is so good to see you". Her smile was as radiant as the sunshine she just stepped away from. I put my right hand to the top of my chest for a second, because I thought I had stopped breathing momentarily. She was the most beautiful woman I think I have ever seen.

CHAPTER FORTY TWO

SARAH

Sarah gave Adam a kiss on the cheek and led him back to his place by her father. "Hi Daddy" and she leaned over to give him a kiss. Simon was smiling at the sight of his daughter. I felt invisible, but that's okay, I'll play the role of the passive, compassionate, observer.

Simon introduced me to Sarah. We said our hello's in doing so she took my hand warmly, she was one of those full contact, her eyes look you in the eyes people on an initial greeting. Adam, Sarah and Simon had a brief conversation on daily events and Adam updated her on his travels. I was beginning to feel invisible again when Simon said, "Sarah could you take Ted down the cafeteria, I have a couple of private matters to discuss with Adam."

"Sure Dad."

Adam said, "When we're finished playing our card game, I mean, talking about private matters, I'll come down to the cafeteria to get you Ted and we'll go. Sarah can come back and spend some time with her father." Adam was smiling.

"Sounds good to me, Simon it was a great pleasure to meet you. Adam was telling me about the time you two had together in the Navy and your adventures in Peru. I am sure there are many stories to tell."

"It was nice meeting you Ted, if this old coot Adam is hanging around you, I know you have some special qualities. Sarah, I'll see you in around fifteen minutes. Thank you dear."

Sarah took charge, "Come on Ted, let's go down to the cafeteria. You want to sit on that wheelchair, and I'll give you a ride, or are you okay to manage on your own?"

I just smiled as we left the room. The cafeteria was newly renovated, it had lots of new tables and lots of natural sunlight streaming in through the large windows. We got two coffees and found a table by a window.

We talked about Adam. My story of the diner and the last seven days. She told me about the enduring friendship that Adam had with her family. Adam was her father's most cherished friend. We talked briefly about Simon's health. The prognosis was not good, he had a number of ailments and he was slipping downhill. Sarah was putting on a brave face, but I could tell it was bothering her. She told me about her job working at a large museum in the city. She did a variety of administrative functions for the Director of Exhibits. She loved her job.

"So what is it that you do Ted?"

"I am in the investment business, a stock-broker."

Sarah hesitated for a moment in her response. Then, she put her hands over her ears and let out a short burst "ding. ding,ding, ding."

"What's that?"

"My warning bell going off. I have to avoid investment people, I have had some horrible life experiences with one in particular."

I decided to avoid the details that Adam had told me "No need to recount the story. I don't seem to be spending much time at my job right now, I am following an Adam Almeida program."

"Are you a student in one of his metaphysical disciplines?"

"I don't know, I guess I am, he is giving me homework assignments."

"Fast track or evolutionary program?"

"You know about that distinction do you. Fast track, because Adam doesn't have time for evolutionary mentoring. How do you know about that?"

"Because I am one of his evolutionary program students, if he hasn't given up on me yet. I have had to spend a lot of time in the last three years, getting my life back into some form of order; marriage disaster, daughter going into University, problem with my son, financial burdens, new job, new house. And now there will be some concerns because dad is ill. The Universe is really challenging me now. That was not on my list of Intentions, but I am managing to deal with it."

"Is everything okay with your son?"

"I don't know." She saw my confusion with her answer, "I haven't seen him in two years, he is in Vancouver, working I think, but he refuses to have any contact with his family or his friends from here. This thing with his father was very damaging. I prefer not to discuss it."

"Understood. What program is your daughter taking?"

"Geology. She loves it. Her grandpa got her interested in rocks and minerals. It seems to run in the family."

"You to?"

"Sort of. I collect crystals."

"I saw two fabulous collections this week. Adam's and we saw a friend of his this week-end, and she has a huge collection."

"Lynette?"

"Yes. You know her?"

"Why yes. She is a friend of mine as well. I spent a week at her house in Peterborough about ten years ago, she was teaching me about Energy Healing using crystals, Reiki and other things. She is a fascinating lady, I haven't seen her since she got married."

"We were at her and her husband Gary's farm this past week-end."

"Adam said he was at a friend's place in Michigan, he didn't tell me it was Lynette.I am going to kick him in the butt for not telling me, he knows that I adore Lynette."

I glanced out the corner of my eye and saw Adam walking over to us, "Well Sarah, if you have your steel-toed shoes on, you can hoof him right now, if you like."

Adam had a bottled water in his hand, he was going to sit down with us. Sarah got up and gave Adam a hug, "Thanks for visiting us, your visits mean so much to dad."

"Sarah can you sit just a few moments before going up to see your father?" Adam had a rare seriousness in his voice, but he maintained the slight smile on his face.

"Sure Adam, is there anything the matter?"

"No my sweet thing. There is nothing wrong. I have a question."

"Sure Adam. What is it?"

"Do you still have the White Sphere?"

"Of course, the Emperor Jade sphere is in a safe place."

"Your father will speak to you about this, but he wants me to take the Emperor Jade back to China."

Sarah hesitated, she looked concerned. "The Emperor Jade has been one of my father's most prized possessions for over fifty years. I guess I don't understand."

Adam continued, "He'll talk to you about this. Your father has been having troublesome dreams for several nights. It is clear to him that the Emperor Jade sphere must return to its home. He is adamant about it. I am sorry."

"No, no. I have no real attachment to the crystal Adam. If anything, I have had feelings that something is not right. Since my mother died I have very rarely looked at the sphere. I will follow my father's wishes. I guess I should go up to his room now, Adam, will we see each other soon?"

"Yes we will Sarah"

"Good, next time I see you I will be wearing steel-toed work boots. Ted will fill you in." She gave Adam a kiss on the cheek, turned to leave, and turned back again to face me. She put out her hand to take mine, and looked directly into my eyes, "I hope to see you again soon Ted. I need to properly warn you about spending too much time with Adam." She looked serious, then burst out into a large smile. She handed Adam a card, "Adam, all my phone numbers and my email address are on there. Contact me soon. Bye for now."

With that, she turned and walked briskly to the exit. Adam turned to me and handed her card to me. "Here Ted. You hang on to this, I have a feeling you will need it."

CHAPTER FORTY THREE

QUINTESSENCE

Back in the car we agreed to drive back to the Diner, have some lunch and I would leave Adam and go to the main office to see Greg about a few business matters. I thought about not bringing the subject up, but I had to ask.

"Adam what is the Emperor Jade?"

"It is a beautiful sphere, a crystal ball if you like, except it is made from white jade, not clear quartz crystal like a perfect crystal ball. Simon gave it the name the Emperor Jade because he knew the ball had historical significance relating to the time when China was ruled by Emperors."

"How did he get it?"

"After Simon returned from Peru, he met Esther. They fell in love, it was a short courtship and they got married. Shortly after the wedding, Simon went on am archeological excursion to Burma, Thailand and Hong Kong. He took Esther, it was like a honeymoon for them. When they were in Hong Kong, they met with an antiquity trader. Esther saw a piece in the collection, a white jade ball, and Simon bought it. What they didn't see clearly at the time of the purchase and the antiquities dealer hadn't noticed it was the ball had green coloring in it, common with white jade, but one or two parts of the green colored crystal appeared to be Chinese like characters. He showed it to a Chinese art dealer friend back home, and the friend would not tell him what the characters meant. But the man said to Simon that he had a very valuable white jade ball, it might have belonged to a Chinese Emperor. Simon did not know what to think. As far as getting a value for it, he was not interested, he had no plans to sell it because Esther liked it so much. He decided to not investigate it anymore, but he began calling it the Emperor Jade."

"Have you seen it Adam?"

"Yes I have, it was a time when Lynette was with me, and we were visiting Simon and Esther. They showed us the Emperor Jade. It was a beautiful piece, unbelievably shiny, it radiated. Lynette touched the ball and mentioned it had enormous energy. She said the vibration was pure. I remembered joking at the time that the ball was quintessential. The energy was of the purest essence."

"It leads back to your metaphysical theories on Quintessence?"

"In a way, I guess it does."

"I still don't understand what you mean when you say Quintessence. I know we had one conversation on the Quantum Trio – the Body, Mind, Spirit in one talk, and the three characters Personality Self, Higher Self and Code-Master in another talk. And at the farm you talked about the linkage of non-physical energy with physical energy and called that Quintessence. Then in the car you were talking about alchemy and the fifth element of quintessence bringing it all together. I still can't see how it all comes together."

"When various pieces line up properly Ted, what word to do you use to describe it?"

"I am not sure. It wouldn't be quintessence. I would probably use the word alignment."

"That is a good word. We'll use that. I am sorry I confused you with my previous explanations. The explanations were all correct in the context of the time. If I asked you now, describe quintessence what would you say?"

"Personally, I like the purest of essence. When someone says quintessential, that is what I think."

"Okay, what is the purest of essence?"

"I don't know. You take the essence of something and find the essence of the essence. That is a silly wild ass guess."

"Not a bad guess. What would you guess to be the purest essence of purity itself."

"I have no idea."

"You know something Ted, I have no idea what it consists of either. Other than it is a pure form of positive energy. You know the five questions – What, Where, When, Why and How? Let's use the description of it is the purest form of energy to answer the what question. Where is it? I am going to ask you to paint a visual in your mind, think of a quadrant. The top two boxes are the two raw forms of energy, on the left is physical energy, on the right, non-physical energy. The bottom two boxes of the quadrant are location boxes, but not physical location. Let's call them the 'In this moment boxes'. The left side box is You. The right side box is Everything Outside of You. Now all four boxes in the quadrant have their labels. The two boxes on the left – You and Physical Energy – we will call your Conscious Moment. The two boxes on the right – Non-Physical Energy and Everything Outside of You – we will call the Collective Unconscious. The relative timing is important and at the same time unimportant because it is relative time, not a specific time. A moment can be a nanosecond thought in your consciousness or it could be this car ride to the diner. The time is relative. Now, looking at this quadrant, where do you think quintessence might exist?"

I was silent for a moment. Or maybe it was a 'relative' moment, certainly longer than a nanosecond. "I was going to cop out and say I haven't got a clue. But let's use some logic from past descriptions. I believe it occurs at the interface of physical and non-physical energy. And we talked about the power of intention of you drawing stuff from outside you to you, if that makes sense. Putting those together, I would say the one spot where quintessence exists is at the point where all four boxes in the quadrant touch."

Adam looked at me quietly for a moment, "It depends."

"How can it depend Adam. I am putting that answer forward on the logic of the information you have given me."

"It depends on the defined relative moment Ted. What we need to add to your visualization is a third axis and have it run through the quintessential point you just defined. In those moments where you, everything outside of you, the physical energy fields that make up you and your surroundings and the non-physical energy fields that make up you and surround you touch each other in a moment of your life purpose and destiny fulfillment, quintessence exists. All the other things could be in place, but if the moment does not have purpose, there is no quintessence. That answers the when question."

"Okay that answers what, where, when. How?"

"The simple how is a one word answer. Purpose. Or another word, Intention. The only way to align physical with non-physical energy, is through intention or purpose. If you don't provide intention or purpose by conscious thought, the alignment happens anyway through default. The default mechanism is the Code-Master interpreting the intentions or purpose for the alignment of physical energies with on-phys-ical energies."

"We are now at the diner, I confess I need more lessons on Quintessence.. But before we leave, the one final question left is why?"

"When you learn to recognize your quintessential moments, and you haven't learned that yet Ted. But after you learn when they happen, you can use them as a guidepost, to recognize that for at those moments in time, you could have not done anything better, for at those moments you have the answer to why? At those quintessence moments you are fulfilling a portion of the reason for you being here on this planet."

I had taken the liberty of parking in the back alley behind the diner. We got out of the car. Adam was smiling again as he turned to me, "And Ted, that moment we just had in the car ride, talking about quintessence, was a significant moment. I felt Quintessence. If it is a quintessential for me in fulfilling my life purpose, it would also be true for you. Take a quick moment to see how you feel"

I felt quiet, then a sudden wave of enormous joy swooshed over and through my body, mind and spirit. I was in a moment of eternal bliss.

CHAPTER FORTY FOUR

THE QUANTUM TRIO IN BALANCE

We ordered soup for lunch. Adam was interested in what was going on with my job. I explained to him, the new work arrangements I had in working at home. I also explained that I had the incredible good fortune of having very loyal and prosperous clients especially Jimmy Wong from Hong Kong. I told him a few Jimmy Wong stories, he enjoyed listening to them.

"Well Adam what is next for me in my program?"

"You are not ready for the next step."

"How can you say that?"

"Because you are asking about it. When you are ready for the next step, you will know what it is; you won't have to ask about it. You are not far from being there. Make sure you do your readings and begin taking notes about Metaphysical stuff, start filling up journals."

"I have a question on what you said in the car."

"Sure Ted. I have to say you are a fast learner because you don't hesitate to ask questions. Keep that up in whatever you do in life. What is your question?"

"You mentioned the big assumption about having Quintessence in your life is that what makes up **you** is in alignment. What did you mean by that?"

"Ah I am glad you raised that question. I keep meaning to have one more Quantum Trio discussion with you, and the discussion is on alignment. To have your Life in proper alignment meaning you have your Vision, Your desires and goals translated into Intentions, and take positive actions every day towards your destiny, you should make sure you are both balanced and grounded. Balancing has different aspects and aspects all are inter-related. Let me look at Aspect One, Spirit-Mind-Body, our Quantum Trio of Higher Self, Personality Self and Code Master. Ted, do you know why I call them 'quantum'?"

"I am not sure. It is a Physics term isn't it – quantum mechanics and all that."

"Yes it is a physics term. A quantum is a subatomic packet of energy. I think Science and Physics in particular are very close to understanding the Science behind Consciousness. I loved some of the work that David Bohm did, and he proceeded with his colleagues wondering if he was on the lunatic fringe. Dr. Edgar Mitchell has also published some work on the quantum hologram. I have read some of his papers over three times and I am still trying to understand the concept. I just figured out his use of the term non-locality to describe instantaneous energy transfers over long distances, is the same thing that mystics have discussed for thousands of years in the concept of 'oneness'. Anyway, I am digressing from talking about the quantum trio. My term for the three components that make up you or me. They are not three separate components, but one cohesive Consciousness. I divide into three because I know these three areas have to be in balance if I am going to maximize my potential – be as healthy as I can be, be as creative as I can be, be as joyful as I can be, to learn and share my wisdom as much as possible, to draw the events and people into my life that will help me realize my full potential and fulfill my mission on this planet in this life of mine. If I treat my Consciousness as one, I can't adjust and correct parts of my life as easily. My Quantum Trio is my Quantum hologram, the smallest imaginable 3-D replica of me."

"What do you mean by balance?"

"Balance has different meaning depending on the trio member, and overall, in balance means the three members work in harmony. Let's use an analogy and treat them like people. Higher Self looks for nothing in this World other than for me to try to do the best I can in the circumstances I am given. Higher Self is loving and wishes that I don't get hurt, and also wishes that I don't hurt other living things with my thoughts and actions. Higher Self wants to be my guide, if I want Higher Self to guide me. In regards to balance, Higher Self only wants to have his voice heard through my intuition. Higher Self wants me to have quiet moments every day, where the chatter in my Mind is silenced, so Higher Self can speak to me. Higher Self can provide guidance or loving support if I need it. Code Master performs all the programming tasks of the body. Code Master was really busy at my moment of conception. Imagine starting this project, imagine Code-Master standing inside of my mother's egg, 'let us see here, we have one strand of X chromosome that Mom has in her egg, and what did dad deliver?, ah, a Y chromosome, so we have a boy in the making. Now lets wrap these strands together in a coil, there you have it our first DNA double helix, now the fun part encoding this youngster's DNA, okay first chromosome, we'll take this characteristic on Y, next one Y again, now X,' and Code Master does this right down the whole genome. By the time he finishes, it is time to replicate the cell, then his next decision from one to two, let's make both these cells stem cells until I can decide whether to leave them stem cells or give them one of the other 216 cell types. Then the replication pattern continues, from 1 to 2, 2 to 4, 4 to 8, 8 to 16, 16 to 32, and he starts giving out new cell type assignments. Okay you are a bone cell, let's tweak the DNA for this, you are my first tissue cell, I'll assign you to the heart organ, a couple of tweaks on the DNA, there we go. After only forty-seven replication cycles or doublings, the human is created in miniature form ready to be released on the world. Code master has setup the original code, and his job function now turns into reprogramming codes and some management of the cell death and creation process. Ted, as we sit here, we are not the same people as we were nine years ago. 99% of our cells are new in that time period. As we speak my Code Master is telling a liver cell to split, and telling Part A – now terminate, part B you are the liver cell for an 87 year old man. Part B has already inherited a lot of moleculic crud from the original cell, so it is not hard to act like an existing cell for an 87 year old. You get the idea of what Code Master does. For balance, you think that a healthy body would be the prime requisite for Code Master, but, get this, it is not. The Mind needs a healthy body for proper balance, so it doesn't have to be pre-occupied with pain and worries dominating the thought stream. Code Master really doesn't care if your body has cancer or not, he has no opinion on your health, he just works with the instructions he has been given and the environmental events that the body has encountered. In some people who are smokers, you can see him going, 'okay smokes a lot, I guess a few DNA's are going to change, that is want person wants, my job is to deliver. Looks like that cell in the lung is going to mutate into a cancer cell. In a person who has a calorie intake greater than what is expended, Code-Master goes, 'Okay, lots and lots of food energy here, can't metabolize it fast enough, so I guess I better set-up some more fat cells, decisions, decisions, where do I put them, on the gut or on the butt.' Person has a lot of stress, my buddy the subconscious has had to release a lot of chemicals, what do I do here, I am going to have to speed up the aging process in a lot of cells, there we go, tweak the DNA's when we replicate. Okay, new heart cell, you are the heart cell of a sixty year old and I know Person is only forty, but I gotta do what the program outline tells me.' Well Ted, I have digressed from the balance point for Code Master. The Code Master needs only one thing to stay in balance. Clear instructions on his programming job. He will determine his instructions communicating with Unconscious Mind Node because he knows Unconscious Mind Node handles communications with Personality Self, Higher Self and the Subconscious. If Code-Master gets mixed signals on his required programming, he will generally select signals that lead to a quicker demise of the body. Code-Master knows his job is finished when body has to shut down and moves from being organic cells to inorganic molecules and atoms. Code-Master knows that ultimately the Higher Self wants to merge with Personality Self, but this is usually accomplished when the body dies. That leaves us with the toughest balancing act, Personality Self and the realm of the Mind. There are several items that need to occur for balance. One – quiet the chatter in the mind, consciously recognize that ego and the emotives are the main source for this chatter or noise in your consciousness, and they should be asked to stay quiet. Two – take actions to prevent disease and poor health in the body, the best action is to have 'I am healthy' thoughts. Three – eliminate clutter in the Mind, finish bothersome little tasks. There is a correlation between clutter in your surroundings and clutter in the Mind. Leading a more simple life removes a lot of clutter. Four – maintain consistent values. I love *the Four Agreements* given to us by Don Miguel Ruiz 'Be impeccable with your word, don't take anything personally, don't make assumptions, always do your best', although use different words for points two and three because the Unconscious Mind node has trouble under-standing 'don'ts', it thinks of them as do's. Five – connect with Higher Self with prayers or silence. Six – work on the posi-tive energy flow. We have talked about the program we have in place with positive thoughts and power of intention. And Ted, there is more, but I don't want to risk overloading or clut-tering your mind."

He looked at me to speak. "Wow Adam I wish I had my tape recorder going here."

He smiled, "You did. Your Unconscious Mind node re-corded everything. Take some quiet moments later today, and ask it to rewind to this conversation."

"I hesitate to ask, but I will anyway, what is grounding?"

"Literally and figuratively it is contact with Earth. When you exhale your breath, you have the potential to ground yourself, assuming your feet are touching the ground and complete that big old energy circuit for non-physical energy.

Some times during the day, and it only takes seconds, both feet on the ground or floor in a building, visualize yourself exhaling bad energy with your breath and at the same time sending away bad energy through your legs to Mother Earth. Visualize that dark molten center of our Earth, Mother Earth wants all living entities to send their bad energy there."

"Thanks Adam that was a load."

"You are welcome Ted. By the way, when are you talking to Jimmy Wong again?

"Maybe tomorrow, why do you ask?"

"Ask him if it is okay for you to come visit him, three weeks from now."

"Well I do need to visit, but I also need to scrape up the cash for the trip."

"Don't worry about the money, I'll pay for the trip, you set up the visit time."

"Oh Adam I can't make money from you."

"Consider it a payment for services."

"Services, what have I done for you."

"Well you drove me to Michigan, you drove me to the nursing home, and you are going to help me find some Antiquity Dealers in Hong Kong."

"Antiquity dealers. How will I do that?"

"I am not sure, but we'll help you."

"We?"

"Yes, Sarah and myself."

"How will you do that? On the Internet or something?"

"No, we are going to come with you."

CHAPTER FORTY FIVE

THE UNFOLDING UNIVERSE

After leaving the Diner, I went over to Kunlow Investments, and spent the afternoon there on work matters. I had dinner downtown, and as I was leaving the restaurant recognized that I was across the street from a huge bookstore. Thoughts were running through my mind, about all the names of people that Adam had mentioned, and books to read, I knew I had five or six unread books at home, but it doesn't hurt to browse. I wandered through the Science and Philosophy sections, why was I here? Okay. Let's peek at the New Age stuff, the name 'New Age' bugged me. I found the section, and was scanning the shelves, when a sudden urge came upon me to turn my head. There to my right was Sarah Sparling. A city of 4 million people, and the one I wanted to see the most was five feet away, synchronicity in action.

She seemed thrilled at our chance encounter. We carried the moment, by deciding to have a coffee or at least I did while she had a latte. We had a fabulous talk until closing time and then we agreed on a tomorrow lunch date, I would meet her at the Museum.

Sarah was going to give me a lesson on antiquities in preparation for the Hong Kong trip that she was extremely excited about. For some reason I had glanced at a book on clouds earlier in the evening. The first page I turned to talked about the nineteenth century British education system having a textbook that described the ten types of clouds. The big fat fluffy one, the cumulonimbus was cloud number nine. I felt like I was riding on cloud number nine, Sarah had a way of elevating my energies to the cloud riding level.

I got up at 3:30 AM the next morning to call Jimmy Wong. Jimmy was excited that I was coming to Hong Kong. I mentioned that I had two traveling companions coming and he wasn't phased at all. His company owned a five-bedroom guesthouse, and he insisted that we would be his guests for the time we were in Hong Kong. I had to email him our itinerary, and he would set up the accommodations and travel. I decided to not go to the Diner that morning, and spent time instead getting caught up on some work. My boss Greg made it clear the previous day that I would be expected to bring in some new clients soon. I was working on a prospecting list of old clients from previous positions. I was also going to put the soul mate intention in second place behind my new prime intention of 'get new clients for work'.

Later on at the Museum, Sarah gave me a quick tour of her offices and we had lunch at the Cafeteria. During lunch, Sarah had a chance encounter with a friend, who joined us for lunch. Mrs. Wilson was an elderly and lively lady; she came to the Museum at least once a week. Mrs. Wilson had asked what I did for a living and I told her. She went into a story about her investment broker being a rude young man, and impatient with her questions. I gave her my card and said when she was comfortable with it, she could call me to discuss our company services. Later that day, Mrs. Wilson called me, I went to her apartment at 4 PM for tea, at 5 PM, I had a new $1 million account. I was thinking my non-physical energies must be harmonized with the Universe. I called Sarah to thank her for the introduction, and we talked for over four hours. I think she was also on the same cumulonimbus cloud that I was on. In our conversation, we made plans for dinner the next day.

For the next week, Sarah and I had incessant conversations and get to-gethers. I met her daughter Jaden, and we got along really well. Jaden was very much like her mother, strong, independent, hard-working, compassionate, intelligent, and beautiful. The only downer over the week, was her father's health. Simon was declining, but the news about taking the Jade Emperor to Hong Kong delighted him. He had provided Sarah with a list of people, mostly dealers, to contact when we arrived in Hong Kong. The only paperwork he kept in the nursing home was his address book. Adam was returning from Sedona on Thursday, and we had arranged to have dinner with him at a downtown restaurant.

Adam and I were standing in the restaurant foyer waiting for Sarah, she had gone to see her father prior to coming to dinner. My cell phone rang, it was Sarah. Her father had a stroke. Adam and I drove to the nursing home and spent the evening with Sarah and Simon. Simon passed on early Friday morning. The next few days were very tough on Sarah. The arrangements for Simon were made, and carried out, but her son Richard refused to come to the funeral. Adam provided her with a lot of comfort, he had the gift of being able to take away grief and burdens.

Gary and Lynette came to the funeral and we had a chance to catch up on things with them. Gary had sold the retail part of his business, they had landed a major outsourcing contract from a large business located an hour away from their office, so no one lost their job. Lynette had designed and put into production and distribution a new set of tarot cards, a major book chain had signed a purchase agreement for 10,000 sets. She signed the deal when she was in Sedona with Adam. They had built a dam and now had a large pond in the back meadow. Trees were being cleared to build a log cabin.

I was amazed at how rapidly these events were unfolding. Simon had passed on and the Universe was unfolding at hyper-speed all around me. I was sad at his passing. Later on at the wake, Sarah took my hand, she knew what I was thinking.

"It is alright Ted, he knows, and he is very happy about it."

"What's that darling?"

"Dad knows that we are in love and almost everything in our Universe is in harmony."

I smiled warmly at Sarah and embraced her. When I looked up, I saw Adam walking towards us, he was with Jaden and leading a very handsome young man to us. The young man was crying. Sarah felt an instinct deep inside her and turned quickly.

"Richard!"

The young man ran to her and clasped her now sobbing body. "Mother, I am so sorry. Will you please, please forgive me."

CHAPTER FORTY SIX

LIVING YOUR BEST LIFE

It was mixed emotions for the next few days, lingering sadness about Simon's passing, but happiness with Richard's return. Richard had mentioned that Adam had called him several times, updating Richard on his grandfather's health. The conversations always ended up being a listening session where Adam was able to get Richard to open up and talk about his fears and misgivings, his resentment of his father which he had transferred to his mother. Richard talked about his bouts with depression, his use of drugs, and his inability to keep a job or to have close friends. Richard smiled as he recounted the one time on the phone when Adam had challenged him to name as many Beatles songs as he could, knowing that Richard loved "old" music from the 60's and Adam loved "new" music which happened to be released in the "60's". Adam had beaten Richard very easily. The contest had transitioned into a discussion about favorite Beatles songs and Adam told him about his realization and insight that 'Let It Be' was his song of choice when it came to forgiveness. Richard had queried him further, and Adam had said that he used to think the way to deal with the hurt of past transgressions was the traditional "Let it Go", assuming the hurts would go away. Then he came to the realization, that past mistakes, transgressions and failures would never go away, and it was a waste of energy to even focus on a Let It Go mindset, it was better to recognize their existence, but don't disturb the pile of crud. Let It Be. Think of the world you want to have or be in, and take those small steps every day to make it happen. He asked Adam if his relationship with his mother was going into the 'Let It Be' category, and Adam convinced him that Sarah only loved him, and it could be nothing else.

I caught up with Adam at the Diner. We were very close to leaving for Hong Kong, all the travel arrangements were made, and I was getting very excited about the trip. I was getting to see my good friends Jimmy and Rebecca, meet their children, and I was traveling with the love of my life and my good friend and mentor, Adam.

"Adam, I want to thank you for what you did for Sarah and Richard."

"That is no problem Ted. Their reconciliation was destined to happen, I knew the discussion on a Beatles song would speed up the process, it always does."

"How do you do it Adam?"

"Do what Ted?"

"How do you always know what to do, what to say, where to go when you need to go. How do you do it?"

"I have been blessed. I have made a lot of mistakes in my life that I have finally learned from. There is no shortage of lessons in this life.I have encountered a lot of wonderful people who have helped me a long the way. I have made use of the lessons I have learned on non-physical energy, I have gotten myself into the flow, and I am lucky the flow is going where I want to go, so I haven't had to use much energy to adjust my course. I have chosen to do a little good every day. It seems very simple to me. There really isn't anything hard or amazing about it."

"After we get back from Hong Kong, where are you going Adam?"

"I am going to find that Lemurian mother-lode of clear quartz crystals."

"Huh?"

"My ultimate destination is the one I had when I was eight years old. Find a giant clear quartz crystal. But along the way, I am going to help people in the walks along their pathways, some need guidance, others need help in moving boulders on their path. My immediate task is journey to Asia is to help a dear friend find the proper home for a lost treasure. I am also going to help some other friends – Ted and Sarah – in their quest for knowledge. Some day Ted and Sarah will help others do the same thing."

Adam seemed to be relaxed and more vibrant than I have ever seen him.

"Can I ask you just one more question on your Quantum Trio understanding of Consciousness? Maybe two or three questions depending on your answer?"

"Sure, I will try to answer. It is like anything, I think I have a simple understanding of a complex subject, but if I have to go into a lot of detail to explain it, it becomes as complicated as the original subject. I will try my best."

"When you were talking about the Code-Master, I had the feeling Code-Master was disconnected from Life itself, and he operated in this little world of the body reprogramming DNA and deciding what each cell should do. Is that accurate?"

"No. First, Code-Master is integrated with Personality Self and Higher Self. His role is different than Personality and Higher Self, a trinity, if you want to use that terminology, but they are all the same guy. Second, one half of Code Master's job is programming physical matter, cell structures and DNA. The other half is managing the "in and out flow" of non-physical energy that provides the life force to each cell, making them organic. Our living entities are specks on the massive grid of life force energy. The non-physical life energy doesn't stay forever with each cell, it is constantly exchanging with other quanta of non-physical energy that comes from near and far, time and space are irrelevant. The most fascinating part of Code-Master's job is the quanta energy exchanges in the cells we call neurons, most of which are in the organ called the brain. A portion of these quanta exchanges make up the thing we call Consciousness. Don't let my other metaphor of the Conscious Mind node data stream with the Unconscious Mind node confuse you, that exists, but in a physical matter context, the neural pathways and the electrochemical processes are the physical reality of thoughts. In those cells that act as the stimulators of charges and those cells at the synapses a very subtle non-physical energy information exchange is occurring. Code- Master manages that based on the previous instructions given to him for DNA programming and current instructions that he picked up at the Unconscious Mind Node and some programmed codes can be traced back to your Conscious Mind intentions."

"The big set of original instructions, or codes for a human life form, is that from God?"

"Yes, but it is not a big set of instructions, I prefer to think of them as sets of probabilities, more or less in line with the Physicists understanding of quantum theory. I like the year 1916 Ted, you know why?"

"Nice change of subject Adam, but I am not sure why, it is the year before you were born."

"Technically correct, Ted.But during 1916, the Master of all Quantum Trio's sparked several little Quantum Trio's in their flows in the massive non-physical energy field. One of those sparks was in Madagascar and took place in a fertilized ovum in Marie Almeida's womb. A set of probabilities accompanied that spark of energy. Code-Master was in charge of the cell division plan and DNA coding of the boy, Higher Self looked on in interest, and Personality Self had a sleep until his moment of wakening in 1917. There were also little sparks released for Marcel Vogel, David Bohm, Indira Gandhi, John F. Kennedy, and Arthur C. Clarke, all of whom have touched me in a way. All these folks had a set of probabilities on whether they would use their talents or not, and to what degree they would use them."

"Have you used your talents to the highest level dictated by the laws of probability Adam?"

"I don't know. I only discovered a few weeks ago, that I have expert driving skills and I am fearless. Maybe, I should have been a Formula 1 racecar driver. Any of us will never know that we used our talents to their highest probability. We need to discover our talents, and those which help others, focus time on them"

"Thanks Adam."

"Ted, how long is your apartment lease?"

"I am paying month to month, why do you ask?"

"I have recently done something that I have never done before in my life. I bought a huge five-bedroom home, an older house, I only need one room for sleeping, another for my personal stuff. The rent will be cheap, if you are interested, let me know. Tell Sarah, she knows the house, 23 Stornoway Place."

"How does she know it?"

"She grew up there, it is Simon's old house."

CHAPTER FORTY SEVEN

SPECIAL GIFTS

I could understand more than ever what Adam had meant about the flow of the Universe. I felt like I was more than in a flow, never before in my life had things moved so quickly, I actually felt like I was surfing the big wave. Adam cautioned me that in any flow it usually acted like tides, so if you have some flow, you can also expect a few ebbs or setbacks along the way. And what if I was riding the big surf, I had asked him. He cautioned me to not fall off the board, and to do that I need to listen to my intuition and not my ego. Enjoy the ride because it won't last forever, and I would have some work ahead of me to paddle out to catch the next wave. Everything came together for the trip to Hong Kong. Sarah was able to get off work for a week, I had informed Greg I would be away for a week, he was very happy to see I was visiting a large client, and he wasn't paying travel expenses. The flight was going to be over twenty hours and I was very happy when I got the tickets and saw Adam had booked us into Business Class on Cathay Pacific. It should be a nice flight, but nonetheless tiring. We were leaving midnight on Tuesday and arriving 8 AM Thursday morning local time.

Jimmy had emailed me that he would meet us at the airport. Jimmy told me on the phone that he recently had an exciting event happen to him, and it was good and bad for him. On a trip to Shanghai, he finally located his long lost grandmother. His father and grandfather had come to Hong Kong in the 1950's, but grandmother could not come. His father searched in vain to find his mother (Jimmy's grandmother) and could not find her, they presumed she might have passed away. Jimmy's father died at a young age, 46, and one of his regrets was not to see his mother again. Jimmy was not really looking for his grandmother but at a business meeting in Shanghai, the person he was negotiating a contract with was talking about family and when Jimmy told the man about his grandfather, they started tracing family origins and realized that his new business associate was a distant cousin. The astounding news was the cousin told him his grandfather's wife was still alive and living with another cousin. Jimmy was ecstatic to locate his grandmother, but the sad news was she was ill. Jimmy had still managed to arrange permits and transportation for his grandmother to come to Hong Kong and she was placed under the care of a private nurse.

On the flight to Hong Kong, Sarah and I took turns sitting beside Adam, he was more or less our personal guru, but we not call him that to his face. I had to ask Adam more questions on the metaphysics of non-physical energy fields.

"Well Adam, do you think we will find a home for the Jade Emperor?"

"We will find a home for it, but the right home, it's true home, I am not sure. We will get it closer to where it wants to go, eventually it will find home."

"I would like to thank you again for the plane tickets, it was very kind of you."

"Absolutely, no problem Ted, I am delighted we can share this journey together. I made one change in my personal travel schedule I did not tell you about. I am staying in Hong Kong for an extra day, then I am flying to Madagascar."

"Oh my goodness, that is a big change."

"Yes, I had the calling again."

"The calling?"

"The Lemurian quartz crystal. I keep dreaming about it. I think it wants me to come find it. I don't know how long it will take, but I will see if I can find her in a two week search. Can I show you another toy of mine?"

"Sure Adam."

"Well a few weeks back, I had never bought a house in my life, property yes, but a house to live in no, and I bought one. Last week I bought a lawn mower for the first time in my life, and here in my bag is another first time purchase." He pulled out a cell phone.

"Your first cell phone!"

"Yes, and not just any phone, a Satellite phone. Expensive, but I need it because I am a new home owner and I have got to check with you to make sure everything is okay on the home front. I don't imagine there are many pay phones in the tropical rain forest or the big hills and mountains of Madagascar." Adam was smiling.

"Next thing you know, you will be buying your first car or an ATV"

"Oh no. Not taking any driver tests, you saw me on the ATV and the mountain bike, there is no way I would pass the test." He was chuckling.

"Adam, I have made a lot of notes on non-physical energy, Mind and Consciousness, I have even started reading some of the work done by Dr. David Bohm and Dr. Edgar Mitchell. I get caught up on trying to understand the change process. The Power of Intentions and thoughts I understand, but how do we change and have the new situation stay that way? It is like a diet, once it is over, we have a tendency to go back to our old weight."

"Patterns."

"What do you mean by patterns?"

"Once you have an established pattern, your Unconscious wants to maintain it, and sends signals to the Subconscious, the Code-Master and the Conscious Mind Node – 'this is the pattern we need to maintain' on the thousands or maybe millions of patterns you have in every aspect of your Life. I will use some examples. Your golf swing, the way you put a key in a lock, the ways you smile and the trigger points for your smiles, the way you think about your boss, the natural pace of your walk, the way you drive a car, your metabolism, your heart-beat rate at rest, your tendency to put-off what you don't like doing, even though you shed your skin all the time that one blemish keeps appearing in the same spot, your fondness for jelly beans, your addiction to coffee, and on and on. These are all patterns. The Unconscious Mind works in conjunction with the Code-Master to help maintain the patterns, and it takes disciplined effort to change them. Some of the big patterns, like your body form and operational capacity at different stages of your life get programmed into your DNA. Most patterns can be adjusted or changed, but it has to happen for both your physical and non-physical energy, and non-physical energy is more important than physical energy if you really want to change your patterns. The Code-Master adjusts non-physical energy. Each cell of your body is made up of molecules, each molecule is made up of atoms. An atom is 99% empty space. The nucleus is a very solid little ball made up of protons and neutrons and way out in space are the orbiting electrons. There are hundreds of analogies for describing an atom and comparing it to a real life situation but I like the physicist William H. Cropper's description because it gives a reference to weight and dimensions. Cropper said an atom is like a giant cathedral. The outer perimeter of the cathedral are the orbiting electrons, or the energy waves of electrons, but inside the cathedral is a single fly representing the nucleus, not only is the nucleus small, but the weight of the fly is the same as the entire weight of the cathedral. A nucleus is small, dense and heavy. The electron has relatively no weight, and is not really a particle or an identified shape. The end conclusion of discussion A, is atoms are over 99 % empty space, they make up molecules, that make up cells that make up you, so you are also 99% empty space. In Discussion B, my premise is back at the tiny little atom, is a quanta of invisible non-physical energy of information providing some basic information to the nucleus, but providing on-going information to the electrons – go this fast, go in this orbit, leave this proton etc. all the elements of change. The non-physical energy quanta carries one message from Code-Master, if a change takes place with the electrons, it comes as a result of Code-Master telling the one quanta it is being exchanged with a new quanta with a new message. Non-physical energy is married to physical energy. If you need to change the patterns of physical energy whether it be the functioning patterns in your physical body or the functioning patterns of your thoughts and behaviors, or the functioning patterns of the physical events coming into your Life you need to change the functioning patterns of the non-physical energy. Crude example, you have a cancerous tumor. It is growing. In physical reality the cancer is a healthy new cell, multiplying like the new cells in a growing fetus. For some weird and wacky reason Code-Master has received instructions or interpreted instructions from the Unconscious Mind Node that this cancer should grow and Code-Master has arranged the non-physical energy patterns to keep it happening, the non-physical energy that carries information to tell it's counterpart physical atoms what to do, new atoms assemble in a specific location to make new molecules that get lumped into the healthy cell in time for its division from one cell into two cells. And being a perceived healthy growth situation, parent cell A does not self-destruct like it would in a normal cell division scenario. It hangs around to multiply again. Eventually the growth of this healthy cancer is going to cause big problems in its specific location in the body, unless Code-Master receives instructions to change. These instructions might be external introductions of radiation or chemicals (chemotherapy), but Code-Master being the objective guy he is applies the new destruction instructions to cells and molecules in the vicinity, the healthy body cells and the cancer cells, causing new problems in the body. There are ways in energy healing of telling Code-Master, 'hey buddy, instruct the non-physical energy quanta in the atoms that make up the molecules of those new guy cells human calls cancer to buzz off". When quanta goes, the atoms go, braking up the molecules, causing the cells to stop dividing and eventually break up themselves, and the local region returns to an old pattern which is a more healthy state. The specific instructions are converted into new non-physical energy information that gives new instructions to the components of physical energy."

"Wow, what an incredible story. Adam you tell good stories used for explanations to hard to answer questions."

"The Power of Transformation, even self healing resides within everyone. But most of the time people will need to have contact in person or at a distance with another person with a gift of healing using their abilities to instruct non-physical energy to provide new information to the components that make up the cells of our bodies."

"Do you have the gift of healing Adam?"

"To some extent, but it is not a special gift for me."

"Do you know your special gift Adam?"

"I think so, it is a gift of noticing things and how they work, and telling others about the strange things I notice. I see things that no one else sees. I have to make up little stories like Quantum Trio's and Unconscious Mind Nodes, and Quintessence so that people can understand the weird and wonderful things that I have noticed about energy fields. I have also noticed the gifts in other people even when they haven't noticed their special gifts themselves."

"Really?"

"Yes, when I have had enough exposure to the person."

"Do you know me well enough to tell me my special gift? And if you do, will you tell me?"

"Yes to both."

"And?"

"You don't know this Ted, you have almost the same gift I have, you can notice things about energy that others don't seem to realize. I am a good storyteller, but my stories are like the one Socrates told, he didn't write them down. When you get around to telling your stories you will be more like Aristotle, you will write them. And, I hope you will write down some of my stories."

CHAPTER FORTY EIGHT

A SHORT STOP IN HAWAII

Our journey had a planned stop in Hawaii. The stop-over was for about one hour, we had time to get off the plane and go into the airport lounge. I almost immediately regretted that we didn't build a two day or more stop off in this fantastic location. We decided to buy some snacks and sit at a table in an open eating area. I broke out into a smile when I saw that all three of us had brought along our journals.

"Ah you must like being in Hawaii Ted." Adam had picked up on my smile.

"Well yes, but I was smiling about the fact that all three of us have brought our journals with us for this short stop-over."

"Terrific. This feels like the perfect time for a lesson review with my two prized pupils."

My first impulse was to object, I wanted to gaze out the window, but I was now mastering the skill of stopping to assess my first impulse, and seeing if the impulse made sense from both a point of rationality and "gut" feeling. In a one second delay assessment, both my mind and my intuition informed me in unison that this time with Adam and Sarah was special, and a terrific learning opportunity was at hand. "Great Adam. Sarah, are you up for some Adam teachings?"

"Absolutely. I had a feeling we would be doing something like this, that's why I brought along my daily lessons journal."

Adam was smiling broadly, "Ted, you already have a lesson in women's intuition, which is generally stronger than men's intuition, but the male species is catching up in intuitive skills, slowly but surely."

"I will mark that down in my journal as Lesson One for today's session Adam."

"No, that is not Lesson One Ted. Sarah tell us what Lesson One is. And today is a review session on Lessons we have learned."

Sarah did not hesitate. "Lesson One, is to be open and aware at all times."

Adam had shifted to his teacher's voice and mannerisms. "Why is that Sarah?"

Again, no hesitation. "If we are open and aware, we can find new opportunities for both learning and experiencing joy. We will find answers to problems or challenges that are confronting us. The open and awareness techniques, once mastered, can be used to open up our intuitive channels and to also help us interpret our dreams."

Adam, pressed on with another follow-up question. "What is the greatest obstacle to becoming more open and aware?"

"I am not sure if this is the greatest obstacle, but I think it is our self-imposed mind barriers, such as strong beliefs and judgment on what we think is right or wrong. It could also be the clutter in our minds from the activities in our hectic lives is blocking us from being more open and aware."

Adam was nodding. "Both obstacles exist, among others. Ted, can you think of something that will help us to be more open and aware, a code we all need to adopt to become open and aware enough to at least get to an assessment stage of any new idea or experience?"

I was caught slightly off-guard, and my mind was frozen with the question. In a nano-second, my mind flashed to a visualization of my first long conversation with Adam and some of the first advice he gave me. "Weird is good."

Sarah started to laugh. "Why, that principle helps me a lot, especially, around Adam."

Adam smiled, but he still pressed on in teacher mode. "Okay, enough for Lesson One summary on constantly being open and aware. As you evolve, a constant state of openness and awareness will move from helping you with daily life, to one that opens the door to a continuous experience of joy and wonderment. Lesson Two, is associated with Lesson One, and is a practical requirement for beginners on the pathway to enlightenment. Any ideas?"

Sarah paused in reflection, and I had an opportunity to speak first. "All new ideas and experiences need to pass through a BS test."

"Well Ted, you remember our chat in the car ride to Michigan. In a crude way, your answer is partially correct. All new ideas and experiences discovered in moments of open awareness, do have to pass, at some point, some hurdles before they should be accepted as useful as a concept, a fact, the truth or a belief. One hurdle, which you mention, is to maintain a healthy skepticism, especially for new ideas. Does the new idea have some logic behind its presentation? If no evidence, we have to decide whether we accept the idea on the principle of faith. A danger here with faith. Some people accept things in faith which is based in the trust of others who are presenting or supporting the idea. This might be okay, but the ultimate test for faith, is your own intuition. If no hard facts. logic or evidence exists, how do you feel about the idea? Intuition, once properly developed, is actually a stronger force than logic. Ted and Sarah, open your journals to a blank page. Mark down Lesson One – Be Open and Aware and Lesson Two – Develop a reliance on your Intuition. Any thoughts on Lesson Three?"

Sarah was focused, and a much quicker, neater journal writer than me. "Adam and Ted, I would propose Lesson Three be to constantly focus on and visualize your desires."

"I'm okay with that Sarah. Adam, as our great teacher, and master of order, does this make sense as Lesson Three."

Adam's hand was gently under his chin, in a thinking pose. "Yes. Our order for the Lesson lay-out is relevant, but only to the students and their stage of learning. Both of you are in a process of quickly transforming your lives to a higher state of abundance and joy, the most important requirement for manifesting your desires is 'visioning' your desired state of existence. But the visualizations are part of a larger process for manifestation. Some desires require a large shift in energy vibration, and may require a lot of variables currently outside your control to almost miraculously come together, other desires are short-term by nature, and will be realized with a short burst of intention. Let me suggest the following. Lesson Three – Know Your Desires. Lesson Four – Always frame your desires as statements of Intention. Lesson Five –

Visualize your desire as a final finely detailed outcome. Lesson Six – After a moment of visualizing your desire, move on to performing the next most important task at hand which is not related to the desire. In essence, detach yourself from the desire's fulfillment. Questions?"

I was busy scribbling the lessons in my journal, with glances over to Sarah's journal as she clearly wrote down the lessons without hesitation. Fortunately, she was sitting closely beside me, so it was easy for me to be a copy-cat. I did require some clarification. "Adam, what do you mean exactly by knowing your desires? I thought that is self-evident."

"No Ted, this is one of the lessons that most people treat too casually. Desires need to be more than a list of goals and objectives. If you ask some people to write a list of their prime desires today, and then write the list again a week later, or even a day later, and the list will probably be different. If that happens, there is a question on how serious those written desires really are for that individual. The key word in the lesson to focus on is '**know**'. This word needs to be more feeling than a written statement. And at the highest level of knowing, the desire is already fulfilled. It exists. It has already happened in your mind, there might only be a slight time delayed reaction for it to exist in your living reality."

"Thanks for the clarification Adam. I have no other questions."

Sarah spoke up. "The only thing missing in the manifestation process description is some description on how the desire turns from thought into reality."

Adam continued smiling. "Yes Sarah, you are absolutely correct. There are two aspects of desire fulfillment, which occur consciously and unconsciously. Lesson Two helps a little as you follow your intuition. But, let us make Lesson Seven – Connect to the God-force on a daily basis. Could each of you please provide me an example of a way to connect to the God-force."

I spoke first. "Pray every day?" I didn't intend for my definite answer to come out of my mouth sounding like a question.

"Yes Ted. Prayer is one method. Sarah, another example?"

"I have three - meditation, quiet reflection, and gratitude."

"Yes to all of the above. Now, let me put this Lesson in context. The two concurrent methods of transforming your desires into physical world reality are - one, taking actions yourself, and two, connecting to the God-force to release your desire to Supreme Power which will assist you in making the desire become a reality. All four methods you mentioned have value. Prayer is a specific and powerful method to bring forward a specific intention to the Creator, as long as you maintain faith, no doubts in your mind, that the Creator will act in a way that is best for all. Meditation is a practice that is very useful in cleaning up clutter in your conscious mind, if you ever manage in meditation to free your mind up completely from any daily world thoughts, you release stress, and at special moments you are completely connected with the God-force. Quiet reflection, can take place at any time during the day, and the best times for inspiration, and note the word inspiration is comprised of 'in spirit', occur when you are performing a routine task – such as having a shower, washing the dishes, driving the car. My favorite connection to the God-force is through gratitude. When you express thanks, as long as it is heart-felt and sincere, you connect to the God-force. You have a special feeling, which is in truth, a connection to the higher power. Let me give you a special Lesson related to gratitude, make it Lesson Eight – Daily express gratitude for all that you have now, and for the fulfillment of your desires. The moment you wake up in the morning, and the first two words out of your mouth, maybe as you spin to get out of bed, first foot on the floor 'thank' and as your second foot hits the floor 'you'. Thank you. Use it freely and sincerely through out the day. Back to Lessons Five and Six, visualizing your desires and releasing them into the Universe for fulfillment. Express gratitude to the Creator for helping to realize your specific desire which is the subject of the visualization."

I couldn't contain maintain myself. "Wow, what an incredible strategy. A direct connection to God as you send off your intention into the Universe for fulfillment!"

"Not a strategy Ted. A way of living."

Sarah continued. "Thank you Adam. Those were eight powerful lessons. And we haven't even mentioned anything about the Quantum Trio. Is there anything we need to add?"

Adam paused. "I am conscious we are going to have to get on the plane shortly. The Lessons we have just discussed all relate to manifesting your desires. There are other Lessons that relate to living your best life and to improving your understanding of the both the physical world and the metaphysical realm. Lesson Nine – In your daily living optimize and harmonize Body, Mind and Spirit. In that order. You need a healthy body to live your most joyous and longest life. Eat healthy foods that provide toxin free proteins, carbohydrates and fats. Eat foods that help cleanse toxins and combat free radicals in your physiological system. Allocate sufficient time for sleep and exercise. Maintain a healthy body weight. Avoid as much as possible the introduction of toxins into your body from the air you breathe, the water you drink, the food you eat, and the things you come in contact with. Cigarettes have over 3000 toxins, no need to ask me my thoughts on smoking, and second-hand smoke. Optimizing your Mind as part of the Trinity is the most complex set of activities. I will only summarize. Always stay positive, even in the biggest pile of doo-doo look for the positive aspects. Find work, study or a career that you enjoy doing, because if you enjoy it, you have less stress and your horizons expand. If you don't enjoy your work, realize that this is a temporary situation, assuming you want it to be, and think of the positives about your work. Make use of your talents in your work and hobbies. In work, always do your best at any task at hand, and do more than what is expected of you. These two attributes will almost guarantee that your career will advance and/or income will rise rapidly. Remove as much clutter as you can in your daily surroundings, and your mind. Find ways to spend time in nature as a way to relax, to remove clutter in your mind and to connect with Spirit. Understand that the Mind is powerful, and your thoughts can become reality if framed as intentions, the old metaphor applies 'be careful about what you think about, you actually might get it'. Understand your talents are special to you, and you have an obligation to use them, and to share them with others. And, the third part of the Trio is Spirit. Understand that the prime substance of Spirit is Love.

Love yourself first. Love, forgive and help others in need if the need is sincere and you have both the opportunity and heart-felt desire to provide support. Love and protect God's greatest creation – our natural world. Understand that these comments about a harmonized Body, Mind and Spirit relate to our physical world. Underneath, surrounding and throughout all things in our physical world, is a twin metaphysical realm where the Quantum Trio exists and acts. The Quantum Trio is one, the non-physical energy that provides life and direction to the atoms that make up the cells of your body. Two, the subconscious mind that quietly without your conscious awareness carries out the orders and follows and adjusts the pre-set codes of both your DNA and your behavioral mindset. Three, the Divine expression of Spirit, a metaphysical particle of God-force, always present and existing as part of the Trio to provide guidance for transformation, and is the connection to all else in the Universe and beyond. The Quantum Trio cannot at this moment, be seen in our physical world, it is Divine substance, comprised of sub-atomic vibrations of light, universal consciousness and love."

The instant Adam finished speaking, we heard our airline associate's voice on the loudspeaker announcing that our flight was boarding.

Adam smiled "My timing is impeccable."

CHAPTER FORTY NINE

GRANDMOTHER

Our plane landed in Hong Kong on schedule. We were all very tired as we got off the plane, went through Customs and Immigration and claimed our bags. Jimmy and Rebecca were there to greet us. I am normally a handshake guy, but I had to give both Jimmy and Rebecca a hug. We packed our bags into Jimmy's van and the driver took us on a drive through the congested streets to the guesthouse. Jimmy showed us to our rooms and said he and Rebecca would be back with the two boys about three o'clock. He had accurately guessed that we would be very tired and would like to get some more rest. Jimmy introduced us to the housekeeper, Mrs. Cheung, and told us she would get us anything we needed.Sarah and I were up about 1 PM, had our showers, got dressed and came down to the main room.

Adam was at a table looking at the white jade crystal ball.

I could see an empty bowl. He either had Mrs. Cheung make him porridge or he had his own.

He looked up at us, "I am not sure if consecutive days of eating porridge streak is broken or not. I managed morning pages and prayers in the past 24 hours but it has been 40 hours between meals of porridge. I think the streak is over. Oh well."

He didn't appear sad at this event; he had a big smile on his face. Sarah went over to the table and put her hand on the Jade Emperor, "I love to feel you Jade Emperor. You have such high energy. I hope we find your home." She was speaking to the ball and not to us. Mrs. Cheung came into the room and saw the ball. Mrs. Cheung was elderly, but moved with a quick step. She had a pleasant smiling face.

"Greetings kind friends. I hope you had a nice rest."

Adam spoke for us, "Yes Mrs. Cheung, we did, I hope you don't mind, I used your kitchen to make some porridge."

"No problem kind sir. I would help you next time." We had to insist that Mrs. Cheung call us by our first names. We saw that she was anxious to ask a question. "Adam, Ted and Sarah. This white Jade ball is very nice. Where did you find it?"

"It has been in Toronto Canada for over the past fifty years. We believe it may have a new owner some where in Hong Kong or China." Adam spoke for us.

"Mr. Jimmy Wong's father, Mr. Joseph Wong, would love that crystal ball if he was still here."

I had to ask, "Was Jimmy's father a collector?"

"Oh yes, he seemed to search for Jade balls all the time. He has over one hundred, would you like to see them? We keep them here."

"Why yes, if it is not too much trouble", Sarah was the first to speak our group feeling.

Mrs. Cheung took us downstairs to a lower level. There was a room at the end of a hallway. She opened the door into what looked to be an office, there was extensive artwork in the room, paintings, sculptures and a large mahogany cabinet with shelves and a series of green, white, clear, rose and a variety of other spheres, some large and some small. It was an extensive collection. "Mr. Joseph Wong never said why he liked the balls made from precious stones, but he looked for new ones all the time. Did Mr. Jimmy Wong tell you that his grandmother is here? She is at the hospital right now, but she will come tonight. She is Mr. Joseph Wong's mother and he did not see her for a very long time. His mother was very sad to hear that he died. She is very happy to meet her grandson and even more happy to meet her great-grandsons. Grandmother spent much time looking at these balls. She asked me about the white jade ball, and I said I did not know it. When I saw the white jade ball upstairs, my first thought, Grandmother will want to see and touch that ball. Grandmother is a very nice lady. She is kind and wise. She has trouble walking, so she is in a wheelchair. Mr. Jimmy Wong loves his grandmother, we are all blessed to have her with us."

"Well is that ever interesting, I wonder what the story is there?" I had asked the question, Sarah had gone over to the collection. Adam was standing by a painting of a lotus flower. He appeared to be looking at the painting, but his eyes showed that his mind was off and away somewhere.

We had a look at the collection, and Mrs. Cheung gave us a tour of the guesthouse. It was for business guests, it had a nice kitchen and large dining area, five bedrooms, sitting areas, offices and meeting rooms. Another office had a computer and internet hook-up so we could pick up our email.

When we went up to the main floor, Sarah took Mrs. Cheung over to the Emperor Jade.

"Mrs. Cheung, I would like you to look closely at the ball, right here, you see that, deep in the jade are some green jade markings, they look like Chinese markings, almost like writing, do you see them?"

"Ah yes, Sarah, I see them, they look very special, but I have a hard time to know what they mean, they are not clearly letters of my language, they look like ancient script. Grandmother may know what these are, she asked a question to Mr. Jimmy Wong if he knew where the white jade ball with markings had gone. It was a gift she left his father when he left the home to come here for safety. When she said markings, I thought she meant carving on the ball, I think Mr. Jimmy Wong thinks the same thing. My thoughts were that the ball was lost, or Mr. Jimmy Wong's grandfather had sold the ball in his trading business, but I do not know for sure. Mr. Joseph Wong, after he had very much money, might have been looking for the ball that was lost or sold. I think that the white ball might have been a family treasure. Maybe Mr. Jimmy Wong will buy this ball from you?"

Adam had been silent for a long time, "We will not sell the white jade ball to Jimmy Wong."

I looked over at Adam, I was going to protest this unilateral decision. Sarah seemed shocked as well.

Adam spoke again, "The ball already belongs to grandmother, we are just returning it to her."

I looked to Sarah, she was nodding her head in approval.

Mrs. Cheung was smiling broadly, grandmother will be coming soon, the men from the hospital will bring her. Mr. Jimmy Wong, Rebecca and the boys are also coming. We will make dinner here, one big happy family."

I had some questions to ask on customs and manners. "Mrs. Cheung, what do we call Grandmother Wong? Do we say Grandmother or Grandmother Wong?"

Mrs. Cheung stopped for a moment, "I think you can call her Grandmother, or if you like you can use her real name, which is Li Wu."

CHAPTER FIFTY

THE JADE CRYSTAL MARKINGS

It was like an electric shock hit me. Could this be the same Li Wu that was Adam's long lost love? It had to be. I looked at Adam.

Adam had already knew my question without me asking it. "Yes it is Ted. Li Wu is the wonderful woman I met in Paris in 1959. I knew it when I came to this house; I could feel her presence. Until now, however, I didn't know that the energy I felt had a physical body or not, I might have been sensing her lingering spirit."

Jimmy, Rebecca and the boys had arrived. We had time to have a nice chat and tell Jimmy and Rebecca Adam's story before Li Wu arrived. Jimmy was astounded at the story, and the sight of the white jade ball.

"I don't know if this is the same ball or not that my grandmother talked about. She gave her husband and her son, my father, several family heirlooms that were passed down through her family. The most precious heirloom was the white jade ball. This ball was for my father to pass down through his family and to continue its heritage. The white jade ball was a gift for the Emperor Wu when China was divided into three dynasties sometime around 270 AD. When China was united into one dynasty, in 280 AD, the Wu family lost their royal status and fled to safety. The ball was given to a son, and passed on through the family. Some say, bad luck would fall on the family if the ball is lost, my father and mother died at young ages. My grandfather died shortly after he sold the ball to a customer from North America. My father made several trips to the USA and Canada looking for the jade crystal. On one of his trips he set up our investment company, Crystal Gardens. Ted, you have been the faithful guardian of those trust funds. Only my grandmother will know for sure whether this is the treasure we speak of."

From my vantage point on the sofa, I could see through the blinds and see a white ambulance pull up in front of the guesthouse. Some attendants helped a lady get into her wheelchair, she was wearing a very nice black dress, when the wheelchair got to the landing, I could see her insisting to stand, the doorbell rang. Jimmy went to the door to greet her. We could them talking in Chinese and we could here a soft gasp from grandmother. She walked on her own slowly into our room. Adam went to her and embraced her. I could see her crying, as we stood up, I glanced at Adam, it was the first time I had ever seen him with tears in is eyes, yet he had his perfect smile on his face.

Li Wu could not speak English but it was not a hindrance. We had a joyous afternoon and evening. Jimmy would translate what Li Wu was saying. She and Adam would speak together in French. There was some other language they spoke together through their eyes. The Jade Emperor was indeed the lost family heirloom. It sat as a centerpiece during dinner.

Li Wu was growing tired, and it was decided she would spend the evening there.

The next day, Jimmy and I had a business meeting, Rebecca took Sarah to a Museum and I suspect they did some shopping as well. Adam and Li Wu spent time together, when Li Wu had to rest, Adam returned to his journaling. To help matters in communications, Mrs. Cheung would help translate when needed. I noticed on the second night, Li Wu was holding an emerald crystal, a gift from Adam.

We had a wonderful week and I was wondering if Adam was going to change his plans for the trip to Madagascar, so he could spend more time with Li Wu. I asked him about it, and he said he talked to Li Wu and she was insistent on him going on his quest while he had the good health to do so.He was slightly sad when he told me that he could see in her aura and spirit that her time was coming close to the end. She had told him that she did not have much time left, and that her three biggest wishes – to find her family, to know what happened to Adam, and to find the white jade ball – had been fulfilled. She was incredibly happy that the white jade would be passed on to her descendants.

We were getting ready to leave for the airport when I managed to pull Adam aside for a few moments. "You want me to call you on that fancy phone of yours, or will you call me Adam?"

"Let's agree that whoever needs to call who, will make the call?"

"When you find your big quartz crystal in Madagascar are you coming back to Toronto or going over to Hong Kong?"

Adam hesitated, "I will be going home Ted. Now that I have seen Li Wu, I only have two lifetime Intentions left on my list. One – find my Lemurian mother crystal. Two – get someone to write a story about any of my Life adventures. I have all my journals placed in my new house. Are you going to move in?"

"Well, it hasn't been decided. I gave my notice on my apartment, but Sarah has her own house. I will have to see."

"My vision and my perfect desire is to have both you and Sarah at 23 Stornoway Place. Talk to her about it."

"I will."

"Will you help me with the written story?"

"What is your vision or your desired perfect outcome?"

"That you write the story, when you are ready. I know your business will occupy you for a while, but you have a talent that you need to use."

"I will think about it Adam."

"Okay. I guess you better get going or you will have a hard time catching your plane on time."

Li Wu sat passively watching us with a smile on her face. Before going out the door, Sarah remembered something important. She rushed over to the dining table and picked up the white jade crystal ball and came back over to Li Wu. Sarah said nothing, and pointed to the green markings. Li Wu said something in Chinese. We looked at Jimmy. "Grandmother says that those markings are ancient Chinese symbols and names for the unifying energy that makes up the entire Universe."

"What is that?"

Jimmy spoke in Chinese to his grandmother. She smiled and looked directly into Adam's eyes.

"Lumiere et Amour"

I don't know much French, but I do know the French words for Light and Love.

Sarah decided to sell her house, and move into 23 Stornoway Place with me. We would be Adam's tenants.

I got a call from Adam that he found a huge clear quartz crystal in a River Valley in a mountainous area. He had hired a crew to excavate the crystal by hand, crate it and fly it by helicopter to the capital city. A freight forwarding company was hired to handle the paperwork with the Madagascar government and ship the crystal to Canada. Adam said he wanted to continue his explorations. He would be home before the crystals made it to Canada.

A week later, Jimmy Wong called me to tell me that his grandmother had passed away. Before she died, she wanted Jimmy to know she was the happiest woman on Earth, she was fulfilled.

A week after that, two men from the RCMP came to the house, my first thought was 'Oboy, there is some paperwork hassles with that rock, can you believe that' but they sat me down to tell me that the Canadian Embassy was trying to find relatives of Adam Almeida, they believed he was on a helicopter that crashed in the mountains of Madagascar. The remains in the crash could not be identified, but they were able to recover a satellite phone registered to him and a leather bag with some articles that belonged to him. I was in shock but I said I did not think Adam had any relatives, I had the name of his lawyer in Toronto, perhaps he would know.

A week later, Sarah and I were called to visit Adam's lawyer. The lawyer said that he could not tell us about Adam's will because it had not been confirmed that he had passed away, but he said that Adam had a living will which he wanted to be invoked in case he was incapacitated or missing. The lawyer made the comment on how he thought it was unusual that Adam had requested that 'missing' be added to his standard form. In any case, Sarah and I were assigned his house to care for, and it would become ours upon Death notification. All his belongings in the Diner would be given to Lynette. The shares of the company that owned the Diner, part of the Diner business and some adjoining property would be assigned to the current Diner employees. All of his possessions at 23 Stornoway would be assigned to me, and I would use or dispose of them at my discretion. I knew Adam had cases of stuff stored in a room at the house.

It was over a week later before I could go into the closed room that held Adam's possessions.

He had clothes in his closet. There were 23 cases that had black journals in every case, and there was one case that had miscellaneous items in it, some pictures, a little bag filled with emeralds, another bag with a variety of other crystals, and a single black journal that was not filed in the other cases. I could see it was almost filled with writing. I opened the journal to the first page. There was only one word on the page.

QUINTESSENCE